European Culture Since 1848

"This is an outstanding, comprehensive survey of modern European culture. It concisely describes the main ideas of every important 'ism' of the last 200 years, giving readers an introduction to the creative individuals as well as the cultural movements and social contexts that have made such 'isms' so influential in the modern world. But the book also looks beyond the most famous European thinkers to identify the imaginative artists, musicians, filmmakers, and photographers who have shaped modern and postmodern Western cultural life. Writing in a clear, accessible prose, Winders carries readers from the arcane theories of complex philosophers, poets, and novelists into the latest experimental films and the rhythms of contemporary rock music.

"This book differs from other introductions to modern European culture by linking the intellectual themes of critical social theorists to the creative works of avant-garde artists and by stressing the remarkable cultural innovations in late 20th-century European societies. *European Culture since 1848* provides a fascinating guided tour of modern thought for students, teachers, and travelers who want a new historical approach to the diverse, multicultural creativity of contemporary Europe."

—Lloyd Kramer, University of North Carolina, Chapel Hill

"A vibrant mosaic of ideas and portraits both elite and popular, James Winders's new volume is a creative and spirited challenge to the traditional notion of the intellectual history survey 'textbook.' With special emphasis on developments at the end of the twentieth century, Winders's linked essays and synoptic discussions propel the reader through a hundred and fifty years of European cultural and intellectual expression from Romanticism and Ranke to Foucault and Fluxus, from Darwin to Derrida and Wollstonecraft to Wenders. Multiple sources in scholarship and literature, media, film, photography, art, and all kinds of music anchor this engaging balance of great men and women, critical philosophies and movements, and idiosyncratic examples from Restoration newspapers to European hip-hop."

—Matt K. Matsuda, Associate Professor of Modern European History at Rutgers University, author of *The Memory of the Modern*.

" . . . an amazing book, a survey of recent intellectual and cultural history that one can assign to a class of undergraduates without embarrassment. Winders has given us a book that for the first time treats the 2nd half of the 20th century as an integral part of modern cultural history. He has in effect redesigned the way we will teach intellectual history in chapters that reflect the most recent scholarship. And he has pitched his material consistently to the readership of contemporary undergraduates. A great textbook!"

—Carl Pletsch, Associate Professor of History & Office of Teaching Effectiveness, University of Colorado at Denver

European Culture Since 1848

From Modern to Postmodern and Beyond

James A. Winders

palgrave

First published 2001 by
PALGRAVE
175 Fifth Avenue, New York, N.Y. 10010 and
Houndmills, Basingstoke, Hampshire RG21 6XS.
Companies and representatives throughout the world

PALGRAVE is the new global publishing imprint of St. Martin's Press LLC
Scholarly and Reference Division and Palgrave Publishers Ltd (formerly
Macmillan Press Ltd).

ISBN 0–312–21416–2 hardback
ISBN 0–312–22873–2 paperback
ISBN 978-0-312-22873-6

Library of Congress Cataloging-in-Publication Data
Winders, James A., 1949-
European culture since 1848 : from modern to postmodern and beyond /
James A. Winders
    p.   cm.
  Includes bibliographical references and index.
  ISBN 0–312–21416–2—ISBN 0–312–22873–2 (pbk.)
   1. Europe—Intellectual life—19th century. 2. Europe—Intellectual life—
20th century. 3. Civilization, Modern—19th century. 4. Civilization,
Modern—20th century. I. Title.
CB204.W55 2001
940.2'8—dc21

2001021940

A catalogue record for this book is available from the British Library.

Design by Letra Libre, Inc.

First edition: September, 2001
10 9 8 7 6 5 4 3 2 1

Printed in the United States of America.
Transferred to Digital Printing 2008

To my mother and father

Contents

Acknowledgments

Each year, for most of my academic career, I have taught a course on modern European intellectual history. I have been privileged to enjoy the intellectual stimulation of many remarkable students, a number of whom remain very good friends. Their ideas and insights have much to do with the nature of this book. Over the years students have suggested frequently (especially since both they and I have been critical of the survey accounts we have used) that I write a book like this. Typically I would change the subject, but I did write a book some years ago that ended with the observation that intellectual historians who had been inspired by new currents in historical scholarship and cultural theory should take up the task of writing new surveys. In a way, I am belatedly taking up the challenge my students set for me and that I issued in such a general way. Another boomerang victim.

As is the case with any book, many friendships and valuable professional associations contribute abundantly to its realization. But I must certainly specify the importance of conversations with Michael J. Moore, who suggested at just the right time that I should write such a book as this. Michael Flamini of Palgrave has consistently offered his encouragement and intelligent suggestions, for which I am also grateful. I also appreciate the help I have received from Rick Delaney and Amanda Johnson of Palgrave. Thanks also to the Department of History, the College of Arts and Sciences, the Office of International Programs, and the Office of Academic Affairs of Appalachian State University for their support.

With love and gratitude this book is dedicated to my father, Jack Winders, and to the memory of my mother, Wilma Comerford Winders.

Introduction

Although the twentieth century has ended, students of European cultural and intellectual history have had access to no survey account of that history that does justice to its second half. That is one reason for this book. Also, in recent decades historical study has expanded to include topics of gender, everyday life, and a broader notion of culture more in keeping with the insights of cultural anthropology, a direct influence on the new cultural history. That is a second reason to offer a book such as this. Finally, the subdiscipline of European intellectual history has been challenged by these same demands to encompass more than its traditional emphasis on influential ideas and the figures who introduced them, and has received this challenge in the midst of great theoretical upheaval involving language, meaning, texts, signs, and discourse. To these new challenges also this book is a response.

Thus this volume is intended for use by both undergraduate and graduate students not only in European history courses but also in literature, comparative literature, languages, art history, film studies, philosophy, anthropology, and more broadly defined interdisciplinary domains like women's studies or cultural studies. The topics explored herein are inherently interdisciplinary. To correct the familiar tendency of survey accounts of modern European cultural or intellectual history to emphasize heavily the period up through 1945 or so while offering thoughts on the last half of the century as a kind of coda or anticlimax, this book tilts the balance in the other direction. The reader will find deliberately heavy emphasis on the second half of the twentieth century, and, after a brief summary of some important cultural trends pertaining to the years from 1789 to 1848, we begin in earnest at that point, roughly the time that modern European culture begins to define itself.

The chapters are largely thematic in organization, although chronology still receives its due. The familiar drama of "the history of ideas" does not disappear in this book, but shares an arena with literature, art, music, photography, and cinema. The definition of culture used here includes both "elite" and "popular," and many chapters feature both emphases. Occasionally topics of popular culture, including photography, are treated in greater depth in separate chapters. The arts of photography and cinema dominated twentieth-century culture, and their inclusion within the domain of cultural history is long overdue.

Except for the first brief chapter that summarizes some themes in the immediate background to 1848, all chapters close with a short list of suggestions for further reading appropriate to the themes of that chapter.

Chapter 1

Background to 1848:
Legacies of the Enlightenment and Romanticism

The period from 1789 to 1848 has been called an age of revolutions, meaning not just the political revolutions of 1789, 1830, and 1848 but the intensifying industrial revolution that began in the mid-eighteenth century in England and also the revolution in the arts summed up under the term "Romanticism," emerging first in Germany and still flourishing in France when the 1848 Revolution broke out. It was the period of the Napoleonic Wars, of a prosperous middle class making significant political gains, of new political theories and movements in opposition to industrial capitalism, of the first railroads, of the birth of modern chemistry and biology (and the brand-new sciences of geology and paleontology), of such modern institutions as the medical clinic and the prison, of a growing sense of the separation of art and the artist from the rest of society, and of an increasingly literate public eager for newspapers, magazines, and printed books—the subject of the next chapter.

While this was largely a time of political reaction, including much reassertion of monarchy, revolutionary uprisings broke out in France in 1830 and 1848, and there were groups more or less underground in various parts of Europe interested in radical political ideas, often tied to emergent nationalist movements, as in Italy. Even though officially the politics of the French Revolution were denounced and regretted, the more radical ideas of that period found new expression through the emerging critiques of industrial capitalism.

In this way a combination of influences gave rise to early nineteenth-century Utopian socialism, as represented especially by Henri de Saint-Simon (1760–1825), Charles Fourier (1772–1837), and Robert Owen (1771–1858). Utopian socialists originated some of the ideas that would be taken up by later socialists, including Karl Marx and Friedrich Engels. Unlike the latter two, they did not expect workers themselves to take the initiative in replacing capitalism with socialism. They dreamed instead of its establishment by enlightened benevolent persons. They shared the Enlightenment faith in human perfectibility and progress, and helped to transmit that faith to the nineteenth century.

Saint-Simon, descendant of a French noble family, criticized some of the specific ways workers were made to suffer under capitalism and envisioned a socialist utopia managed by a body of able technocrats, almost like some latter-day version of Plato's "philosopher kings." He was fond of ambitious architectural and engineering schemes, and through his followers directly influenced Emperor Napoleon III of France. Fourier, a lonely visionary who worked for years as a traveling salesman, offered a model of decentralized workshops called "phalanxes" around which society would be organized. His ideas included overcoming the monotony of industrial labor by rotating tasks throughout the day as well as by arranging for the gratification of all the worker's needs and pleasures. Owen, owner of a textile mill in Scotland, financed his own social experiment by seeing to his workers' housing, education, and other essentials. When he realized greater profits through his benevolent efforts, he advocated his approach as a universal one. His anticlericalism was not popular in Scotland, and he tried a similar experiment in the United States that met with little success. Owen's followers included many early English feminists.

For European women, the early nineteenth century was an unpromising time. Feminists had sought to play a role during the French Revolution, rallying to the example of the English writer Mary Wollstonecraft (1759–1797), whose *Vindication of the Rights of Woman* (1792) asked pointedly whether the revolutionary "rights of man" included women and went on to lament the squandering of human resources caused by failure to educate women and to encourage them to develop their talents. The male revolutionaries answered the question Wollstonecraft and her French sisters raised resoundingly in the negative, especially during the Terror. At that time (1793–1794) women's political clubs were banned and some prominent feminists were guillotined.

With regard to women's roles, the ideas of the French *philosophe* Jean-Jacques Rousseau (1712–1778) exercised considerable influence. In his writings, for example in the wildly successful novel *Julie, ou la nouvelle Héloïse* (1762, *Julie, or the New Heloise*), women were criticized if they strayed from what the philosopher regarded as their natural maternal domestic role. Deferential to men, especially to her tyrannical father, Julie embodied all the correct feminine attributes, as Rousseau saw them. Rousseau, much the philosopher of virtue, imposed on women the special burden of representing virtue in the family sphere. One of their principal tasks, in his view, was to instruct their children in the essentials of morality. The German philosopher Immanuel Kant (1724–1804), much influenced by Rousseau, concurred and saw women as uniquely qualified to be guardians of the ethical dimension of life.

The sexual ideology that saw the family as woman's destiny was reinforced by newly established medical opinion, which, at the dawn of the modern period, greatly exaggerated the differences between the sexes and represented women as physically weak and necessarily dependent on men. It was almost as if men and women were separate biological species, quite a contrast to the view that held sway a century earlier, in which male and female were variations on a common theme (although the masculine model was the defining one). Also a century earlier, the bourgeois nuclear family enclosing the wife and mother within domesticity was far from the norm. Philosophical and medical opinion had come to play supporting roles in a social revolution, one that enshrined the new model of family and rationalized the polar opposition of gender roles within it as "natural" in much the same way that late eighteenth-century political economists like Adam Smith had rationalized the capitalist economy as perfectly in keeping with an unchanging human nature.

But if there is one thing historians of the European family have established in recent years, it is that there is no one "natural" or inevitable pattern of family organization to be discerned in the past. Even the concept of childhood as a special period of life requiring particular kinds of parental nurture and educational strategies had been established only by the Enlightenment period (and as a result such ideas became part of the chorus of opinion urging mothers to sacrifice more of themselves to child rearing). The family itself as bastion of protectiveness against the harsh "outside" world, where a unique kind of domestic intimacy reigned and private feelings were shared with the understanding they were not to be broadcast beyond the home, was of recent vintage, just as was constructing homes with private bedrooms. Greater secrecy attached to physical intimacies of all kinds, increased privacy of basic bodily functions, and growing intolerance of the smells, sights, and sounds of others' exercise of those functions were all relatively new phenomena.

It was to this new institution, the discreet family sphere where private sentiment reigned, that new forms of artistic expression by a new type of artist were addressed. Romantic art, emphasizing powerful emotion made sublime by art, was perfectly suited to the new affective individualism nurtured by this emergent kind of family. Just as the family increasingly defined itself as a zone removed from the larger society, so the Romantic artist was self-defined as a lone creative force, of necessity acting beyond the codes and confines of established society. In many ways Romanticism created the idea of the artists as a bohemian, sexually unconventional, perhaps taking drugs, living as a kind of vagabond, claiming the right to an existence forbidden others.

But this in turn was related to a kind of artist as scapegoat, the suffering creative misunderstood genius, what French literature understood later as the *poète maudit,* the poet as cursed or damned by an uncomprehending society incapable of the degree of sensitivity necessary to empathize with the artist or to understand the creative product of his suffering. In its extreme form, this kind of artistic stance resulted in the simultaneous claim that one's work could not be comprehended except by those with sufficiently refined taste and the demand to receive more notice and recognition.

Yet Romantic artists were not uniformly aristocratic. For every aesthetic elitist there was a populist. One important strain of Romanticism was the effort to learn and preserve as much as possible of folk culture, which led to such activities as collecting the traditional ballads and tales found in the countryside. No matter where one looks, it is impossible to generalize about the politics of the Romantics. Some, such as the French writer Chateaubriand, espoused reactionary monarchist views, while other such as Percy Bysshe Shelley proclaimed the cause of the people rising up against their oppressors. Like the highly successful novelist Sir Walter Scott, one might dream of medieval glories, or, like Karl Marx, one's response to Romanticism might well be to denounce the indignities people suffered as a result of the emergent industrial economy. And just to show how the contradictory strands of Romanticism wound around each other, one of Marx's favorite writers was Scott.

Marx observed that the industrial division of labor was reproduced throughout society, and certainly the new social roles and categories for literature or art during the first decades of the nineteenth century seem to fit this pattern. An English literary and cultural critic named Raymond Williams pointed out in several studies that words like "culture," "art," and "literature," began to take on their modern highly specific and delimited meanings during the period from the late eighteenth century through the early nineteenth century, at the same time that "social" or "society" came to be used in the modern sense. Feminist historians and others working on social and cultural history topics have shown as well

that modern European culture brought about a highly exaggerated separation between public and private life. Whether such arguments imply
a preference for premodern culture or not, it must be said that even
though the Enlightenment project for human perfectibility based on
universal notions of rights and reason now addressed itself to a much
more complex and compartmentalized culture.

The literate members of that culture, growing in number, responded
to writers steeped in the Romantic spirit and working within newly
defined practices in publishing. These aspects of nineteenth-century
European culture are explored in the next chapter, the first of a series
of thematic explorations.

Chapter 2

The Growth of Literacy and the Popular Press in the Nineteenth Century

Early nineteenth-century Europe experienced profound changes in the nature of publishing, the status of literary genres, and even the act of reading itself. Literary scholarship in recent years has expanded beyond themes of celebrated authors and canonical texts to consider a "history of the book," including a consideration of the changing role of the book in Western culture. Such study teaches one not to take for granted any aspect of the nature of reading. For example, it has become apparent that silent, solitary reading was not always the norm. When literacy rates were low, it usually fell to those able to read to read aloud to others gathered around, a reminder of proximity to the oral tradition.

When it comes to common publishing practices, including standard treatment of authors, much of what has been taken for granted in the contemporary world actually emerged during the years from roughly 1790 to 1830. During this time, most Western nations adopted some type of copyright law. Authors also benefited from the growing trend of publishers paying them royalties, whereas previously they had been vulnerable to unscrupulous publishers who could pirate manuscripts and profit from publication that would not benefit the author monetarily, especially since the actual author's name was of negligible consequence unless it was already famous (in which case the publisher stood to benefit handsomely). During the eighteenth century it was not yet standard practice for authors to sign their works, so a publisher might say whatever he liked about a text's authorship.

Under the patronage system, there would be no particular reason for authors' names to be publicized, and aristocratic authors, by definition not dependent on literary activity for their livelihood, might have wished to avoid the "scandal" of subjecting their names to public scrutiny. For that matter, as long as the reading public was small and dominated by social elites, guessing the author of a new title was a favorite parlor game. Eighteenth-century *philosophes* were the first to try to support themselves through the sale of their writings, although even Denis Diderot (1713–1784), who lived the life of a literary "hack" for a time, eventually accepted the generous patronage of Tsar Catherine II. But by the early nineteenth century, as books began to circulate more widely and the reading public grew larger, and as publishing practices gave authors some guarantees, the expectation that their names would be clearly identified grew apace.

The New World of Publishing

Important economic and technological changes, accompanied by new structural changes in the world of book publishing, took hold as the market for published books, newspapers, and magazines expanded. These transformations were profound and long in developing, so that the world of publishing and the prominence of the printed word looked vastly different by the end of the nineteenth century. At the century's outset only a minority of the population was literate, but by the century's end it was a substantial majority. In between, most European nations adopted universal mandatory public education, and books and periodicals became affordable for the majority of the population.

The cost of printing dropped dramatically in the first part of the nineteenth century, and prohibitive duties on paper were removed, for example, in England by midcentury. Publishing houses were in a position to profit from this, for one significant change was an end to the separation of publisher and bookbinder. Previously, book publishers had bound only the least expensive editions, leaving it to bookbinders and private book dealers to arrange for the particular kind of binding preferred by their well-heeled customers. The historian Robert Darnton has described the intricate negotiations engaged in by a wealthy eighteenth-century reader who specified in great detail exactly the appearance he wanted for his personal editions of his most beloved author, Rousseau. By the mid-nineteenth century book publishers were able increasingly to offer less costly editions, concentrating their resources on one standard appearance per publication.

A number of British publishing houses pioneered in the introduction of low-cost editions for what was becoming a mass readership, particularly as the appetite grew for novels of all kinds. The "Railway Library" of novels published by Routledge and priced at a mere shilling apiece ran to well over one thousand volumes during its half-century run that ended in 1898. Even more affordable editions of literary classics became available later in the century from such publishers as H.G. Bohn and Cassell's, whose "Cassell's National Library" totaled more than two hundred volumes. These could be had for a price of threepence or sixpence, depending on whether one bought the title in paper or cloth. On the continent, German publishers in particular emulated these practices, as in the highly successful Reclams Universal-Bibliothek, a series beginning in 1867.

Nineteenth-Century Newspapers

A related change, one that affected the way books were sold, was in the nature and availability of newspapers. The eighteenth century saw the emergence of newspapers as important vehicles for the dissemination and formation of opinion, along with reports of current events. *Philosophes* had written quite consciously for the milieu of the coffee houses, where businessmen (indeed, gender-specific) met to smoke their pipes, consume the newly available and hugely popular stimulating beverage, and discuss the latest. The "newspapers" at their disposal were found uniquely in such establishments, usually in the form of brief broadsides containing a variety of public notices. The contemporary German philosopher Jürgen Habermas, an important influence on cultural historians, has emphasized the significance of this development in creating a "public sphere" that enables modern democratic debate and dialogue. The number of newspapers proliferated greatly during the last decade of the eighteenth century, especially in Paris during the Revolution.

Even after daily newspapers became more affordable and easily available for purchase one issue at a time, readers still did not necessarily retreat to the confines of their homes to peruse them. Cafés remained favorite spots for the leisurely reading of newspapers. One nineteenth-century paper, *L'Evénement,* targeted café habitués, as depicted by Paul Cézanne in his 1866 portrait of Louis-Auguste Cézanne. His subject sits in a café, reading *L'Evénement.* By 1866, one could purchase a paper from the nearest *kiosquier* before making one's way to the café of choice. But for the first half of the nineteenth century in France, newsstands or kiosks remained unknown. Nearly all sales of newspapers were in the form of individual subscriptions, priced out of reach of most individuals. Thus, to read newspapers one needed to frequent what were called *cabinets de lectures,* reading rooms

that charged a modest entry fee and offered access to the leading periodicals, typically with multiple subscriptions to the most popular
items. Here a visitor might have reached for *La Presse* or *Le Siècle,*
popular dailies founded in 1836. Both papers ran serialized novels (*romans-feuilletons*) on their first two pages, a practice that increased
newspaper sales through the growing popularity of novels, and one on
which novelists and their publishers came to depend.

This was the period in France of the July Monarchy, named for the
uprising of 1830 that drove Charles X from the throne and brought to
power Louis Philippe, the Duc d'Orléans, who presided over what was
to be a constitutional monarchy, complete with a legislature. But the
constitution continued to be postponed, and demands for reform were
frustrated. Although the danger of censorship always existed, opinion
critical of the regime could be found in many newspapers of the day. In
fact, most French newspapers were identified with particular political
stances, a tendency that has become more pronounced over time. Older
male readers were partial to *Le Constitutionnel,* while reform advocates
preferred *La Caricature* or *Le Charivari,* papers founded by Charles
Philipon (1806–1862).

Himself a journalist, lithographer, and caricaturist, Philipon hit upon
the idea of devoting an entire publication to caricature, including the art
of the political cartoon. Founded in 1830, *La Caricature* became the target of government suppression. Philipon's way of outwitting the censors
was to launch a series of new publications, each one offering an irreverent spirit and liberal political opinion. In 1835 he introduced the new
daily *Le Charivari,* featuring a fresh caricature each day. This influential
paper, a direct influence on the English publication *Punch,* provided a
forum for the greatest caricaturist of the century, Honoré Daumier
(1808–1879), who would make his mark as well as a Realist painter. Occasionally Daumier spoofed other newspapers or, more particularly, a
particularly gullible kind of reader who was easy prey for journalistic
sensationalism. *Le Constitutionnel* was a frequent target. In one Daumier
Charivari cartoon, an elderly couple are seated together by a lamp. The
woman knits, while the man, reading *Le Constitutionnel,* exclaims in terror that the newspaper reports the sighting of a sea monster. The humor
in the cartoon depends in part on an association between that particular
newspaper and elderly men. In another cartoon, Daumier depicted a
man who was so engrossed in his reading of *Le Constitutionnel* that he has
wandered off his woodland path and into ankle-deep water.

Daumier's biting satire became quite familiar to readers, as in his famous caricature of bloated, complacent legislators in *Le Ventre législatif*

("The Legislative Belly"). But when he pilloried the king himself with a most unflattering cartoon, Louis Philippe was apoplectic with rage, and the outcome, in 1832, was a six-month prison sentence for Daumier. The king was known popularly as *Le Poire* ("The Pear"; the slang term also connotes dull-witted stupidity), a comment on his rather distinctive body shape. Philipon had been the first to lampoon the Orléanist king in this graphic way, and he encouraged other caricaturists to adopt the practice. Daumier's deliberately grotesque version incurred the royal wrath like no other.

Censorship remained a much greater threat in a monarchy, and generally speaking Continental countries were more restrictive than Great Britain. But even so censorship lessened by midcentury, and this factor along with the growth of a literate market for newspapers was behind the establishment of a number of prominent European newspapers, including *Le Figaro* (1854) in France, *Die Frankfurter Allgemeine Zeitung* (1856) in Germany, and the *Corriere della Sera* (1876) in Italy. And even where censorship was greater, a writer's fear of prosecution often was outweighed by the advantage of favorable publicity owing to a signed newspaper article. A French law adopted in 1850 required writers to sign such articles.

A new era dawned in French newspaper publishing in 1863 with the appearance of *Le Petit Journal,* the first daily to be made available throughout France in quantity, bearing the attractive price of one sou (five centimes). Like *La Presse,* it carried serialized fiction and stories, and soon had its imitators throughout the country. The new papers targeted rural readers and not just Parisians, featuring stories that would entertain the former. The combination of this emphasis and the use of *romans-feuilletons* sounded the death knell for the long-standing book-peddling trade that had flourished especially in the countryside. This Europe-wide enterprise, called *colportage* in France, had long been a means of getting relatively inexpensive books and periodicals into the hands of rural people.

A typical book peddler's (*colporteur*) stock included religious tracts, primers, some works by classical authors, and some of the novels most in demand. When Paris newspapers, for example, began publishing novels in installments, it posed no immediate threat to the *colporteurs,* since theirs was not an urban clientele. But with the advent of newspapers like *Le Petit Journal* appearing in all parts of the country, *colporteurs* no longer had a unique service to provide. In areas without bookstores or lending libraries, they had been the only recourse for isolated readers. Now, however, they were shouldered aside by the hot-off-the-presses latest novels available in inexpensive newspaper form.

The Role of Magazines

Nineteenth-century magazines employed some of the same strategies that newspapers did to gain readership, such as serialization of novels. One innovation that was to prove immensely popular was the use of illustrations (and eventually, to be sure, photographs). The first magazine to experience a dramatic increase in sales as a result of profuse illustrations was *The Illustrated London News,* which made its debut in 1842. Eventually this weekly would employ artists to make on-site drawings as a form of reporting the news. Its success spawned imitators, including the popular monthly *English Illustrated Magazine.* Magazine publishers in other countries followed suit with *L'Illustration* (France), *Die Woche* (Germany), and *Harper's Weekly* (the United States).

Literary magazines and reviews were important to the careers of nineteenth-century writers. The British Isles boasted a significant number of such magazines. Edinburgh was home to several, including the *Edinburgh Review* (founded in 1802), the *Quarterly Review* (1809), and *Blackwood's Edinburgh Magazine.* The latter, founded in 1817, enjoyed a run that lasted until 1981. London was home to *London Magazine* (1820), *The Examiner* (1808), *Bentley's Miscellany* (founded in 1837 with Charles Dickens [1812–1870] as its first editor, *Oliver Twist* running there in serial form), and *Cornhill Magazine.* This last, whose astonishing success included being the first literary periodical to attain a circulation of 100,000, was founded in 1860 with novelist William Makepeace Thackeray (1811–1863) as its first editor. Science and politics were subjects of successful magazines. *Nature* (1869) served to popularize scientific ideas, and its contributors included Charles Darwin and Thomas Huxley. With its clever illustrations, the satirical weekly *Punch* (1841) became an institution in British political life.

On the Continent, writers faced greater threat of censorship, and so serious magazines steered relatively clear of political commentary. Noteworthy French magazines of a literary bent included *Revue des Deux Mondes* (1829), which published such writers as Victor Hugo (1802–1885) and the eminent critic Charles-Augustin Sainte-Beuve (1804–1869), and *Revue de Paris,* a competing review that published Gustave Flaubert (1821–1880). *Die Literarisches Wochenblatt* was a successful weekly German literary magazine founded in 1820. Politically to the right and left of it came, respectively, *Deutsche Rundschau* (1874) and *Die Freie Bühne* (1890). The latter two appeared after German unification had been achieved. Italian reviews of similar prominence, emerging during and after that country's unification, were *Nuova Antologia* (1866) and *La Cultura* (1881).

Women readers provided an important market for magazines. Newspapers had established an association with public life, but that realm was coded increasingly as "masculine," the more domesticity was imposed on women. Women's magazines of the nineteenth century addressed a public assumed to occupy a private domestic realm, in need of advice on household matters or child rearing, and eager for literary diversion and entertainment. Magazines treating such topics existed earlier in the century, but the first truly inexpensive woman's magazine to attain a mass market was *The Englishwoman's Domestic Magazine,* a monthly that appeared in 1852. This publication placed primary emphasis on instructing women in the domestic arts, such as dressmaking. Not long thereafter in England, fashion became a major theme of women's magazines, as with two that first appeared in 1875, *Myra's Journal of Dress and Fashion* and *Weldon's Ladies Journal.*

London was taking its cues from Paris in this case. The first French publications devoted to feminine fashion had begun to appear by the end of the previous century. In 1825, the *Journal des Dames* debuted as a showplace for *haute couture. La Mode* (1829) introduced the widely imitated practice of publishing literary works in addition to reporting on fashion. Honoré de Balzac (1799–1850), Eugène Sue (1804–1857), and Victor Hugo (1802–1885) were among the prominent authors whose works appeared in its pages. The list of additional women's fashion magazines is long, but no publication could boast a more substantial subscription base than *Le Moniteur de la Mode* (1843). By the time it folded in 1913, it claimed some two hundred thousand subscribers and was published in eight foreign-language editions, including one in the United States.

The Novel as Dominant Genre

One of the most decisive cultural transformations assisted by the popularity of the new newspapers and magazines was the establishment of the novel as the principal literary genre for readers of every taste. This was the culmination of a process that had been under way for a century, beginning in the mid-eighteenth century. At that point, novels were gaining popularity but enjoyed little critical acceptance. Established literary opinion, especially as enunciated by the Académie Française, held that the novel was a debased form that in no way approached lyric poetry or verse drama in aesthetic quality, and of course not at all in moral or didactic properties. Eighteenth-century aristocrats may have indulged a taste for novels in secret, but they were not about to accord official sanction to a literary form that, because it portrayed a less-than-ideal world through an emphasis on characters of modest social station (or worse), was held to be devoid of uplifting value.

By the following century the aristocratic objection had become increasingly irrelevant, and readers seldom felt compelled to apologize for their taste for novels. Not that some worries did not remain, including the fear that a steady diet of novels amounted to an escapist avoidance of the real world and misled impressionable (especially young and especially female) minds, feeding fantasies and creating unrealistic expectations of life. Some expressed worries that almost seem to prefigure more recent warnings about substituting television viewing for a more immediate experience of life. This was at least one of the themes of Gustave Flaubert's novel *Madame Bovary*. Despite having been written at a time when apologies no longer needed to be made for the genre, it was in part a story of a young woman whose disillusioned outlook stemmed from excessive consumption of novels.

Popularity remained the most salient justification for the novel's central role in European letters, and the *roman-feuilleton* and its equivalent in the popular press of other countries made writers of novels by far the most (commercially) successful writers of the nineteenth century. In France, no novelist enjoyed more dominance than Honoré de Balzac. He wrote ninety-one novels or novellas during a relatively short career, and the *roman-feuilleton* was both blessing and a curse: a blessing because it fed his popularity and increased sales of his books, and a curse because his prodigious debts and the many manuscripts he promised publishers required him to adhere to an absurdly arduous daily regimen of writing that ruined his health and shortened his life.

Balzac was a founding figure of literary realism, a movement that had its counterpart in the visual arts (see chapter 5). In his imposing collection of novels under the title *La Comédie humaine* ("The Human Comedy"), he populated a world with a vast array of characters. As would be true of Charles Dickens in England, it was a world the reader seemingly could enter, one whose inhabitants seemed at least as real, if not more so, than those who made up one's own world. The habit of publishing novels in segments in newspapers may further have blurred the line between fiction and nonfiction, between reporting and fictional narrative.

The realist writer was someone able to use fictional description of a most recognizable social world to call attention to societal ills and injustices, much like an investigative reporter. Historians generally credit the early novels of Dickens with helping to spur Victorian reform efforts. Not a few readers responded to writers of *romans-feuilletons* as readers of a later era might have responded to a "muckraking" investigative journalist. The French novelist who most played such a role for the newspaper-reading public in the early nineteenth century was Eugène Sue. He painted melodramatic scenes sympathetic to the urban poor of Paris, in a sentimental style that made him popular with readers of his day, but consigned him to oblivion as far as later critical opinion and literary history were concerned. His novels *Les Mystères de Paris* (1842–43, *The Mysteries of Paris*) and *Le Juif errant* (1844–45, *The Wandering Jew*) were published as *romans-feuilletons* in the newspaper *Le Journal des Débats,* where legislative sessions received full coverage. Each of the 150 episodes of *Les Mystères de Paris* closed with the promise *"La suite au prochain numéro"* ("to be continued in the next number"), the method many newspapers used to keep readers eager for the next installment, and thus to guarantee continued sales.

The public that eagerly awaited the latest offering from Eugène Sue likewise supported George Sand (1804–1876)—the nom de plume of Aurore Dupin, a writer of Realist novels informed by a Romantic spirit, and one also imbued with string sympathy for workers, peasants, and the poor. A writer of the late Restoration and July Monarchy periods whose sentimental, sensational style was especially suited to serial publication in newspapers was Paul de Kock (1793–1871), whose cleverly plotted novels verged on the pornographic, so that some worried about the effect such literature could have on impressionable young minds. A popular cartoonist known as Cham depicted a mother horrified to find her daughter reading Paul de Kock. Expressing her shock in the caption of the cartoon, she hears her daughter respond by protesting that she needs to find "instruction" and that she is learning some things she did not already know about (the mother's fear, exactly).

Adventure stories were also quite popular. The wildly successful novels *Le Comte de Monte Cristo* (1844–45, *The Count of Monte Cristo*) and *Les Trois mousquetaires* (1844, *The Three Musketeers*) by Alexandre Dumas *père* (1802–1870) first made their impact as *romans-feuilletons.* By later in the century, the futuristic fantasies of Jules Verne (1820–1895) would captivate readers in a similar way. Already in the nineteenth century, America loomed as a source of exciting adventure stories. German readers especially gravitated toward the fiction of James Fenimore Cooper (1789–1851). As did readers everywhere in the Western world, German readers also avidly consumed the historical novels of the English writer Walter Scott (1771–1832).

English Women
as Authors and Readers

Some of the most admired English writers of the nineteenthth century were women, and their success also was related to the popular press. The currently much-esteemed novels of Jane Austen (1776–1817) and the Brontë sisters preceded the boom in newspaper and magazine publication that helped later writers gain exposure. One such writer was Elizabeth Gaskell (1810–1865), known in part for her close friendship with Charlotte Brontë (1816–1855), whose literary reputation she helped establish, albeit posthumously. Known for novels that portrayed the desperate condition of the poor in England, Gaskell's first publication, "Sketches Among the Poor," appeared in 1837 in *Blackwood's Edinburgh Magazine.* She went on to publish two of her novels and some short fiction in *Howitt's Journal* but found her widest audience in *Household Journal,* to which Dickens asked her to contribute. Mary Ann Evans, better known to the world as George Eliot (1819–1880), did not publish such acclaimed novels as *Middlemarch* or *Adam Bede* in serial form, but her early work did appear in literary magazines. *Scenes of Clerical Life,* the first work she signed with her famous pseudonym, was published initially in *Blackwood's Edinburgh Magazine.* Late in life she also contributed to *Cornhill Magazine.*

The place of the novel in European literature, including the distinction achieved by women as novelists, was closely linked to woman's role in society, a society that decreed woman's proper sphere to be the domestic one. Her role, epitomized by the Victorian "angel of the hearth," was to nurture her family and provide a proper haven for moral instruction. Women novelists typically depicted domestic scenes and skillfully described complex interactions among principal characters. This, after all, is what women were socialized to do—to be extremely attentive to the moods and demands of those around them, able to react to the slightest nuance. The nineteenth century was one that brought about a sharp distinction between the public and the private, two realms seen as gender exclusive. Not only did novels portray this reality, the very act of reading novels, typically carried out within closed domestic space, manifested the interiority of woman's assigned role. If man was fated to act and to shape reality, woman was fated to adapt to his actions and to observe, without expectation of similar power of agency. Thus went the sexual ideology of the day.

In an era when access to education was extremely limited for women, the reading of novels was viewed as an appropriate outlet for those who were intellectually curious. By the end of the century, when the first women's colleges were established, the study of literature, the domain within which the novel had established its dominance, was seen as highly appropriate for young women, both to cultivate appreciation for literary refinement and to enhance the understanding a woman needed of human character and behavior. And, as was openly acknowledged, reading might elevate and make more agreeable the conversation of a wife, the status that was held to be the ultimate goal of all young women.

The Novel and Time

One further way in which the cultural prominence of novels may seem symptomatic of nineteenth-century European culture is in that century's preoccupation with time. Politically, Europeans were preoccupied with chronological processes of national development. Industrial labor processes insisted on schedules and punctuality. New sciences of geology and evolutionary biology challenged age-old conceptions of elapsed time. Dramatic improvements in technology and transportation made time an ever more urgent concern. As opposed to poetry or classical theater, where actions were circumscribed by the Aristotelian requirement of twenty-four hours' duration, the novel allowed for the steady accretion of many episodes, and for patient development of character and plot worked out over the period of a lifetime or several lifetimes. Consciousness of the long, slow, relentless workings of chronology made possible appreciation of the novel, just as it heightened a new awareness of historical time. It is most appropriate that the culture shaped by these tendencies should have given rise to modern historical study, one of the principal themes of the next chapter.

Suggestions for Further Reading

Barker, Hannah. *Newspapers, Politics, and English Society, 1695–1855*. New York: Longman, 2000.

Chartier, Roger, ed. *The Culture of Print: Power and Uses of Print in Early Modern Europe*. Trans. Lydia G. Cochrane. Princeton, NJ: Princeton University Press, 1989.

de la Motte, Dean, and Jeannene M. Przyblyski, eds. *Making the News: Modernity and the Mass Press in Nineteenth-Century France*. Amherst: University of Massachusetts Press, 1999.

Gilbert, Sandra M., and Susan Gubar. The Madwoman in the Attic: The Woman Writer and the Nineteenth-Century Literary Imagination. New Haven: Yale University Press, 1979.

Chapter 3

The Reorganization of Knowledge
and the Human Sciences

The period from roughly the last quarter of the eighteenth century through the first quarter of the nineteenth century, one of tremendous growth and consolidation of the industrial capitalist economy, created not only more pronounced division of labor in the workplace but also produced sharper delineations in the cultural sphere among the various arts as well as an intellectual "division of labor" that grew to exaggerate the isolation of areas of human knowledge. Throughout the nineteenth century, the various fields or disciplines came to be organized professionally, most often in relation to the evolution of the modern university. The era of the polymath—the learned individual conversant with a wide range of intellectual and cultural pursuits—was on the wane and greater specialization, marked by specific disciplinary terminologies and taxonomies as well as by distinctive forms of professional identification, was part of the elaborate process of transformation seen throughout economic and social life.

Beginning with the "new" discipline of history in the 1840s, the "human sciences," as they have been known in Europe (including linguistics, history, sociology, anthropology, psychology), constituted themselves with the goal of studying and describing "man" in the various spheres and categories not covered by biological science or medicine. From the outset, the new disciplines sought to claim a "scientific" foundation for themselves. This desire grew stronger as the cultural prestige of science rose, but the belief that the study of humanity could attain the level of science had roots in the previous century, when the jurist and philosopher Giambattista Vico (1688–1744) argued in his *La Nouva scienza* (*The New Science*) that human beings could understand and interpret society accurately because they had fashioned it. And Immanuel Kant had envisioned what he called a "social physics" that would be as capable of describing culture as the physical sciences were of describing nature.

One of the most profound and influential efforts to understand the cultural shift that brought about such an emphasis was made by Michel Foucault (1926–1984) in his 1966 book *Les Mots et les choses: Une archéologie des sciences humaines* (*The Order of Things: An Archaeology of the Human Sciences*). He called his book an "archaeology" because his method was to examine the period during which the human sciences emerged in archaeological, spatial terms, that is, to try to show where the new disciplines fit in the new order of things and what role they played in the changed worldview that made their status possible. The most important foundation of all, Foucault argued, was a preoccupation with "man" that was neither inevitable in Western history nor destined to reign forever as the given of our worldview. In fact, it had a specific history, beginning with Renaissance humanism, and was related to a major change in the way language was regarded. Language had come to designate "things" in the same way that oil painting made possible dramatically accurate depiction of three-dimensional objects on a single plane. Previously, however, language had been a separate activity, intervening in the world and operating according to its own rhetorical procedures, competing with rather than objectively representing the phenomena one assumes (if one inhabits the mind-set Foucault attempts to dissect) it must serve.

The modern human sciences take for granted that language is a neutral set of tools available for describing, naming, and classifying the objects of their respective studies. They are not necessary intellectual enterprises in accordance with the operations and capabilities of the human brain, but contingent ones, with specific histories and important links to other cultural processes. They are not unaffected by economic and political developments and agendas, but take their places at specific sites in a complex social system within which their pronouncements perform significant tasks that have much to do with power. In Foucault's definition (formulated in his later work), power both affirms and denies, supports and excludes. Each of the human sciences developed its own set of objects and phenomena (Foucault went so far as to argue they "produced" the realities they pretended to analyze) that constituted its raison d'être but also defined itself by what was excluded from its field of vision.

The Early History of "History"

Foucault's analysis focused on comparative linguistics, political economy, and morphology, but his interpretive scheme can be a useful one to apply to the discipline of history, in some sense the founding human science. But although "history," in the sense of knowledge about the past, is as old as humanity, the professional activity known by that name did not emerge until the 1840s, in a time and place (Prussia) that had everything to do with the great political drama of national unification. The location was the University of Berlin, the leading educational institution in the Kingdom of Prussia, and the driving force was Leopold von Ranke (1795–1886), who founded the first historical seminar. Under his direction, historical scholarship was defined in a modern form that distinguished it from its predecessor, philology. From the outset, history as a discipline was defined both by what it offered and by what it excluded.

Ranke (the aristocratic "von" was bestowed in 1865) was an extremely prolific researcher whose books ranged from ancient Roman history, to Reformation-era Germany, to studies of modern European nations, including England. An ardent Prussian nationalist (although not ardent enough for many in his country), he assumed the nation-state to be an essential organizing principle for the study of history, and he had imbibed the German idealist tradition in philosophy that reached full flower in the thought of another great Prussian nationalist, G. W. F. Hegel (1770–1831). Like his eighteenth-century predecessor the philosopher Johann G. Herder (1744–1806), Ranke assumed that the nation must always be defined in terms of a particular individual character, ethnic (Herder's view) or otherwise. In fact, for Ranke the appropriate topics for historical research were individual people, national groups, and specific time periods. Even though he himself ranged widely over a broad sweep of history, each specific book was an exercise in intensive examination of each period. He encouraged his own students to limit their studies to manageable spans of time.

The twin keys to historical professionalism were immersion in the archives and the closely related historical seminar. These became fixtures for advanced historical study at leading universities throughout the world. Ranke's seminars were to serve as models for generations of historians. Ranke placed heavy emphasis on archival research and enjoyed unprecedented access to state documents and papers. He would secure a trove of these for his seminar and set students to work poring over them. The goal of such research, Ranke asserted, was to devote sufficient attention to the minutiae of the past to be able to know it *"wie es eigentlich gewesen"*—"as it actually happened." The paramount goal was objectivity: to describe what one discovers as a historian dispassionately and judiciously. From the viewpoint of contemporary historical study, this was not an effort to present the past in all its aspects. Nearly exclusive emphasis was placed on political and diplomatic history, which of course tended to be the subject of those documents deemed worthy of preservation.

Limiting historical study to politics, diplomacy, and warfare excluded from legitimacy topics dealing with families, social life, customs, popular entertainments and diversions, and details of everyday life, all of which had been the province of amateur historians, particularly during the eighteenth and early nineteenth centuries. Many of these "amateurs" had been women, often privileged women of intellectual curiosity and the means to devote themselves to research and writing. A major example had been the Swiss-born French writer Germaine de Staël (1766–1817), who was keenly interested in what would be recognized today as sociology of literature: literature understood in relation to the society and culture around it. Excluding such topics from legitimate historical research had the effect of excluding women from the profession, whether that was consciously motivated or not. Certainly no female faces were to be found around Ranke's seminar table. What one now realizes is that the current interest in social and cultural history actually represents a return to an older emphasis in historical scholarship. What Ranke set in motion could now be seen as a kind of detour, and the exclusive emphasis on national political histories as a product of nineteenth-century fascination with nationalism and national unification efforts.

France was home to some major figures in nineteenth-century historical scholarship, not unrelated to the turbulent history of which the dates 1830, 1848, and 1871 remind us. Perhaps the greatest of all French historians was Jules Michelet (1798–1874), who like Ranke explored a vast number of historical topics and filled many shelves with the books he produced throughout a very hectic life. Unlike Ranke, he made no fetish of objectivity but trained the full force of his charismatic personality on the topics of his research. Fervently anticlerical and politically progressive, Michelet ran afoul of the authorities under the July Monarchy, losing his chair at the Collège de France, only to regain it with the Revolution of 1848. His official prominence ended, however, when he refused to take the oath of allegiance to Napoleon III in 1852.

Michelet was inspired by the Revolution of 1789, one of the many historical topics to which he devoted his labors (a seven-volume history, in this case). The older he became the more he embraced a belief in *le peuple* ("the people"), the title of one of his books (1846). Taking advantage of the access to archives he enjoyed during those periods when he enjoyed official favor, he embarked on his *Histoire de France,* which, by its culmination in 1867, would total eleven volumes, covering France from earliest times to the eve of the Revolution. Giving full rein to his emotional nature, he described himself as being overcome by the voices calling to him to tell their story. Michelet believed emphatically that the historian should hold back nothing of his personality and desire to commune with the past, which he restores through an imaginative process of reconstruction. In his last years, working closely with his wife, Michelet embarked on a series of unusual, highly poetic studies of the natural world and on women.

Whereas German historians led the way in establishing the distinct nature of the profession, in ways to be emulated both in England and the United States, French historical scholarship in the nineteenth century remained closer to literary and philological fields. Literature as a topic for historical study was the speciality of Hippolyte Taine (1828–1893), who until relatively late in his life worked independently of any academic institution. In sharp contrast to Michelet, Taine sought to avoid emotionalism and speculation, which he associated with the "Eclectic" school of philosophers who held sway during his student days in Paris. Taine wished to apply Positivist principles to the study of cultural history, epitomized by his four-volume work *Histoire de la littérature anglaise* (1863–64). In it Taine argued that a writer must be considered in relation to the three-part scheme of *race* (his ethnicity), *milieu* (his cultural environment), and *moment* (the particular historical juncture at which he operates). Taine was a far more pessimistic interpreter of French history than Michelet. Although like Michelet, he was deeply saddened by the French defeat by Prussia in 1870, he placed the blame on a deficiency bred in French political life especially by the legacy of the Revolution, which he argued had instilled even greater bureaucratic rigidity and centralization in French life than had the old regime. This argument runs through his six-volume *Les Origines de la France contemporaine* (1876–1893).

The methods of philology, the science of verifying and interpreting ancient texts that preceded the establishment of history as a discipline, were kept alive by Ernest Renan (1823–1892), another very complicated and intriguing nineteenth-century French intellectual. Like Taine, Renan was impressed by Positivist ideas and in fact sought to apply them to his particular area of interest, the history of ancient religions. A religious skeptic whose political ideals were closer to Taine's pessimistic conservatism than to Michelet's populist idealism (although identifiable with neither position), Renan was able to attain an appointment to the Collège de France despite the shock waves produced in clerical circles by his monumental *Vie de Jésus* (1863, *Life of Jesus*). In this work, Renan applied his exceptional knowledge of biblical languages to a critical, historically accurate biography of Jesus. The offense, of course, was in treating what many regarded as a divine figure as a mortal historical character. Renan remains an extremely compelling example of the conflicted bourgeois intellectual, eager to define an alternative to an increasingly weakened theological claims on human knowledge and understanding. Intentionally or not, history as a discipline had contributed to the marginalization of those claims.

The same could be said of the emergent disciplines of sociology and anthropology, two human sciences that developed much in tandem. In fact, for some decades it was difficult to find a clear line of demarcation between them, especially before fieldwork became standard practice in anthropology. As human sciences they also shared a strong need to establish themselves as scientific pursuits, seeking energetically to define methods of study and interpretation that would adhere as closely as possible to scientific method.

Early Sociology

The very concept of "sociology" as a science of society implies a highly developed degree of abstraction that is symptomatic of the growing separation of modern cultural life into isolated spheres to be designated "society," "economy," "art," and so on. The very idea of establishing a means of obtaining reliable knowledge about the workings of human society owes much to Enlightenment thought, including Vico's demand that intellectuals seek to understand human society as thoroughly as scientists have the natural world. Indeed, the French philosopher Auguste Comte (1797–1850), who coined the term "sociology," was the intellectual heir of such *philosophes* as Condorcet and, more immediately, to the Utopian thinker Saint-Simon. Comte is remembered more for his philosophy called "Positivism," (See chapter 4) developed in his six-volume work *Cours de philosophie positive* (1830–1842, *The Positive Philosophy of Auguste Comte*). Comte viewed the sciences as a hierarchy, resting on the foundation of mathematics, the most reliable but the narrowest in scope of them all. Ascending the hierarchy, the succeeding sciences grew more complex and ambitious (although more divorced from mathematical certainties). Atop them all sat sociology, queen of all the sciences in Comte's view, for its aim was knowledge of all aspects (including both "static" and "dynamic," in his terminology) of human social experience, which must be understood to contain all that biology and the other sciences seek to know. Although most subsequent sociologists have coveted the label of science for their discipline, no one has sought to justify that designation more elaborately than Comte.

Comte was not the only sociological theorist to seek to borrow the growing prestige of science for the new field. The British philosopher Herbert Spencer (1820–1903) famously applied Darwinian evolutionary theory to society. In fact, it was he (in his 1864 book *Principles of Biology*) and not Darwin who first used the phrase "survival of the fittest." Spencer began a series of works under the collective title *Descriptive Sociology* in 1873, but the complete series would remain unpublished until many years after his death. But even this was only a small part of his overall project, for he was every bit as intellectually ambitious as Comte. And even more than Comte, he took an "organic" view of society, likening its operations to those of the natural world, both in static and evolutionary terms. But whereas for Comte sociology reigned over other sciences, Spencer envisioned what he called the "synthetic philosophy," a vast array of fields of knowledge that would include biology, psychology (he began his series *Principles of Psychology* in 1855), and philosophy.

The person whose ideas were to prove most immediately useful for sociologists was Émile Durkheim (1858–1917), who exerted a profound influence on an entire generation of French intellectuals through his teaching at the Sorbonne as well as through his influential books. Far more unassuming than intellectual predecessors such as Comte or Spencer, Durkheim approached sociology through a combination of philosophical speculation and empirical study. He authored a general guide to sociological research called *Les Règles de la méthode sociologique* (1895, *The Rules of Sociological Method*) and founded the important journal *L'Année sociologique* in 1896. For the most part, however, Durkheim addressed specific social and cultural problems in his studies.

Quite unlike Comte and Spencer, Durkheim had reservations about the bright promise claimed for science and technology. In two very important and original works he took the pulse of contemporary culture and found the patient ailing. In *De la division du travail social* (1893, *The Division of Labor in Society*) he described the threat to existing social structures, ethics, and morality of a labor process that threatened community among workers and kept persons isolated from one another.

Durkheim's analysis was reminiscent in some ways of Marx's critique of industrial capitalism (see chapter 5), but he added a new concept he called *anomie* to describe the sense of rootlessness and disorientation being produced by modern social existence, as traditional social structures broke down without being followed by satisfying replacements. This could lead to feelings of such extreme estrangement that suicide, the subject of his 1897 book *Le Suicide,* could be the result.

Although he did no fieldwork of his own, Durkheim was fascinated by ethnography and incorporated research on totemism and other traditional practices of aboriginal peoples in his last great work, *Les Formes élémentaires de la vie religieuse* (1915, *The Elementary Forms of the Religious Life*). It was a founding text of modern religious studies by an agnostic writer, although one deeply respectful of religious observance. Durkheim was a highly principled man who endured severe criticism at times in his life and as a Jew experienced vicious anti-Semitism, especially at the height of the Dreyfus affair (see chapter 6). Then, during World War I, his cosmopolitan outlook (including familiarity with German language and interest in German thought) and his Alsatian origins led some detractors to accuse him of disloyalty to France. This pained him in the extreme, especially as he lost his only son, who died fighting for France in 1916. His own death came not long thereafter. Durkheim's students were devoted to him and to his memory, and a number of them were in the front ranks of French sociology and ethnography in later decades.

The wide-ranging researches and ideas of Max Weber (1864–1920) exerted a profound influence on the establishment of sociology in Germany. Weber began a promising academic career first at the University of Berlin, then at the University of Freiburg, and finally at the University of Heidelberg. While illness forced him to resign his position at Heidelberg, a substantial inheritance that came his way in 1907 afforded him the financial independence to continue his work without university affiliation. He threw himself into the editorship of a journal he started called *Archiv für Sozialwissenschaft und Sozialpolitik* (*Archives for Social Science and Social Politics*), in which he published his influential and controversial study *Die protestantische Ethik und der Geist des Kapitalismus* (1904–5, *The Protestant Ethic and the Spirit of Capitalism*).

This study, in which Weber was wrestling with his own Protestant upbringing, was an intervention in cultural history that argued for a link between the rise of modern capitalism and the Protestant faiths that explicitly gave their blessings to the accumulation of wealth, as long as it was justified by a "worldly asceticism" that forbade hedonistic indulgence. Not only was this a founding text for the sociology of religion, but it launched a historiographical debate that continued for many years, especially among Reformation historians. Like Durkheim, Weber was concerned with ways to define the social phenomena that were emerging in the place that religion had occupied for so long. In such works as *Wirtschaft und Gesellschaft* (1922, *Economy and Society*), he explained that bureaucracy along with a kind of abstracted "rationalization" were becoming the driving forces of modern society. Weber also was the first to use the word "charisma" to identify a kind of aura created in part by publicity that surrounds certain modern leaders, one that seems to be a substitute for older religious cultural motifs. In a way that might seem prophetic in light of later German history, Weber developed this idea in relation to his studies on authority in modern society.

Weber's interest in the traditional role of religion in society was by no means limited to Western civilization, and he became a devoted student of Indian and Chinese civilization. His respect for religions of the world, despite his own freethinking views, was similar to the position of Durkheim. He also shared that French thinker's ethical stand against jingoism and militarism, and incurred the wrath of many Germans when he criticized his country's military ambitions during World War I. And of course both he and Durkheim had attempted to characterize what of social value was lost in the process of modernization.

Although his overall sociological work did not make as substantial a contribution as that of Durkheim or Weber, the German sociologist Ferdinand Tönnies (1855–1936) offered two terms precisely to express this loss that have remained enormously influential in social and cultural studies. The term Tönnies proposed for an older, more organic human community based on solidarity and traditional patterns was *Gemeinschaft*. What had replaced it, he argued, was a new artificial form of social organization, characterized by rational self-interest, that he called *Gesellschaft*. Although he did not use the term, this concept would seem to complement Durkheim's notion of anomie. The modern world, in either case, does not seem "like home."

Sharing in large part the cultural pessimism of Tönnies, Georg Simmel (1858–1918) was an extremely prolific writer and social theorist whose ideas were by no means limited to the field of sociology. A charismatic lecturer whose influence on European thought was to be largely posthumous, Simmel was based in Berlin, where he remained a *Privatdozent* (a lecturer dependent on student fees he had to solicit himself). His failure to obtain a genuine academic position was glaring in the face of the admiration that came his way from contemporary intellectual figures (including, notably, Weber), although at least his financial circumstances made it bearable. Simmel rejected the "organicism" of Comte and Spencer, arguing forcefully that society was no way analogous to nature. Society for him was to be understood as an intricate web of the many relations obtaining among its members, but no "total" attempt to theorize its whole could be successful or desirable. In this, Simmel may now seem like a "postmodernist" *avant la lettre.*

Simmel's ideas ranged widely over a number of topics, and he was an interpreter of Kant and Nietzsche as well as a close friend of the poets Rainer Maria Rilke and Stefan George. (See chapter 6.) One of his most influential works has been his complicated *Die Philosophie des Geldes* (1900, *The Philosophy of Money*), a book with a most misleading title, since, for Simmel, money is far more than a means of exchange. Simmel was interested in the social aspect of money changing hands. In addition, he meant something different from Marx's idea of the "cash nexus" that money creates in place of traditional social relations. What mattered most to Simmel was money's central role in creating an overly rational (here he was close to Weber) impersonal kind of society.

The Foundations of Modern Anthropology

In addition to the factors already described that gave rise to the human sciences, two in particular provided impetus for the new human science of anthropology, a word that meant the study of *anthropos*—"man," the human species. One development that spurred on the would-be science of anthropology was the discovery, beginning early in the nineteenth century, of the fossilized remains of various early ancestors of modern *Homo sapiens.* As the collection and study of these artifacts unfolded at roughly the same time that Europeans were intruding on the far corners of the earth where people they deemed inferior lived, a version of anthropology called "physical anthropology" held sway and was used often to support various racial theories. (See chapter 5.) The colonial conquest that made possible encounters with living humans their observers viewed through the lens of an evolutionary racial hierarchy was this second development.

In practical terms, European incursions into territories where previously unobserved human communities dwelled potentially made possible the fieldwork that became obligatory for ethnography (i.e., writing about the various ethnic groups among whom observers lived for a sufficient time). At first, however, anthropological theorists were by no means schooled in the field. Most early anthropologists, whether they were physical anthropologists or not, were evolutionists, tending to see the remote human communities that interested them as examples of earlier evolutionary stages. Paul Broca (1824–1880) was a leading French physical anthropologist, devoted primarily to the study of the brain, samples of which he collected and dissected. Attempting to draw conclusions about human types based on the structure and size of preserved brains was closely related to anthropometry and other pseudosciences that played major roles in the formulation of racial theory. (See chapter 4.)

Anthropologists figured at the center of a cultural debate that pitted "monogenecists" against "pangenecists." Monogenecism was the theory, persuasive to many religious believers, that one unique human type was created, whereas polygenecism held that several were to be found. Such a view lent itself easily to racial hierarchies. As evolutionary theory gained ground with the spread of Darwin's and Alfred Russell Wallace's theory of natural selection (see chapter 4), the terms of the debate were redrawn. Suffice it to say that anthropologists lined up in the evolutionist camp. They applied these views in various ways to earlier stages of human history. For example, the Swiss legal theorist and historian Johannes Bachofen (1815–1887) argued that the study of ancient myths could be used to demonstrate the existence of a first stage in human development marked by group marriage. This later was overthrown in favor of matriarchal rule and families based on matrilineal descent, which was in turn defeated by the establishment of patriarchal rule and monogamous marriage. The American Lewis Henry Morgan (1818–1881) elaborated these ideas more extensively in light of his research on native North American peoples. The most influential work in this same interpretive tradition was *The Origin of the Family, Private Property, and the State* (1884) by Friedrich Engels (1820–1895), who was inspired directly by Morgan and worked on this topic in the years following the death of his intellectual partner Karl Marx.

Feminist scholarship in recent anthropology has revived these questions and elaborated these interpretations further. Probably the most influential contribution for later anthropologists to emerge from the ranks of the evolutionists was the concept of "culture" argued by Edward Burnett Tylor (1832–1917), a British archaeologist who chose his profession and became a committed Darwinist as a result of an 1855 voyage to the West Indies and Mexico. There he became fascinated by pre-Columbian civilization, and developed his ideas into a work published ten years later called *Researches Into the Early History of Mankind and the Development of Civilization*.

Tylor believed strongly in the mental unity of the human species, past and present, and regardless of race. This was a bold claim to make in its time. His definition of culture, announced in volume 2 of his *Primitive Culture* in 1871, was similarly inclusive, taking in the full range of human activity, from the everyday to the most exalted expressions of art and ideas. This view of culture has been the basis for cultural anthropology especially and more recently has informed the field of cultural history. Tylor's appointment to a professorship at Oxford University at the age of sixty-four (1896) signaled the embrace of anthropology by the academic establishment. His influential concept of culture helped to define ethnology, or the social and cultural areas distinct from physical anthropology.

British anthropologists were among the world leaders in placing fieldwork at the center of their discipline. Two of the most important early twentieth-century "reinventers" of anthropology, both of whom emphasized social anthropology, were A. R. Radcliffe-Brown (1881–1955) and Bronislaw Malinowski (1884–1942), the latter born in Poland and emigrating to England in 1910. Radcliffe-Brown, who did fieldwork among the aboriginal tribes of western Australia, argued for the need to use scientific means to study what he called the "collective consciousness" of a people. He influenced a number of later anthropologists by singling out kinship patterns as keys to understanding the mental world of so-called primitive people. His books *The Andaman Islanders* (1922) and *Social Organization of Australian Tribes* (1931) display what has been termed a "functional" analysis. Radcliffe-Brown tried to show that the scientific study of kinship, something common to all human groups, could be the basis for a general science of society. Eventually Radcliffe-Brown went to the United States, to the University of Chicago. Through his teaching and writing he became one of the great influences on American anthropology, together with his American contemporary Franz Boas (1858–1942).

Malinowski, another pioneer of functionalism, extended the domain of social anthropology to include all social institutions, rituals, and ceremonies. He was greatly influenced by the French school of social theory following Durkheim, but he was wary of the abstract tendencies of French thought. A meticulous observer who attained fluency in the languages of the South Pacific peoples he studied, Malinowski excelled as a field researcher. He shared Radcliffe-Brown's interest in aboriginal peoples but specialized early on in the study of the ethnic groups that inhabited islands near Australia, especially the Trobriand Islands.

Malinowski's most famous work based on this research was *The Argonauts of the Western Pacific* (1922), in which he announced that the point of fieldwork was to observe thoroughly enough to be able to penetrate completely to the mental outlook of the people one studied. Every detail to be observed was significant, and even the most seemingly minor feature of social life should be understood to play a vital function. He acknowledged that fieldwork was often a lonely task, and wrote poignantly in his diaries of his loneliness and sense of isolation, something nearly every anthropologist has experienced at one time or another. Malinowski was a highly influential teacher at the University of London and met many leading people in a variety of intellectual fields. Later in his career he became interested in African cultures. In 1938 he accepted an invitation from Yale University to participate in a research project involving indigenous peoples of Mexico. He remained in the United States when World War II began, and died in New Haven, Connecticut, in 1942.

French ethnology remained close to sociology and the influence of Durkheim in particular. Lucien Lévy-Bruhl (1857–1939), a colleague of Durkheim's at the Sorbonne, was a philosopher, psychologist, and ethnologist who, in his early work, sought to keep alive the positivist spirit of Comte. Reflecting the progressivist assumptions of the Comtean view, Lévy-Bruhl's 1910 book *Les Fonctions mentales dans les sociétés primitives* (*How Natives Think*) opposed a "prelogical," mythical "primitive" thought to modern logical mental processes. He refined his ideas in *La Mentalité primitive* (1922, *Primitive Mentality*) and other later works. To his defenders, Lévy-Bruhl's investigations of what he deemed the "primitive" mentality served to demonstrate alternatives to overly rational modern thought, but critics argued that his terminology was pejorative. Lévy-Bruhl's *Carnets posthumes* (1949, *Posthumous Notebooks*) show that he had taken this criticism to heart, and sought to explain that his terminology was meant to describe two enduring types of thought found in all human groups. Put another way, he viewed the mythic nonlogical cast of mind not as a rejection of logic but as an alternative.

Some of the most thoughtful objections to Lévy-Bruhl's use of the term "primitive" were raised by Marcel Mauss (1872–1950), Durkheim's nephew and intellectual heir. Mauss was an active man of the French Left, supporting Dreyfus during the great struggle surrounding the unjust accusations against him and helping to found the radical newspaper *L'humanité* with the French socialist leader Jean Jaurès. As a teacher and writer his influence was immense, and not only in France. He first distinguished himself as a Sanskrit scholar and involved himself in Indian studies. He traveled to England and established ties with Malinowski, influencing both his work and that of Radcliffe-Brown. Mauss rose to the top of the French academic establishment, becoming a professor at the Collège de France in

1931, although he was forced to resign in 1941 due to the imposition of the anti-Semitic Vichy laws.

Even more so than his relative and predecessor Émile Durkheim, Mauss was a sociologist whose ideas deeply influenced French anthropologists. He synthesized many of the insights of Franz Boas and Bronislaw Malinowski, especially those having to do with the fascinating ceremony of the "potlatch" found in Melanesia and in the far Pacific Northwest. Where the potlatch was found among isolated tribes, whether in a benign or a rather aggressive form, it involved elaborate procedures of gift-giving and the deliberate squandering of wealth. Mauss seized on this practice and elaborated the ideas behind it in his most famous book, *Essai sur le Don* (1925, *The Gift*). This essay presents a general theory of "gift economies" found among indigenous peoples, implying an alternative practice as critique of a political economy based on competition through accumulation of wealth, removing valuable items from circulation. The idea of endlessly circulating wealth and gift-giving for the purpose of forming social bonds has had wide appeal to ethnologists and more generally to critics of advanced capitalism.

The French sociological tradition epitomized by Marcel Mauss exerted great influence over early twentieth-century ethnographers, many of whom were associated with the Paris museum and library of ethnography and anthropology called the Musée de l'Homme. By the twentieth century France had established an empire that included possessions in Africa and Asia. As was generally the case throughout the early history of anthropology, French researchers were closely tied to their country's imperial designs. The Musée de l'Homme, eager to collect artifacts and information, dispatched ethnographers to specific locations in the French empire.

One of the most ambitious of the French government-sponsored undertakings of this kind was the Dakar-Djibouti expedition of 1931 to 1934, which followed an itinerary through fifteen African countries, traversing the continent from west to east. Researchers studied previously unknown languages and collected much data during this expedition. Two of the most significant researchers involved were Marcel Griaule (1898–1956), who directed the enterprise, and Michel Leiris (1901–1990), appointed "secretary-archivist." Leiris went on to enjoy a long career as a multitalented man of letters, with ethnography being but one of the genres he explored.

Both men had ties to the French Surrealist movement (see chapter 7), which shared the general interest in African art found throughout the history of the modernist avant-garde. In 1936 the Surrealist magazine *Le Minotaure* published a special number devoted to the exhibition of African artifacts at the Musée du Trocadero, many of them collected during the recent expedition. Both Griaule and Leiris brought a highly personal style to their ethnographic writings, often describing their discomfort as would-be sympathetic observers who nevertheless represent a dominating colonial power.

This theme had emerged even more in the ethnographic writings of Victor Segalen (1878–1919), who documented his Asian travels as a French naval physician. Segalen made a memorable visit to Tahiti, where he examined some of the last sketches and writings of the artist Paul Gauguin, who had died just before his arrival. Segalen became deeply interested in Chinese culture and became involved in an archaeological expedition in China that was halted by the outbreak of World War I. After military service in Europe, he returned once more to China, then contracted the Spanish flu upon returning to France in 1918 and died the following year.

The effort to study other cultures and languages was central to the development of the human sciences in Europe, including of course anthropology. It was also inextricably linked to colonial ambitions and foreign interventions that rested on common assumptions about the inferiority of the people to be both subjugated and studied by the new scholars. As the human sciences formulated their views of "man" from their various disciplinary positions, the claims they made were always related to these "others" being discovered around the globe. Excellent examples can be found in the writings of the many British officials whose presence in India afforded them close contact with the cultural traditions of that continent. One such person was the English historian Thomas Babington Macaulay (1800–1859), who was appointed by the East India Company to the Supreme Council of India, where he served from 1834 to 1838. He is famous for having remarked, after having become acquainted with Indian languages and literature, that one shelf of English literary works was worth more than all that had ever been written in Sanskrit or other languages of India. But even with the most sympathetic European observers, processes of affirmation and exclusion spiraled around each other. The dual processes of scholarly study and ethnocentric condemnation especially can be seen in the nineteenth-century development of what has come to be called Orientalism.

Orientalism

To Europeans in the nineteenth century, especially to the French, "the Orient" meant what elsewhere and at other times would be called the

"Near East" or what contemporary Americans call the "Middle East." For our purposes here the term will mean the Levantine and North African countries bordering the Mediterranean Sea, an area long of concern for Europeans, beginning with its absorption into the Islamic world and European attempts to conquer the "Holy Land" during the Crusades. Of course, this is still a part of the world that receives much attention and about which many observers from afar express great concern. Regrettably, interpretation of the political or cultural lives of the people there is too often distorted by stereotypes of one kind or another, especially those that hold Muslims to be violent, irrational, or excessively zealous where religion is concerned.

A contemporary writer who has devoted himself to exposing the distortions caused by these prejudices is Edward Said (1936–), a Palestinian-born American professor of literature whose 1978 book *Orientalism* has founded a whole new way of reexamining the relationship, political as well as cultural, between Western civilization and the Islamic world. Said provides an intellectual history of the formation of the scholarly disciplines (linguistics, history, anthropology, etc.) that, so to speak, "constructed the Orient" as a topic. The process began at least as early as the Napoleonic invasion of Egypt in 1798, which set in motion not only the plundering of the conquered territory for objects that ended up in the collections of European museums but the scholarly effort to decipher the ancient inscriptions on the famous Rosetta Stone.

The first generation of Orientalists specialized in linguistic studies. Silvestre de Sacy (1758–1838) was the resident Orientalist in Napoleon's foreign ministry after 1805 and became a professor in the Collège de France the following year. He prepared Arabic grammars and performed a number of translations. Another important early scholar of Arabic was William Lane of England, whose book *An Account of the Manners and Customs of the Modern Egyptians* (1836), with its lurid descriptions of the customs of the harem, the practices of dervishes, and episodes of violence, fascinated and titillated European readers, including the young Gustave Flaubert. Like many young men of comfortable means, Flaubert made his "grand tour" of "the Orient."

The second generation of Orientalists included Sir Richard Burton (1821–1890), the English explorer of Africa and adventurer who mastered the Arabic language and specialized in penetrating the Islamic world as no European had done before, as when he successfully made the *haj,* or pilgrimage to Mecca, in disguise. Ernest Renan turned his philological abilities to the study of "Oriental" languages, demonstrated in his *Histoire générale et système comparé des langues sémitiques* (1863, *Gen-*

eral History and Comparative System of Semitic Languages). Renan was the first to use the term "Semitic." The influence of his and other Orientalist studies was such that stereotypes of "the Orient" as exotic and mysterious were well entrenched throughout Europe by the late nineteenth century. It is no accident that such studies grew in importance at precisely the time that European cultures were busy defining themselves in their modern form. Suggested comparisons and contrasts could be benign, but at other times they resembled the racial theorizing that often took place at the intersection of science and culture, in part the subject of our next chapter.

Suggestions for Further Reading

Clifford, James. *The Predicament of Culture: Twentieth-Century Ethnography, Literature, and Art.* Cambridge, MA: Harvard University Press, 1988.

Foucault, Michel. *The Order of Things: An Archaeology of the Human Sciences.* Trans. A. M. Sheridan-Smith. New York: Pantheon Books, 1971.

Frank, Manuel. *The Prophets of Paris.* Cambridge, MA: Harvard University Press, 1962.

Orr, Linda. *Jules Michelet: Nature, History, and Language.* Ithaca: Cornell University Press, 1976.

Said, Edward W. *Culture and Imperialism.* New York: Knopf, 1993.

Said, Edward W. *Orientalism* New York: Pantheon Books, 1978.

Smith, Bonnie G. *The Gender of History: Men, Women, and Historical Practice.* Cambridge, MA: Harvard University Press, 1998.

White, Hayden. *Metahistory: The Historical Imagination in Nineteenth-Century Europe.* Baltimore: Johns Hopkins University Press, 1973.

Chapter 4

Science and Culture:
Gender and Race, ca. 1850 to 1900

The eighteenth century had been a time marked by the popularization of the scientific theories introduced in the age of Descartes and Newton, but the nineteenth century was the time of real growth and more advanced professional development of the modern sciences. Before the century had advanced very far, the word "science" was taking on its talismanic properties, signifying knowledge, certainty, and authority for an increasingly admiring civilization. Driven by the Newtonian paradigm, modern physics was the first to establish itself. Next came chemistry (having adopted the atomic theory late in the eighteenth century), and then biology.

Biology and medicine were still in relatively crude condition at the beginning of the nineteenth century, a century that would see the discovery of the cell and the establishment of the Darwinian theory of evolution. Readers of today who take for granted the enormous cultural prestige physicians enjoy can gain a sense of just how much their image has changed by attending to passages in works of fiction, even up through the mid-nineteenth century. One finds doctors portrayed as pretentious buffoons, spouting a few Latin phrases, prescribing questionable treatments, possibly even appearing inebriated. But by the end of the century, medicine had become far more reliable, and its professionalization had transformed its social status significantly.

The historical terrain on which these very general trends played out was populated by hundreds of people working in very specific areas to tackle the most pressing problems posed by the new sciences. To do justice to the many important European scientists and scientific theories and accomplishments of the nineteenth century would require at least an entire book by itself, let alone a detailed chapter. Instead of surveying all of that, the purpose of this chapter is to examine something of the impact of science on European culture during the second half of the century and to show how science was sometimes abused and applied inappropriately to social, cultural, and political life.

The prestige science enjoyed in the nineteenth century was symptomatic of a buoyant cultural optimism, especially pronounced in such Western European nations as Britain and France, which itself was a legacy of the progressive outlook of the Enlightenment age. No matter what cultural differences could be demonstrated between the era of the *philosophes* and the period on the other side of the historical divide that had included the Revolution of 1789, Napoleon, or the Romantic movement, the Enlightenment faith in progress through the application of reason remained strong. Victorian English culture certainly was imbued with such a faith, and one of its most representative figures, whose intellectual development had been tied closely to the legacy of the Enlightenment, was John Stuart Mill (1806–1873).

John Stuart Mill

Mill was a child prodigy, subjected by his father, James, a member of the late eighteenth-century philosophical movement of Utilitarianism, to a daunting educational regimen through which he mastered Greek while still a young boy, going on then to read the Greek and Latin classics in the original by the time he was ten. John Stuart Mill's knowledge of languages, history, philosophy, and political economy was without parallel. He also became much involved in the world of politics and business. He was head of the British East India Company for twenty years beginning in 1836 and served for a time as a member of Parliament. Mill was an intellectual heir to the Enlightenment belief in human progress, and more immediately had inherited from Utilitarianism the belief that the most necessary enterprises were those that contributed to human happiness.

Like a latter-day *philosophe,* Mill wrote on a wide variety of topics. He wrote treatises on political economy and on democratic and socialist theory, including *On Liberty* (1859) and *Socialism* (1870), and collaborated with his wife, Harriet Taylor, in essays on feminism. After her death he wrote *The Subjection of Women* (1869). His major work on logic was *System of Logic* (1843), and his contribution to the Utilitarian movement was the book *Utilitarianism* (1863). From 1835 to 1840 Mill edited the magazine *Westminster Review,* and he contributed regularly to other British periodicals. He published his *Autobiography* in the last year of his life (1873).

Mill was a great admirer of French culture and died while visiting Avignon in southern France. Like most nineteenth-century social theorists, he was interested in the work of Auguste Comte (see chapter 3), and found much of merit in Comte's "positive philosophy." He particularly admired Comte's effort to establish what he called positivism, basing knowledge on the scientific method. Comte, as we have seen, devised an elaborate scheme for ranking the sciences according to a hierarchy founded on mathematics and extending eventually to the crowning discipline of sociology. Positivism influenced later sociologists and most of the other human sciences emerging during the nineteenth century.

Comte's claims for science were excessive, however, and he went so far as to fashion a kind of substitute religion, modeled on Roman Catholicism (with Comte himself as pope), that would devote feast days to great scientific thinkers and hold ceremonies in honor of scientific achievement and knowledge. Here Mill parted company with Comte, and made it clear that elevating science to the status of a new religion was far from healthy. Unfortunately, a crude kind of Comtean positivism did infect many fields of knowledge in the late nineteenth century, eventually engendering an antirational reaction and mistrust of science. (See chapter 6.)

Charles Darwin

If for an earlier age the name "Newton" often stood more generally for "science," in the latter decades of the nineteenth century the name "Darwin" played that role. It was a name that represented the prestige of the modern science of biology, but also one that referred to an ongoing "culture war" over the philosophical (and, especially, theological) implications of the Darwinian theory of evolution through natural selection. Actually, credit for the discovery of natural selection belongs both to Darwin and to Alfred Russell Wallace (1823–1913), but for a combination of reasons, the name of the former came to represent the new explanation for the evolutionary process.

Charles Darwin (1809–1882) was in many ways an unlikely character to make a name for himself in the scientific field, let alone figure at the center of a strenuous controversy that often pitted fervent religious believers against those who championed Darwin's ideas. He was from a wealthy family and suffered much of his life from poor health. His pursuit of the profession of naturalist was a typical preoccupation for an English gentleman. But it was a decisive voyage from 1831 to 1836 that

gave him the experiences that launched him on the study that culminated in his landmark work of 1859, *Origin of Species*. Darwin signed on
as naturalist aboard the H.M.S. *Beagle*, bound for South America and
destined to sail around and up the Pacific coast to the Galapagos Islands
off the coast of Ecuador.

He was already well acquainted with arguments that greatly revised
the estimates of terrestrial time offered by biblical literalists, for among
the books he carried with him was the first volume of *Principles of Geology* (three volumes, 1830–1833) by Charles Lyell (1791–1875), the
Scottish geologist who held that the geological and other transformations on the planet had needed vast amounts of time to be accomplished. Moreover, he was conversant with earlier evolutionary theories,
which after all dated back to the pre-Socratic Greeks and most recently
had found expression in the ideas of the Chevalier de Lamarck
(1744–1829) of France, who held that organisms change through adaptation to environmental changes.

But he was not prepared for the astonishing discoveries that awaited
him in South America, where he found fossilized remains of shellfish
high in the Andes, or especially in the Galapagos Islands, rich in both
botanical and zoological varieties. If Lamarck had been right about environmental causation of adaptation, how could one explain the existence of significantly different species from one island to another
(islands presumably free of human presence before Darwin's expedition)? Darwin returned to England, was embraced by the scientific
community there, married, and settled down to write his account of the
Beagle's voyage and to ponder the meaning of his observations and the
specimens he had collected. Very gradually, he arrived at the theory of
natural selection, an internal process by which certain traits are selected
for offspring that give them better odds of survival.

Darwin was famously slow at his work and rather reluctant to publish his findings. He was comfortably established and in no particular
need of making a bigger name for himself in the world. Also, partly in
deference to his wife, who was much more religious than he, he inclined toward withholding his theories for fear of antagonizing theological opinion. Then, in 1858, he suddenly received a long letter from
the Scottish naturalist Alfred Russell Wallace, who outlined a theory as-
tonishingly similar to Darwin's. From 1848 to 1852, Wallace had made
his observations in the Amazon basin as well as in the East Indies. It
was an amazing case in the history of science of simultaneous discovery by two people working independently of each other. Darwin's
friends and associates, including Lyell and the philosopher/scientist

Thomas Henry Huxley (1825–1895), rescued him from despair over this turn of events and prevailed on him to publish his findings. They arranged a special meeting of the Linnaean Society in July of 1858 at which both Wallace and Darwin presented papers. But then Darwin published *The Origin of Species* in 1859, and Wallace's name became something of a footnote to history.

The book was an overnight *succès de scandale,* one of those books about which everyone had an opinion (and few had read). It was known as the book that argued that human beings were descended from apes, which was grist for the mills of many a political cartoonist and illustrator. (Actually, it was not until 1870 in *The Descent of Man* that Darwin made explicit human descent from primates.) In the heat of the controversy, many were quick to assume that Darwin's opponents were all biblical literalists and his supporters were gleeful atheists or agnostics. That last word, meaning someone who remains to be convinced of the existence of God but has not ruled out the possibility, was coined by Thomas Huxley, the famous stand-in for the colossally shy Darwin in the many public debates that ensued. Huxley faced down the Anglican bishop Samuel Wilberforce in a much-heralded debate at Oxford University in 1860. Whatever this occasion did to convince the public of Darwin's theory, it certainly contributed to the oversimplified view that all religious believers lined up on one side of the debate and scientists on the other.

In fact, many biologists remained unconvinced of Darwin's theory of natural selection, not out of distaste for evolutionary views but because Darwin could offer no convincing proof of it; could not demonstrate how this mysterious "natural selection" worked. Unbeknownst to Darwin and his contemporaries, the key was in the hands of an obscure Austrian monk named Gregor Mendel (1822–1884), whose painstaking observations of his experiments with crossbreeding varieties of garden peas formed the basis of the science of genetics. Mendel's scientific paper on his experiments remained undiscovered until 1913. And whereas not all scientists embraced Darwin, not all religious people rejected him. Some argued that evolution, Darwinian or otherwise, could be entirely consistent with divine creation, even further proof of God's subtle design.

Darwin went to his grave doubting his own theory of natural selection and regretting his inability to discover the mechanism that made it work. Meanwhile, Darwinian thought was being put to other uses, many of them far from benign. There have probably been few cases in the history of science as it intersects with culture where a theory has been as

abused and distorted as was Darwinian theory. Almost from the very beginning, Darwin's ideas, or some approximation of them, were misap-
plied to society and civilization. And Darwin's friends, so to speak, were
worse than his enemies in this regard. Herbert Spencer's use of the phrase
"survival of the fittest," meant to characterize the ideas found in *Origin
of Species,* lent itself all too easily to racial and class differences observed
in the nineteenth century. In the United States, the Spencerian version
of Darwin resulted in the movement known as Social Darwinism, used
especially to rationalize extreme discrepancies of wealth and poverty.

In Europe, the misapplication of Darwinian thought made for a
major intervention in an ongoing tradition of race theorizing that
served to rationalize the European domination of Africa and that
Southern slaveholders, earlier in the century, had followed with great
interest. This brings us to the strange and tragic topic of race and culture in nineteenth-century Europe, very much at the intersection of science, medicine, philosophy, and simple prejudice.

Racial Theory: Science and Philosophy

"Race" was an invention of nineteenth-century paleontology (the study
of fossils), a new science founded to confront the amazing discoveries
taking place from the earliest years of the century, from dinosaur bones
to the skulls representing earlier stages of human development. As European colonization of remote parts of the globe, especially in Africa
and Asia, took place, the different physiognomies and other slight physical variations observed among the human family were read into the
rigid racial hierarchy already well established in paleontology. The pale-
ontologist (and comparative anatomist) who was the first to propose
such a hierarchy was Georges Cuvier (1769–1832), on whom Napoleon Bonaparte bestowed the title of chevalier in 1811 in recognition
of his work at the Paris Musée de l'Histoire Naturelle.

Cuvier rejected evolutionary theory and attributed the disappearance
of earlier species indicated by fossilized remains to "catastrophism," including the biblical account of the flood in the Noah story. But his
meticulous observations were of great value to the new field, and he de-
serves credit for establishing the science of paleontology. As for the different human types found in the world, Cuvier reasoned that they had
been created simultaneously but that they could be ranked according to
superior and inferior characteristics. He designated three races, which
he termed, in descending order, "Caucasian," "Mongoloid" (Asian), and
"Negroid." It seemed natural to him to regard lighter-skinned Euro-

pean types as superior. At the other end of Cuvier's scale stood the Negro, an object of morbid curiosity and anxiety for him and for later generations of Europeans.

During Cuvier's lifetime Europeans had made little contact with Africans south of the Sahara, but in the period from 1810 to 1815 an opportunity presented itself for Europeans to satisfy their curiosity about African "creatures." In 1810 a twenty-year-old South African woman of the Quena people named Saarje (Sarah) Bartman was brought by an English ship doctor (who promised her she would make her fortune) to London, where she was dubbed the "Hottentot Venus" and kept in a house in Piccadilly and there displayed naked to the paying public. In 1814 she was taken to Paris and became a circus attraction, eventually also being exhibited to medical specialists. Some scientists familiar with Lamarckian evolutionary theory speculated that she might represent what came to be called a "missing link" in human evolution.

Her humiliation was compounded when she was part of the evening's entertainment at a fancy ball in Paris given by the Duchesse du Barry. It was on this occasion that Cuvier met her. When she died after an illness in 1815, he was given her remains, which he dissected and described in great detail. He removed her brain and genitals, which were preserved and eventually placed on exhibition in the Musée de l'Homme in Paris (They were not removed from view until 1990.)

Cuvier's diagrams show elaborate attention to the genitals. He found both the clitoris and the labia greatly enlarged, and presented a series of representations of the various stages of dissection. He concluded that the engorged nature of the genitals was evidence of the greater animality of African women, to whom he attributed a rampant licentiousness he believed to be in marked contrast to Caucasian women. One cannot help but suspect that this was a telltale example of the researcher seeing what he was already predisposed to see, since he started from the premise that he was examining an inferior example of the human species. The "Hottentot Venus" remained popular in the iconography of Restoration France, and indeed the line between grotesque caricature and Cuvier's anatomical drawings is hard to locate. The entire episode most certainly contributed to deeply held cultural assumptions about sexuality and race that would surface again in reactions to modern art. (See chapter 5.)

Later in the century, it would be another Frenchman who theorized about racial differences, this time in an exhaustive four-volume work called *L'essai sur l'inégalité des races humaines* (1853–55, *Essay on the Inequality of the Human Races*). He was Joseph Arthur de Gobineau (1816–1882), an aristocrat who believed in the natural aristocracy of the white man. Gobineau's particular emphasis was on blood and racial purity defined in terms of blood. Miscegenation held a peculiar fascination for him, in ways comparable to the Southern slaveholder. However, Gobineau appeared to condone miscegenation as a means of improving the blood stock of the inferior races. He argued that it was "natural" for a member of an inferior race to seek intercourse with one who was superior.

Still later in the century, after the success of movements of national unification fueled in part by strongly held notions of ethnicity (including the persistent influence of Herder's definition of "nation" as a specific ethnic/linguistic group), and in response to the spread of neo-Darwinian ideas, racial categorization became more complex and soon extended to Jews, whom anti-Semites held to be a race. The theorist whose ideas most encouraged this kind of thinking was an English writer named Houston Stewart Chamberlain (1855–1927). Chamberlain was a dedicated Germanophile whose two-volume *Foundations of the Nineteenth Century* (1899) introduced the concept of the "Aryan" as the ultimate superior human type. By this he meant fair-skinned, fair-haired Teutonic or Nordic peoples, and his argument fed directly into the Nazi propaganda of the 1920s and beyond. Chamberlain renounced his citizenship to become German and married the composer Richard Wagner's youngest daughter. (Both eventually met Hitler.)

The racial theories we have been describing were not mere abstractions, nor were they simply exercises in the establishment of new disciplines and professions. They were intimately tied to practice. Slavery flourished in both the British and French empires during the first half of the nineteenth century. During the second half, Europeans spread throughout Africa for colonial purposes, as well as for missionary work and "disinterested" scientific observation. The crowning moment came with the Berlin Conference of 1885, where the major European powers helped themselves to the as-yet unclaimed African territories. The audacity of their actions, founded on their unshakable belief that the superiority of European civilization made it both their right and their duty to take charge of Africa, is more intelligible when one realizes they believed they had the blessings of science, at least as represented by the theorists just described.

Nineteenth-Century Science and Gender

Explorers of the African continent often used strikingly sexual language to refer to the territory they encountered. Adjectives like "virgin" crop up in their reports and descriptions. Theirs was a language of mastery, very much like the unselfconscious language of men regarding women as objects to be dominated. In fact, recent historical scholarship has demonstrated a striking parallel between the colonial discourse that justified and celebrated the subjugation of colonial subjects and the combination of social, legal, philosophical, and medical explanations for the "natural" domination of women by men. European societies during the nineteenth century more or less universally accepted the view that women were less physically capable than men, less intelligent, less emotionally stable, and by definition dependent on the guidance, protection, and governance of men.

In large part this was the legacy of the Early Modern period. One of the most sweeping cultural transformations accomplished between, roughly, 1500 and 1800 was the marked change in the view held of women: from seeing women as strong, competitive with men, and even sexually rapacious to accepting a stereotype that represented them as feeble, delicate, subservient to men, and deeply afraid of sexual expression of all kinds. Those who were not—prostitutes, feminists, or women of races deemed inferior—were "unnatural" women. It is interesting that the reversal of the stereotype coincided with what historians of the family have described as the beginning, roughly by 1800, of the modern (especially bourgeois) nuclear family, defined by a strong sense of cultivating a private haven in opposition to a harsh, unforgiving public realm. Within this protected space, the housewife/mother was to serve as guardian and exemplar of morality for her spouse and offspring.

At the center of this dramatic cultural process of redefining woman for the modern age stood the medical profession. As physicians ascended in professional status, having benefited from very real advances in biology during the nineteenth century, they flexed their muscle, so to speak, more and more. The area of reproductive biology, as related to gynecology and obstetrics, provided some new opportunities. It had not been so long ago that conception was understood as the work of two different types of spermatic fluid, one male and one female. Once the existence of the ovum was discovered, it was portrayed as the passive receptacle for the invading sperm, and all of female sexuality came to be modeled on this image. And as the professionalization of medicine made greater strides, doctors were successful in wresting control of childbirth away from midwives, turning what traditionally had been a scenario controlled by women into a process of medical intervention by the male-dominated field of obstetrics.

Just as this view of women as needing masculine expertise and assistance in childbirth fostered a sense of female weakness and helplessness, the emergent field of psychiatry came to concentrate on the mental disorders to which women were supposedly (uniquely) prey. In the earliest decades of the nineteenth century, the infant field of psychiatry had few terms available for its taxonomy. The prevailing term for mental disorders was "monomania," later to be expressed by such terms as "obsession" or "complex" or "fixation." By midcentury, the term "hysteria" had come to represent a wide variety of behavioral symptoms believed to be inherently female, including sexual frigidity, excessive emotionalism, or even a kind of catatonic state into which some patients seemed to lapse.

"Hysteria" is an ancient concept, found in the Hippocratic corpus and in Galen's medical writings. It derived from the Greek *hysteros,* meaning "uterus." According to the ancient teachings (formulated at a time when dissection of bodies was taboo), the uterus was an organ that demanded to be filled. When a woman was barren for long, so the argument went, the organ could become detached and move about in the body, causing disturbing symptoms, including erratic behavior (hence, "hysteria"). The only remedy was pregnancy, which, so to speak, provided the necessary anchor. Nineteenth-century psychiatrists, who found themselves more and more inclined to consider the emotional state of women a "problem," grafted their new terminologies and treatments onto this venerable notion. Etymologically and otherwise, "hysteria" had to be viewed as an exclusively female disorder.

As Darwinian ideas gained acceptance, at least one expert theorized that hysteria represented a kind of evolutionary regression whereby a woman lapsed into a kind of animal state. He was Henry Maudsley (1835–1918), an early psychologist who worked in various London hospitals. Major urban hospitals and medical clinics were leading centers for the study of hysteria, thought by some to be more pronounced among urban women. One of the most famous clinics was at Salpêtrière in Paris, under the direction of a neurologist named Jean-Martin Charcot (1825–1893, see chapter 6). He subjected female "hysterics" to relentless examination, often putting them in hypnotic spells where their symptoms (e.g., temporary paralysis) would disappear for the duration of the hypnosis. Many times he directed them to assume various theatrical poses, which he sometimes photographed. The voyeuristic character of these scenarios, where all-male medical audiences gazed on patients who happened often to be beautiful young women, has received ample comment.

These are extreme examples of the general trend whereby women were viewed as "problems" to be solved by medical science and, by extension, civil institutions (including the family) under male domination. Since the medical (including psychiatric) profession enjoyed great prestige by late in the century, its pronouncements in matters involving women, from regulation of prostitution to treatment of wives and daughters whose emotional disorders caused their families distress, were taken very seriously. Often their intervention in judicial proceedings could be decisive.

A compelling example of this can be seen in the murder trial of Henriette Caillaux in 1914, a case that prompted sensational coverage in the Paris press. (See chapter 10.) Madame Caillaux calmly and deliberately shot to death Gaston Calmette, the editor of the Paris daily *Le Figaro*. Her reason was to defend her "honor" as "a lady" after the paper had published negative profiles of her politician husband that included details of their affair together when he was still married to a previous wife. She avowed her act, but nevertheless was tried in a criminal case that would end with her acquittal on grounds of extenuating circumstances. These included her fragile emotional state as a "lady," who could hardly be expected to bear up under the lurid publicity that disgraced her name. Expert testimony of physicians and psychologists figured decisively in the trial, as these witnesses for the defense explained that women were by nature weak creatures without the intellectual or emotional resources to bear up under the glare of contentiousness and publicity that a (by definition) stronger man might be able to withstand. The triumph of a medical and social discourse that exaggerated the difference between men and women was complete.

The point of historical scholarship centered on race and gender is not to provide sidelights to the standard historical narrative, but to show instead how central considerations of racial and sexual difference have been in the construction of that narrative, even—especially—when those considerations have been hidden from view. When nineteenth-century Europeans celebrated the accomplishments of their civilization, they did so in terms that included disdain for civilizations they judged inferior, for racial and other reasons. The language of achievement and mastery was, moreover, nearly always one specific to masculine experience. Whether "the other" was racial or sexual, it was always in view. It always mattered. It was during roughly the second half of that century that European civilization fell deeply in love with itself. But this self-love was not without misgivings. It is to this conflicted love story that we turn in the next two chapters.

Suggestions for Further Reading

Eiseley, Loren. *Darwin's Century: Evolution and the Men Who Discovered It.* Garden City, NY: Doubleday, 1958.

Gilman, Sander. *Difference and Pathology: Stereotypes of Sexuality, Race, and Madness.* Ithaca: Cornell University Press, 1985.

Gilroy, Paul. *The Black Atlantic: Modernity and Double Consciousness.* Cambridge, MA: Harvard University Press, 1993.

Goldstein, Jan Ellen. *Console and Classify: The French Psychiatric Profession in the Nineteenth Century.* Cambridge: Cambridge University Press, 1990.

Gould, Stephen Jay. *The Mismeasure of Man,* Revised, Expanded Edition. New York: Norton, 1996.

McClintock, Anne. *Imperial Leather: Race, Gender, and Sexuality in the Colonial Context.* New York: Routledge, 1995.

Showalter, Elaine. *The Female Malady: Women, Madness, and English Culture 1830–1980.* New York: Pantheon Books, 1985.

Young, Robert J. C. *Colonial Desire: Hybridity in Theory, Culture, and Race.* London: Routledge, 1995.

Chapter 5

The Formation of Modern European Culture,
ca. 1848 to 1885

While Europe remained primarily rural and agrarian, the mid-nineteenth century was a time when energies were shifting in the direction of urban development, especially in the Western countries. London and Paris were proud centers of the new civilization, eager to extol the virtues of industrialism and the market economy. In London this was most evident in the Great Exhibition of 1851, with its headquarters in the imposing "Crystal Palace" in Hyde Park (just for the duration of the exhibition). It was a veritable temple whose acolytes intoned the promises of modernity, assuring the public of the bright future guaranteed by science, technology, and industry. In Paris the public could admire the wonders of the new economy in the splendid arcades found throughout the central city. These were elegant covered spaces enclosing fine shops and boutiques, usually with glass panels in the roof to bathe the interior with light. They prefigured the shopping malls of the late twentieth century.

In such protected spaces members of the comfortable middle class could reassure themselves that all was well in their civilization, which must surely be the envy of the world. Much depended, however, on their ability to ignore the suffering and degradation of the urban poor and the industrial laboring class, afflicted with low wages, poor housing, illness, and lack of education. But such ability was far from lacking.

The self-congratulatory material complacency of this civilization was interrupted and challenged by a growing number of critics, typically themselves members of the bourgeoisie, who sought to expose the flaws and inconsistencies of the industrial capitalist economy and to prophesy dire consequences of its unimpeded expansion. For the most part, these critics were socialists, with socialism being defined as a critique of bourgeois property coupled with the demand that workers share much more equitably in the wealth they themselves created. Some, however, were anarchists, viewing the state as the source of oppression and calling for its abolition and for the establishment of egalitarian, worker-controlled industries. Both socialists and anarchists drew on the Utopian socialist tradition that emerged during the early years of the century. (See chapter 1.)

Pierre Joseph Proudhon, Early French Socialism, and Anarchism

Pierre Joseph Proudhon (1809–1865) was an influential proponent of anarchism, a particularly "Left" variety marked by great hostility to existing property relations and a call for worker-managed cooperatives and workshops. Proudhon hailed from the Franche-Comté, near the Swiss Alps, and, like a latter-day Rousseau, extolled the virtues of rural labor. A gifted writer, he had been a brilliant student made to suffer by callous classmates for his obvious poverty. A lifetime of resentment and passion for reform found expression in the ringing phrases of his most famous work *Qu'est-ce que la propriété?* (1840, *What is Property?*). Proudhon wasted little time in answering the title question. He wrote, *"La propriété, c'est le vol!"* ("Property is theft"). Despite the stirring language, this was less an attack on property per se than an argument about the relationship between wealth and poverty and a critique of bourgeois notions of property.

Proudhon was an activist as well as a writer. Early during the 1840s he was associated with a radical group of silk weavers in Lyon, a city with a history of labor agitation, especially in the weaving industry. He moved on to Paris where he edited a revolutionary newspaper, was elected to the Constituent Assembly after the Revolution and the establishment of the new republic in 1848, but then eventually received a prison sentence for his criticism of Louis Napoleon Bonaparte, the president who would declare himself emperor in December 1851. Proudhon was in prison from 1849 to 1852, suffered harassment by the imperial police in the following years, and fled temporarily to Belgium. But by the time he died in 1865, his ideas had gained a solid following among French workers.

Workers also responded favorably to the ideas of two French socialists who came to prominence at the time of the Revolution of 1848: Louis Blanc (1811–1882) and Louis-Auguste Blanqui (1805–1881). Louis Blanc was a member of the Provisional Government established in 1848, and he proposed the establishment of "social workshops" that would form the kernel of a new socialist society. His idea was somewhat similar to Proudhon's concept of worker-managed production, but it included a recognition that not all workers possessed equal abilities. Instead of arguing for a completely egalitarian socialist economy, Blanc suggested that compensation would be based on the formula "from each according to his abilities, to each according to his needs." This idea had direct influence on Marxism, but unfortunately the workshops, once attempted, were badly managed, probably deliberately sabotaged by Blanc's political rivals.

Blanqui was more an insurrectionist and revolutionary theorist who advocated violence by the workers as a means to taking control. He spent perhaps a third of his adult life in prison, especially under the Second Empire, due to his radical actions and fiery rhetoric during the 1848 Revolution. When the Paris Commune was established in 1871, he was in fact still incarcerated, but many of the radicals of the Commune were inspired by his ideas. The Paris Commune resulted from the Prussian defeat of France during the short-lived Franco-Prussian War of 1870, which ended the Second Empire of Napoleon III. Residents of Paris continued to resist the victors, and Paris endured a prolonged siege. In early 1871 the government of the newly proclaimed Third Republic, established at Versailles, sought to disarm the citizens of Paris. When Prime Minister Adolphe Thiers issued the order to seize the cannon that had defended the city on March 18, his republican troops met with resistance by armed Parisians, who then proclaimed the Commune.

The Paris Commune lasted until May 28, during which time it practiced a politics combining elements of French Revolutionary Jacobinism (including staunch anticlericalism), socialism, and anarchism. During its final bloody week (*la semaine sanglante*), war raged in the Paris streets between the communards and invading Versailles troops, climaxed by a massacre of the "federalists" (*fédérés*), as the insurgents were known, in the Père Lachaise cemetery. (See photograph in chapter 13.) In all, more than 20,000 died defending the Commune, and hundreds more were executed after the defeat. Thousands were imprisoned or deported. The events briefly tempted Karl Marx to believe that the revolutionary proletariat he envisioned for some distant point in the future had surfaced. Blanqui had endorsed the Commune because it was consistent with his view that the revolutionary working class would need to establish a temporary dictatorship and even to practice terror to bring about the necessary transition to socialism. Blanqui's idea appears to have influenced Lenin's Bolshevism and, no doubt, Maoist doctrine.

The opponents of the Paris Commune were scandalized that women has participated in the uprising. They accused women of being *pétroleuses*, or incendiaries, who deliberately set many of the fires that destroyed much of Paris, including the palace of the Tuileries and the Hôtel de Ville. No one woman scandalized bourgeois notions of feminine respectability more than Louise Michel (1830–1905), a poet, novelist, and radical political theorist whose oratory rallied the communards. Her political philosophy combined elements of anarchism and socialism, and like Blanqui she advocated violence. Along with many other survivors of the Commune, she was deported to the French Pacific overseas territory of New Caledonia, but returned to France when a general amnesty was granted in 1880. Imprisoned again during the early 1880s for her subversive speeches, she spent her later years in London.

Anarchists were often at odds with socialists, and purging anarchists from the International Workingmen's Association (or First Socialist International), which lasted from 1864 to 1876, was a top priority for Karl Marx. In addition to Proudhon, two other important anarchists, both of them exiles from tsarist Russia, influenced European workers. One who especially clashed with Marx was Mikhail Bakunin (1814–1876). Bakunin was a fiery orator who enjoyed a considerable following among radical workers in Italy and Spain as well as among those from Slavic lands. He encouraged the formation of conspiratorial groups to disrupt the activity of the state, and he tirelessly accused Marx and the socialists who followed his ideas of an authoritarian, pro-statist streak. Although he attracted much less attention from Marx and the Marxists, the other Russian anarchist whose ideas were influential was Peter Kropotkin (1842–1921), a member of a noble family who renounced his ancestry and embraced a radical anarchism that included the belief that violent acts—"propaganda of the deed"—were sometimes necessary for a revolutionary movement. Marx, and indeed most socialists, dismissed this as irresponsible.

Karl Marx, Friedrich Engels, and Marxism

The most intellectually ambitious effort to study the history and particular nature of capitalism, as well as to provide a thorough critique that combined a kind of static structural analysis with an insistence on the inexorable movement of history, came from the Prussian-born writer Karl Marx (1818–1883). Through nearly lifelong collaboration on these and related topics with Friedrich Engels (1820–1895), Marx synthesized the body of work and ongoing critique that bears his name: Marxism.

Although it owed a debt to earlier socialist theories and drew on French revolutionary politics, British political economy, and German idealist philosophy, Marxism was strikingly innovative and original, with lasting results for political theory and practice as well as for any number of academic disciplines.

Marx began his career as a gifted student in philosophy. Despite completing a doctorate at the University of Berlin, he was denied an academic post due to his radical politics and was forced to take up journalism. In 1842 he began a short-lived career as editor of a newspaper in his native Rhineland, the *Rheinische Zeitung*. His articles critical of the reactionary Prussian regime led to his expulsion from the country in 1843. At that point, having recently married, he and his wife, Jenny, set out for Paris. Although Paris was a favorite choice for European political exiles, the July Monarchy was rather reactionary and any embrace it gave visiting radicals could only be temporary, as would become clear very soon.

In Paris Marx began the most decisive friendship of his life with a fellow Prussian exile, Friedrich Engels. Independently the two men had reached similar conclusions about capitalism, although Engels had done so from a unique vantage point: in Manchester, England, where he became owner of a textile mill, thanks to a family inheritance. While in Paris, Marx threw himself into his writing, particularly a collection of notebooks that remained unpublished for almost a century. These were the *Ökonomisch-philosophische Manuskripte von 1844 (The Economic and Philosophic Manuscripts of 1844)*, and their publication in the early 1930s changed significantly the way Marx's ideas were interpreted. Early in 1845 Marx was expelled from France, the result of Prussian diplomatic efforts. He moved to Brussels, where Engels soon joined him.

There the two men began to collaborate in writings on political, philosophical, and literary topics as well as to make contact with other political exiles. In 1845 they wrote *Die heilige Familie (The Holy Family)*, a work of literary criticism most remembered for its authors' withering dismissal of the sentimental fiction of the French novelist Eugène Sue, (see chapter 2), whose political views they would have been presumed to share. That same year they produced *Die deutsche Ideologie (The German Ideology)*, their critique of neo-Hegelian ideas that contained the famous observation that the ruling ideas of any age are the ideas of its ruling class. Except to make similar points in their very famous *Manifesto of the Communist Party*, they never fully elaborated their concept of ideology, a theme that would receive extensive treatment from later Marxist theorists. Engels typically steered Marx more toward historical and cultural topics, and he explored several of them in his own books. He also addressed themes of gender and the origin of the family as an institution, themes not central to Marx's thinking.

In 1847 a group of German political exiles in London called the League of the Just contacted Marx and Engels and persuaded them to write their manifesto. At Marx's urging they changed their name to the Communist League, and in 1848 Marx and Engels published their *Manifesto of the Communist Party,* a succinct and readable (and always quotable) summary of their views at that juncture and seemingly prophetic given the revolution that broke out that year in Paris and then spread to other European locations. Taking advantage of the changed political landscape, Marx returned to the Rhineland, revived the newspaper he had once edited (it became the *Neue Rheinische Zeitung*), and plunged into political activism anew. But the revolution was swiftly defeated, and in 1849 Marx again took up the life of an exile, this time to London, his final destination.

There Marx remained until his death at the desk in his study in 1883. Although he was to take the reins of the International Workingman's Association he founded with Engels in 1864 (disbanded in 1876), for the most part Marx's life in England was spent burrowing within the massive collections of the British Museum, where he set himself the task of studying thoroughly the history and intricate workings of the capitalist system; poring over account books, invoices, parliamentary reports; and reading history, political economy, and philosophy. The goal was his multivolume study *Das Kapital* (*Capital*), eventually to appear in three massive tomes, although only the first was published during the author's lifetime (1867). The Marx family endured grinding poverty during all their years in England, relieved regularly by the generous support of Engels, who was close to Marx and his wife and daughters. The one source of income (steady but not substantial) Marx enjoyed was the *New York Herald Tribune,* for which he served many years as European correspondent. Occasionally with Engels' help, Marx wrote hundreds of articles on virtually every conceivable contemporary political topic, including the American War Between the States. Marx suffered greatly from illness in his last years, and was little known at his death outside his immediate circle of family, friends, and fellow émigrés.

The Evolution of Marx's Thought

The most immediate source of Marx's political radicalism was the stirring example of the French Revolution. Like others of his generation living under the militarist reactionary Prussian monarchy, Marx looked to France as the source of progressive politics. He was stirred as well by the Romantic movement, and wrote poetry as a young man. He was a lifelong lover of literature and a voracious reader who committed long passages of such favorite writers as Aeschylus, Shakespeare, and Balzac to memory. Marx's first great philosophical influence was G. W. F. Hegel (1770–1831), whose ideas still held sway at the University of Berlin, where he had taught. When Marx became a student there he befriended the so-called Young Hegelians, politically minded students inspired by the philospher's teachings.

Hegel was the great representative of the German Idealist school that included Kant and Johann G. Fichte (1762–1814), and as an idealist philosopher he believed in the necessity of establishing transcendent metaphysical verities that, for him, included the existence of God as an absolute force directing all of human history toward fixed goals. One of the most important goals for Hegel, a nascent Prussian nationalist, was the realization of the state. He regarded the state as a perfect embodiment of the divine ideal. Like other radicals, Marx was impatient with the mystical, implicitly conservative side of Hegel's thought, but he was attracted to its ambitious philosophical range. In particular, he seized on the explanation Hegel gave for historical change—how the wheel of history moves forward toward the grand goal Hegel envisioned.

This Hegel called "the dialectic," a Greek word that means "argument." In his scheme, it was a way of understanding that every thing (every belief, style, tendency) engenders its own opposite. Hegel expressed this by the terms "thesis" and "antithesis." The thesis, that which is dominant at any one point in history, brings into existence its own negation, its antithesis. They become locked in a struggle through which both are destroyed. A new entity results, composed of elements of the two that precede it. Hegel called the new creation "synthesis." His specific language for the stages of this process is complicated and subtle. For example, his German term for the process whereby some elements of thesis and antithesis are destroyed while others are preserved was *Aufhebung,* a word that can mean both cancellation and conservation. Nothing is ever destroyed utterly, and nothing entirely new is ever created. But history moves forward.

For Marx the appeal of these ideas was in their application to the social order: No matter how triumphant capitalism seemed to be, by definition it was bringing into existence the very elements (i.e., the industrial proletariat) that constituted its negation. By the time Marx and Engels wrote *The Communist Manifesto,* this dialectical reasoning would find expression in the idea that history has been a process of continual class struggle (of necessity, to move it forward). But Marx still needed to purge Hegel's ideas of their otherworldliness. He was helped in this regard by the rigorously skeptical, apparently atheistic philosophy of Ludwig Feuerbach (1804–1872). In his *Das Wesen des Christentums* (1841, *The Essence of Christianity*), Feuerbach argued, more or less, that human beings created "God," and not the other way around. Human error consists in the inability to recognize the completely human origins of the major beliefs and abstractions human beings find so very compelling. Marx's earliest writings are filled with the sense of his intellectual grappling with Feuerbach and, through him, Hegel. His brief musings about this were collected as the *Theses on Feuerbach,* the most famous of which is number eleven: that up until that time philosophers had only described the world, whereas after that point it became necessary to change it.

From Marx's early journalistic career and his experiences as a political exile, it seemed clear that what needed to be changed was the material foundation of social existence: industrial capitalism. The influence of Feuerbach had helped Marx to "stand Hegel on his head," as he liked to boast (i.e., to reverse the emphasis of the Hegelian dialectic from its lofty spiritual direction to a profoundly material one). The work in which one can see Marx carrying out this new emphasis, applying his own philosophical synthesis to the ills of the industrial capitalist order, is *The Economic and Philosophic Manuscripts of 1844.* Quite in opposition to claims later made for Marxism, here one can see the humanism and even the Romanticism of the young Marx's background.

Detractors have long held that Marx is bloodless and detached from the human condition, overly intent on demonstrating the scientific reliability of his ambitious theories. But the 1844 work gives the lie to this claim, and it is also not difficult to find passages in such later writings as *Capital* that echo its tone. It is a tone of moral outrage over the insults to human dignity brought about by the labor process under industrial capitalism. The key to this is Marx's concept of alienation, which he explains in several important ways. Human beings, he argues, have a number of different life activities, different ways they can express their humanity. One of these, but only one of many, is the ability to work. But under capitalism, this ability or human quality has actually been purchased by the employer through the wage "agreement." The worker's ability to work, one of his human attributes, now belongs to another. This is as preposterous as the purchase of someone's friendliness or sense of humor.

Marx termed this aspect of alienation *Entäusserung,* which conveys the sense of "divestiture," of something being stripped away from (*entäussert*) another. It now stands as an alienated object (*Gegenstand*) apart from that person. To add insult to injury, the industrial labor process, especially with its highly developed division of labor, makes work repetitive and degrading, and involves the worker in only a small part of the product that is to result. It has no intimate connection to the person who participated in this small part of its manufacture, the way something envisioned and fashioned by an individual artisan might. Through competition and fear of job loss, the labor process also fosters alienation among workers, and certainly between employees and employers. This kind of alienation Marx termed *Entfremdung* ("estrangement"), and he argued that it is replicated throughout the social order, for example, within families, where wives are alienated from husbands and children from parents.

It all makes for a thundering moral indictment, in a tone captured even more memorably by *The Communist Manifesto.* Marx was a masterful prose stylist, taking advantage of the German language's elastic propensity for unusual compound nouns and word coinages, in which he excelled. It can be quite thrilling to read him in the original, and capable English translations exist that capture his powerful tone and characteristic verve. In later works, Marx's critique of capitalism, informed by his exhaustive research in the British Museum, became more detailed in every way. In 1859 *Zur Kritik der politischen Ökonomie* (1904, *A Contribution to the Critique of Political Economy*) appeared, very much a prelude to *Das Kapital.* According to some influential interpreters, these later mature works have the stamp of science whereas, by contrast, the "humanist" earlier writings are so much juvenilia. Yet at several points within *Das Kapital,* for all its technical detail, one finds the kinds of ringing passages of denunciation and visionary descriptions of what may come that resound through the writings of the Paris and Brussels years.

One of Marx's most original concepts introduced in volume 1 of *Capital* was that of the "commodity," his term for what is produced under industrial capitalism. Through clever advertising it is made to appear as if is a treasure that has been bestowed on a privileged public, but it must be understood, Marx argued, as the "congealed" embodiment of the alienated labor that brought it into existence. The commodity therefore has a definite history, one of exploitation and the theft of the surplus labor stolen by the capitalist from the worker (equaling the difference between what the work was worth to the employer and what the worker actually was paid), but this history must remain hidden from view.

To mystify things further, the capitalist learns to present the commodity by association with properties or qualities that are tangential if not downright fanciful, creating the impression that the consumer will acquire these desirable qualities (intelligence, taste, sex appeal, success, popularity, etc.) through purchasing the commodity. Marx called the sum total of these extraneous features used to manipulate consumers "the fetishism of commodities," and he further related this to the opposition he explained in *Capital* between "use value" and "exchange value." According to this idea, anything that is produced presumably has a use value (a shovel, an article of clothing, etc.), but, under relations of capital, also acquires "exchange value." At an immediate level, this means price or what is required for it to change hands. But as capitalism advances, exchange value becomes increasingly abstract and related to the fetishism of commodities. Gradually exchange value overtakes use value entirely. Compliant consumers are motivated less and less by practical considerations and are swept away by superficial considerations that threaten to become the dominant reality.

Such an argument can begin to sound like postmodern theorizing about the age of electronic media, and it can be argued equally that Marx's analysis of capitalism, for all the obituaries bestowed on Marxism in recent years, applies even more to the globalized economy at the turn of the twenty-first century than it ever did to modern industrialism. Marx provided no timetable for the collapse of capitalism and argued forcefully—even in the seemingly apocalyptic the-revolution-is-at-hand tone of the *Manifesto*—that processes of capitalist development would need to spread globally before conditions necessary for its dissolution could begin to emerge. Marx also made it abundantly clear that he admired capitalism for its resilience and innovative character, even if it was a grudging admiration and one necessitated by his and Engels's "materialist conception of history."

While Marx was a vigorous polemicist who staunchly defended his ideas in debates with other socialists, he did not superimpose rigid conceptual schema on his many and varied writings. His historical writings demonstrate this clearly. In such brilliant interpretations of specific events as Louis Napoleon's 1851 coup and establishment of the Second Empire (1852, *The Eighteenth Brumaire of Louis Bonaparte*) or the Paris Commune of 1871 (1871, *Class Struggles in France*), Marx set aside terms like "bourgeoisie" and "proletariat" in favor of more nuanced, piecemeal analysis of subclasses and temporary sociopolitical alliances. After Marx's death, Engels had occasion to complain about a new generation of Marxists who advocated a rigid kind of economic determinism whose dogmatic character later detractors would use to portray the essence of Marxism.

Marxism remained an ambitious program of critique and system of thought, too ambitious even for writers as prolific as Marx and Engels to carry out. Like all such ambitious systems, it can suffer from over-simplification and reductionism at the hands of overzealous or single-minded followers. Marxism remains daunting in practice because it encompasses so much. Not only does Marxism seek to comprehend all of social and economic reality, but it seeks as well to understand that all of it is developing in time, subject to the vicissitudes of history. Thus it is at once a static and a dynamic exercise. The single most useful, and perhaps most strikingly original, Marxist concept is the concept of the "relations" (*Verhältnisse*) of capitalism. Not only does this term suggest the interrelatedness of all aspects of capitalist society (something the intellectual division of labor embodied in different disciplines mitigates against), but it also implies the changing character of these relations over time. Such is the connotation, in part, of the German noun, which conveys a state of tentativeness. In Hegelian-Marxist thought (the rediscovery of the 1844 manuscripts led to extensive commentary of the persistently Hegelian aspects of Marx's thought), these relations change through internal dialectical processes. This of course cannot be witnessed any more than Darwinian natural selection—prior to the science of genetics—could be observed.

Later Marxists and Socialists

In the decades following Marx's death, as his ideas found a small but determined following in the unlikeliest (least industrialized, most primitive) country of all—Russia—they were cited with honor by the theorists of the major European socialist parties while in practice those parties quietly adapted themselves to pragmatic bourgeois politics. The most striking example of this was in Germany, where the SPD (Sozialistische Partei Deutschlands, German Socialist Party) leaders embraced what they took to be orthodox Marxist theory publicly but showed through their actions they were persuaded by the "evolutionary socialism" of Eduard Bernstein (1850–1932). In his book *Die Voraussetzungen des Sozialismus und die Aufgaben der Sozialdemokratie* (1899, *Evolutionary Socialism*), Bernstein took exception to Marxist revolutionary theory and especially to the assumption Marx made of the increasing economic misery of the proletariat. Wages were rising for many German workers, and Bernstein argued for a gradualist or evolutionary socialist politics that took advantage of the political system where possible.

The impact of Marx's ideas on his country of exile appeared negligible until well into the twentieth century. Nineteenth-century English socialism derived from Romantics like Blake and Shelley, and drew as well on an older native radicalism whose heyday was the English Revolution of 1642 to 1649. Many of the complaints intellectuals lodged against industrial capitalism were aesthetic in character, however much they may have sympathized with the plight of workers. This was true of the influential art critic John Ruskin (1819–1900), who argues in works on the Gothic cathedral and the beauty of Renaissance Venice that no civilization based primarily on the material values of the market could produce great art. More obviously socialist was William Morris (1834–1896), a writer, artist, and designer whose "Arts and Crafts" movement was an attempt to recover the beauty of artisanal accomplishment that had been compromised by industrial mass production. Like Ruskin, Morris was a medieval enthusiast, and founded a press called the Kelmscott Press dedicated to producing books inspired by such sources as medieval illuminated manuscripts.

Probably the most influential group of English socialists, though once again decidedly non-Marxist in their outlook, were the so-called Fabian socialists, including the couple Sidney (1859–1947) and Beatrice Webb (1858–1943). The playwright George Bernard Shaw (1856–1950) was also a member of this circle. The Fabians preached a gradual path to socialism, emphasizing the need to participate in Parliament. They attempted to influence the policies of the Labour Party and also dedicated themselves to economic and labor history. This last area was probably their greatest contribution, stirring up historiographical debates about the history of capitalism in Britain and stimulating later scholarship on such topics.

With the stunning success of Lenin and the Bolsheviks in Russia, Marxism by the early twentieth century was coming more and more to be subsumed within Marxist-Leninism. However, the unanticipated rediscovery of Marx's earlier writings in the 1920s followed by their publication in the early 1930s stimulated new interest in his humanist thought and in Hegel's decisive importance in his intellectual formation. The foremost Marxist theorist who pursued this direction was the Hungarian philosopher and literary critic György Lukács (1885–1971). In 1923 he published *Geschichte und Klassenbewusstsein* (*History and Class Consciousness*), which introduced his concept of "reification" as an enormously important aspect of ideology.

The term Lukács offered refined Marx's concept of the commodity, clarifying more specifically how the commodity is made to obscure the labor process that produced it. Lukács argued that a major impediment to class consciousness is the effectiveness with which bourgeois ideology presents complex temporal processes as "things" or essences, history reworked as myth. He described this practice of arresting (or, we might say, "freezing") ongoing developments as "reification" and found it at work throughout capitalist society. A critic and theorist of the nineteenth-century Realist novel, Lukács went on in later years to apply his concept through criticism as ideology critique. His influence on later Marxist literary and cultural criticism (for better or worse, the hallmark of twentieth-century Western Marxism) was considerable.

Literary Realism and Naturalism

The preference Lukács showed for the Realist novel was typical for readers who admired its ability to expose social problems and raise necessary political questions. The tremendous popularity of the novel as a literary genre (see chapter 2) corresponded almost exactly with the ascendance of the Realist movement. The novels of Honoré de Balzac (1799–1850) seemed to open a window onto French society in the years of the Restoration and the July Monarchy. Those of Victor Hugo (1802–1885), by far the most beloved writer of nineteenth-century France, portrayed the suffering and the struggles of the poor—especially his novel Les Misérables (1862). Hugo was also a poet and playwright whose long career spanned the Romantic and Realist era in literature. Certainly he was admired for his political courage, seen especially in his outspoken opposition to Napoleon III.

Great political courage also remains associated with the name of novelist Émile Zola (1840–1902) for his intervention in the Dreyfus affair. (See chapter 6.) Zola represents the shift from Realism toward Naturalism, which probed the more sordid aspects of social life, dwelling on disturbing themes meant to rouse people to awareness and action. His long series of novels collectively titled Les Rougon-Macquart (Chronicles of the Rougon-Macquart Family) portrayed the less pleasant side of France under the Second Empire. They included notably Nana (1880), the story of a famous courtesan, and Germinal (1885), a harsh look at the lives of coal miners. Zola's importance for literary naturalism in literature was as great as that of the Norwegian playwright Henrik Ibsen (1828–1906), whose plays A Doll's House (1879) and Hedda

Gabler (1891) portrayed the unhappiness of women trapped in stifling bourgeois marriages.

Realism in the English novel focused on industrial urban society, especially London. By far the most popular and successful novelist of the century was Charles Dickens (1812–1870), whose vivid descriptions of urban poverty and degradation in such novels as *Oliver Twist* (1837–39), *Our Mutual Friend* (1844–45), and *Hard Times* (1854) were credited with instigating parliamentary hearings and spurring reform legislation. His novel *David Copperfield* (1860) was semiautiobiographical and an example of that staple of nineteenth-century fiction, the *Bildungsroman,* or novel of development, in which the reader follows the efforts of a central character to make his or her way in society. French novelists like Balzac, Stendhal, and Hugo similarly produced examples of this type of novel. William Makepeace Thackeray (1811–1863), considered a possible rival to Dickens, was best known for his vast novel *Vanity Fair* (1847–48). Thackeray was skilled at describing the social foibles and pretensions around him, especially in London society. Like Dickens, he advanced his career as a novelist by publishing his books serially in magazines. (See chapter 2.)

The theme of life in the English countryside, beginning to be eclipsed by urban industrial civilization, was central to two other much-admired Victorian novelists, George Eliot (Mary Ann Evans, 1819–1880) and Thomas Hardy (1840–1928). Eliot, another novelist who gained exposure through publishing first in magazines, devoted such successful Realist novels as *Mill on the Floss* (1860) and *Middlemarch: A Study of Provincial Life* (1871–72) to the tragic lives of rural people, although she shifted gears late in life to write *Daniel Deronda* (1876), a very political novel about London and its climate of anti-Semitic prejudice. Hardy invented a rustic locale known as Wessex, modeled on his native Dorchester. His first success as a novelist was with *Far From the Madding Crowd* (1874), first published in serial form. He continued to add to the lore of his fictional Wessex in *The Return of the Native* (1878) and *The Mayor of Castorbridge* (1886). Except perhaps in his first novel, Hardy in no way romanticized the often harsh lives of his characters. His late novels, *Tess of the d'Urbervilles* (1891) and *Jude the Obscure* (1895), veered toward Naturalism, with the former tackling the subject of sexual hypocrisy women faced and the latter painting a gloomy picture of the efforts of a laborer to improve his condition through education. Harsh criticism turned Hardy toward poetry at this point.

Gustave Flaubert and the Turn
Toward Literary Modernism

By far one of the most significant nineteenth-century novelists, and the one who most pushed the novelistic genre in the direction of literary Modernism, was the French writer Gustave Flaubert (1821–1880). He pursued a vision of literary creation that often ran afoul of contemporary taste and mores, and enjoyed relatively little recognition during his lifetime. Fortunately for him, he came from a comfortably well-established family and did not have to endure the economic hardships so many writers faced. The son of a successful Norman physician, after a spell of travel as a young man Flaubert settled into a life of relative solitude dominated by the rigors of writing, made more painful by his legendary perfectionism. He worked slowly and deliberately, painstakingly crafting his sentences.

His letters to his mistress (to her chagrin the affair was largely carried out through their correspondence), the poet Louise Colet (1810–1876), give a vivid account of his creative agony. This was true in particular of his breakthrough novel *Madame Bovary* (1857), which he worked on assiduously from 1851 to 1856. It was published as a *roman feuilleton* in the *Revue de Paris,* but five installments were singled out for condemnation, and Flaubert and his publisher were brought to trial in 1857 on charges of offending public morality. Flaubert was acquitted on the charges, but the novel was far from the *succès de scandale* that experience might have produced.

For the most part, the literary public did not know what to make of this grim tale of an unhappy housewife whose adulterous affairs and spendthrift ways bring her to ruin and, eventually, to suicide. The moral ambiguity of the novel confused and troubled readers and critics. Flaubert never seemed to condemn her behavior on moral grounds, although she does die at the end. Asked to clarify his position relative to his famous protagonist, Flaubert replied famously and enigmatically, "Emma Bovary, c'est moi." And what made the novel difficult for contemporary readers was that it operated stylistically at levels far removed from the conventions of either Romantic or Realist fiction. The novel is marked by narrative indeterminacy: Sometimes the reader sees through Emma's eyes, at other times through those of a seemingly reliable narrator, but often from a shifting, disembodied perspective that remains deliberately elusive. Flaubert's letters indicate his desire to write a novel "about nothing," or one that was pure style, the kind of exercise in literary expression for its own sake we associate more with the experimental writing of twentieth-century Modernists.

Flaubert published several other novels, but with mixed results. Critics have admired greatly his 1869 novel *L'éducation sentimentale* (*A Sentimental Education*), very much a *Bildungsroman* about a young man coming of age at the time of the 1848 revolution, but it met with little success when published. The one work the public did embrace, the only commercial success Flaubert enjoyed, was his collection of three novellas called *Trois contes* (1875, *Three Tales*), written at a time of mounting family debts when he very much needed a best-seller. At his death he left unfinished a satirical novel called *Bouvard et Pécuchet* (*Bouvard and Pécuchet*), about two small businessmen who strike it rich and decide to retire to the countryside and devote themselves to learning, exhaustively compiling information as if in some parody of the eighteenth-century editors of the great *Encyclopédie*. They seem the perfect target for Flaubert's well-known scorn for the bourgeois middle-brow mentality (*la bêtise*), yet it is not hard to find passages where the author shows affection for these well-intentioned bumblers. Such ambivalence is characteristic of Flaubert. He remains a major transitional figure in the history of modern literature, rooted in late Romanticism, operating according to an apparently Realist aesthetic, yet anticipating Symbolism and subsequent chapters in literary modernity.

Symbolist Poetry

The poet Charles Baudelaire (1821–1867), Flaubert's contemporary, was less fortunate with his trial for offending public morality with a book published the same year as *Madame Bovary*. The book was a collection of poems called *Les Fleurs du mal* (1857, *The Flowers of Evil*), and Baudelaire was fined and he and his publisher ordered to remove six offending poems from subsequent editions of the book. Baudelaire had been trying to make his name as a poet, although this was not quite the way he had wanted to go about it. His earliest writings had been art criticism, including essays on Romantic artists such as Eugène Delacroix (1798–1863). Later he helped to publicize the important but misunderstood new artists who would move from Realism to Impressionism.

Baudelaire's most reliable literary activity, from the remunerative point of view, was as a translator of the tales and poems of Edgar Allan Poe (1809–1849). This tragic American writer became a leading inspiration for literary Symbolists as well as the Surrealists who came after them in the following century, and Baudelaire was the writer who inaugurated the particularly French fascination with him. Poe influenced Baudelaire directly in the development of the Symbolist concept of *synaesthesia,* the phenomenon whereby one sensory experience (e.g., a piece of music) can produce one in a different register (perhaps a color or a tactile impression). Baudelaire, who wrote of his own enthusiastic use of wine, hashish, and opium, also shared the notoriously alcoholic Poe's self-destructive tendencies.

The poems in *Les Fleurs du mal* were like nothing else that had appeared in French literature. They broke with the purely Romantic style of poets like Alfred de Musset (1810–1857) and Alphonse de Lamartine (1790–1869), but also steered clear of the lofty aesthetics of the influential "Parnassian" school, so named for the journal *Parnasse* and dedicated to the principle of *l'art pour l'art* ("art for the sake of art"). Elements of Romanticism could still be found but were subservient in several of the love poems to the mysterious effects of obsessive symbols, such as the loved one's hair or an elegant swan. The emphasis was on the effects these private symbols had on the poet's consciousness.

It was far from a happy consciousness. Baudelaire styled himself the *flâneur,* or idle man about town who takes in the urban scenery with no fixed agenda or purpose. Second Empire Paris provided much for his observing gaze. The Paris of Baudelaire's day remains celebrated for its grandeur and opulence, but more often the poet of *Les Fleurs du mal* sees the squalor and misery that could be found there. The poems were to be the flowers somehow able to bloom in this desolate landscape. In a cycle of poems bearing the title "Spleen," the poet observes a Paris whose very gray, leaden skies are filled with foreboding and weigh down on his oppressed spirit. Then there are the depressing scenes of human misery, explored especially in *"Les Yeux des pauvres"* (The Eyes of the Poor) and other posthumously published prose poems Baudelaire prepared under the title *Les petits poèmes en prose.*

Baudelaire's prose poem genre was one of his important legacies to French Symbolism, and went on to inspire modern writers of both poetry and prose. Although he remained close in some ways to Romanticism, as the founding figure of literary Symbolism he was the first to seek to elevate isolated sensory experiences, relayed via poetic symbols, to the level of powerful intellectual experience and contemplation. He attempted to push poetic language to new limits toward this end, and represents a significant step toward a modern poetry that, for better or worse, will become more and more about the power of language itself.

For French culture, concerned as it consistently has been with the writer's relation to society, Baudelaire remains a major figure in that fraternity dubbed by the symbolist poet Paul Verlaine *"les poètes maudits"*—the poets who are damned. According to this idea, there have been certain poets throughout the history of French literature who have achieved a kind of outlaw status, beginning centuries earlier with François Villon (1431–?), who was sentenced to be hanged as a thief. The sentence was commuted and he was banished from Paris. Gérard de Nerval (1810–1855) was an example for the late Romantic era, for he was an unstable character whose life ended in madness. Then after Baudelaire came two more whose renegade reputations made news long after their very brief and turbulent lives. These were the poet known as the Comte de Lautréamont (1846–1870) and his near contemporary Arthur Rimbaud (1854–1891).

Comte de Lautréamont ("Count Lautréamont") was the nom de plume of Isidore Ducasse, the son of a French consular official in Montevideo, Uruguay. Little is known of his life, except that he was educated in France and died in Paris in 1870, possibly as a victim of the siege. He was the author of two works, *Les Chants de Maldoror* (1890, *Maldoror*) and *Poésies* (*Poems*). The first part of *Maldoror* was published in 1868. It was a bizarre book. Lautréamont used a style that blurred the distinctions between prose and poetry, not unlike Baudelaire's prose poems. The spectacularly savage violence of the book resembled nothing else in French literature, with the possible exception of the works of the Marquis de Sade. Its odd juxtaposition of images and symbolic elements made it a favorite with the Surrealists of the 1920s and 1930s. They considered Lautréamont a precursor.

In a similar manner they championed Arthur Rimbaud, although for that matter he has been claimed by nearly every avant-garde or countercultural movement of the Modern era. Initially he was embraced by the Symbolist movement, although he was such an iconoclast that he did not reside comfortably in any one circle. The example of his bohemian, vagabond life has exerted even more influence than his innovative poetry, and in combination this was to make him a favorite of American Beat writers and such rock musicians as Jim Morrison, Bob Dylan, and Patti Smith. Like many twentieth-century popular musicians, his creative period came early and his life was terribly brief. Therefore his neo-Romantic image has remained eternally youthful.

Rimbaud was a prodigy who wrote all of his poems before the age of nineteen. He wrote his first poems at the age of sixteen, then the following year ran away from his home in the Ardennes region of northeastern

France. That happened to be the year of the Paris Commune, whose political ideals Rimbaud fervently embraced. He served as a volunteer with the forces of the Commune but returned to his home before its suppression. The Commune's defeat left him bitterly disillusioned with politics, yet 1871 was also the year of his poetic breakthrough. After he sent some of his poems to the Parisian poet Paul Verlaine (1844–1896), a member of the Parnassian circle who was soon to embrace Symbolism, the latter invited him to visit and sent train fare. Before meeting Verlaine, Rimbaud wrote his long poem *Le Bateau ivre* ("The Drunken Boat"), a remarkable work whose long, languid lines suggest the gentle rocking of a boat on the water. It was a poem filled with remarkable imagery and beautifully realized lyrical expression, more than testifying to the young poet's talent.

Verlaine and Rimbaud inspired each other as poets, but their extremely turbulent relationship was a disaster. Rimbaud behaved like a wild beast, imposing himself on the Verlaine household. The two poets became lovers, which brought an end to Verlaine's marriage. They both drank excessively and quarreled and fought. They parted but then resumed their relationship in London in 1872, where Rimbaud composed his series of remarkable prose poems called *Les Illuminations* (*Illuminations*). These poems refined the genre Baudelaire had introduced, and were filled with evidence of the poet's spiritual intensity.

Again Rimbaud left Verlaine, but the breakup was painful to him, and in 1873 he wrote what turned out to be his farewell to poetry: *Une Saison en enfer* ("A Season in Hell"). He met one last time with Verlaine in Brussels, where he showed him the new poem. Again they quarreled, and this time Verlaine wounded Rimbaud with a pistol. He was sentenced to two years in prison, and he and Rimbaud broke off all contact with each other. At that point, still in his teens, Rimbaud put down his pen, so to speak, and embarked on a life of travel and adventure. He ended up in Ethiopia, made a fortune smuggling weapons, fell ill, and returned to France just in time to suffer the amputation of his leg due to a tumor. Unfortunately this did not eradicate the cancer that ended his life at the age of thirty-seven.

Rimbaud has remained influential as much or more for his comments on the poetic vocation as for his much-admired poems. In a remarkable series of letters to a friend from his hometown named Paul Demeny, Rimbaud described his artistic vision and proclaimed his credo. He proclaimed that the poet must become "a seer" (*un voyant*) in order to create a startlingly new kind of "pure" poetic language. How can this be accomplished? For Rimbaud, the only way was for the poet to subject himself to extreme experiences that would bring about *le dérèglement de tous les sens* ("the derangement of all the senses"). He must, so to speak, step outside his familiar self. As Rimbaud put it in deliberately ungrammatical French, *"Je est un autre"* ("I is an other.") Not only does this anticipate later insights of psychoanalysis about the decentering of the so-called ego, but it approaches a kind of Zen Buddhist sense of deliberate loss of self in order to achieve enlightenment.

Rimbaud's philosophy of poetic language, the theory of which the prose poems especially are the practical application, articulated much of what came to be associated with the aesthetics of symbolism. The poet must manipulate language in such a way as to break its usual boundaries and force it into startling new combinations. Rimbaud's apt phrase for this was *l'alchimie du verbe*—"the alchemy of the word." The words on the page are capable of entering into volatile new combinations, creating effects even the poet could not have envisioned. This remains a vivid statement of what we would now take to be the aesthetics of Modernism, that the artist surrenders everything to the materials with which he or she works, welcoming chance and hoping for new formal realizations. In Rimbaud's formulation, the artist is a kind of sorcerer who unleashes forces greater than his own ability to control them. Presumably he would have been quite pleased that his small body of work has continued to inspire new and adventurous forms of artistic expression, often in the hands of those who share his flaunting of social convention.

Unlike Rimbaud, Verlaine continued to write poetry. He contributed significantly to the Symbolist movement, but he opposed the more radical break with older lyric forms some Symbolists pursued. Verlaine, with a highly refined lyrical sense, was devoted to the musical possibilities of poetic language. For this reason he was reluctant to abandon rhyme. As a result, his style seems much more conservative than that of Rimbaud (not to mention that of his contemporary Mallarmé), yet he was skilled at finding the music, so to speak, in everyday words and patterns of speech. Like Rimbaud, Verlaine moved in a more spiritual direction, which in his case meant a recommitment to Roman Catholicism. He became very proficient in English and both visited England and made translations from the English. Unfortunately, he dissipated much of his literary gifts in alcoholism.

The Birth of Modern Painting in Midcentury France

Quite obviously French writers and Paris in particular play a commanding role in the history of modern culture's origins. That is even truer when we consider the visual arts. Paris had no rival when it came to leading academies and schools of painting, and it was in Paris that the very concept of the avant-garde took hold in painting. Virtually every modern "ism"—Realism, Naturalism, Impressionism, Postimpressionism, Fauvism, Cubism—had its origins there, and the succession of ever newer waves of bold new approaches to painting became almost routine. The twentieth-century German writer Walter Benjamin dubbed Paris "the capital of the nineteenth century," and nowhere does that seem truer than in the field of painting.

As with literature, the newer schools of painting did not announce themselves all of a sudden. They emerged gradually out of their predecessors. For example, Jean Auguste Dominique Ingres (1780–1867) shared many of the themes found in the dramatic canvases of the Romantic master Delacroix, but he pursued a somber, careful draftsman-like approach to painting that would define Realism. The use of oil paints was essential in this regard. Just as this medium had permitted the seventeenth-century Flemish painters to portray the opulent interiors of the successful burghers, so Ingres's portraiture allowed him to present his prosperous bourgeois subjects as people of imposing substance. His portrait of Monsieur Bertin is an example. Looming toward the viewer with just the right balance of light and shadow about him, he is someone to be reckoned with.

Honoré Daumier (1808–1879), best known for his political cartoons and lithographs (see chapter 2), was more obviously dedicated to Realism in painting. For him this often meant portraying ordinary subjects, especially members of the working class whom he endowed with dignity. A striking example is his 1863 painting of a washerwoman (*La Blanchisseuse*) as she trudges up the stairs at the end of her working day. She bears a load of wash (so perhaps her day's labors are not at an end after all) and leads a small child by the hand. But a close examination of Daumier's canvas reveals a delicate play of light and shadow that announces the full-blown Impressionism already emerging in the hands of artists like Claude Monet (1840–1920).

Realist painters, like their counterparts in literature, were dedicated to holding a kind of mirror up to reality. But as was also the case with writers, often they chose to isolate examples around them that emphasized the commonplace, the humble, even the unattractive. In this way Realism gave way gradually to Naturalism. One way this came about was in the deliberately nonheroic, informal pose favored by some Realist painters. Here the great example was Gustave Courbet (1819–1877). Sometimes he shocked with casually presented nudity, as in his *L'origine du monde* (1866, *The Origin of the World*), a detail of a nude in which the viewer sees the woman's bare genitals, thighs, and stomach. But far more unsettling for contemporaries was his large canvas *Un enterrement à Ornans* (1849–1850, *Burial at Ornans*). Here we view a group of people assembled around a freshly dug grave. The priest, attended by his acolytes, performs the rites, and a shirt-sleeved gravedigger kneels nearby. In the foreground, a mourner stands with his dog, which is distracted by something off to the side. The rest of the party assembled for the burial appear to be chatting among themselves, ready for the ritual to be concluded, perhaps looking forward to the meal or the conviviality that awaits them at a nearby tavern. The studied casualness (or should we say the honesty) of what historically would have been an exaggeratedly formal grouping startled Courbet's contemporaries.

It is the same kind of matter-of-factness that made several of the paintings of Edouard Manet (1832–1883), very much a transitional figure between Realism and Impressionism, shocking to gallery-goers in Second Empire France. Manet was a genuine talent who remained steadfastly resistant to any school or academically-approved style, yet he always tried to exhibit his paintings in the semiannual Salon exhibitions of the Royal Academy of Painting and Sculpture. He ran afoul of them in a big way with his 1863 painting *Le Déjeuner sur l'herbe (Lunch on the Grass)*. This exercise in realistic representation shows a party of four at a picnic. In the background, a partially undressed woman wades in a stream. Her three companions in the foreground look casually but candidly at the implied viewer. One is a nude woman seated alongside two fully clothed, rather soberly dressed young men. Her frank gaze seems to say "So what?" to any viewer who might find this disturbing.

It was anathema to the Salon jury, who rejected it emphatically. Accordingly, Manet exhibited it along with the works of other painters who had been snubbed by the Academy at the "Salon des Réfusés," organized for painters whose works had been spurned by the jury. He followed this practice on several other occasions during his career, although, unlike younger Impressionist colleagues such as Monet, he persisted in trying to get his work acknowledged by the artistic establishment. An even greater storm was provoked by the painting Manet chose to exhibit at the Salon of 1865. This was *Olympia,* painted in 1863, and the Empress Eugénie was the most famous viewer who was personally offended. In this painting, a reclining nude woman stares icily at any implied viewer. That itself was already a violation of all conventions of the artistic nude. Her body is bathed in light, and the background shadows are exaggerated. To the right, a Negro servant stands ready to assist "Olympia." She is as chastely dressed and demurely posed as her white mistress is unapologetically naked. This violated yet another convention, one involving race and gender simultaneously. (See chapter 4.) According to the unabashedly racist stereotypes accepted at the time, it would be the black woman, not the white, who represented sexual boldness or lasciviousness.

Beyond the shock effect of certain Manet canvases, it was clear that his primary interest was in the essentials of painting. Juries that rejected his work often cited the "flatness" of his presentation, as if all that interested him was the painted surface. Such an aesthetic would seem to anticipate the Impressionists, and can be found in the work of Gustave Caillebotte (1849–1894). He was associated with Manet as well as with the later Impressionists, whose work he collected. His paintings are Realist on the face of it, but with elaborate attention to what we would now call Impressionistic elements. His painting *Les Raboteurs de parquet* (1875, Floor Scrapers) shows three laborers down on all fours on a floor they are planing. They push their tools toward the viewer, who sees their rippling muscles and senses their strain. But even more noticeable are the wood shavings that accumulate and catch the light from the window behind the men. The light and its play on the particles of wood is the most striking element of the painting.

A similar effect is created in Caillebotte's large canvas *Rue de Paris, temps de pluie, Intersection de la Rue de Turin et de la rue de Moscou* (1877, Paris Street, Rainy Day). It shows a well-dressed couple, umbrella held above them, walking near the Place de Dublin, where several streets intersect just south of the Boulevard des Batignolles, in the neighborhood where several Impressionist artists had their studios. They occupy the right foreground. The real center of the painting is the street with its glistening paving stones illuminated by the light that begins to break through the clouds. Although less recognizably Impressionist than a field of poppies painted by Monet, Caillebotte's large canvas is in many ways dominated by the same fascination with the light refracted on the surfaces he depicts.

Today when Impressionist paintings draw the largest, most admiring crowds at museums throughout the world, it may be difficult to believe that the word itself was once a highly pejorative term. What kind of painting was this, where the artist did not take the trouble to analyze the scene carefully enough to record it exactly, according to the laws of perspective? But Impressionist painters like Monet and Pierre-Auguste Renoir (1841–1919) were perhaps the first to understand that the camera had freed painters from the obligation to perform the equivalent of its task, that is, to capture and record "reality."

The novelist Marcel Proust (1871–1922), in his portrayal of a character modeled in part on Claude Monet, likened the effect Impressionist painters were after to the experience of flinging open a shuttered window on a sunlit day from inside a room plunged in darkness. One would be dazzled suddenly by the shimmering, blurry light on the trees, grass, and sky outside. That—capturing the first light—appears to be the idea in Monet's paintings of flowers and water lilies or Renoir's nudes or groups of festive people partly shaded by trees and foliage while yet illuminated by the sunlight. The "painterly" techniques, more than the subjects chosen, made Impressionist works revolutionary, although Monet for one violated the conventions of landscape painting by including the belching smokestacks of factories in the distance.

Berthe Morisot (1841–1895) was a member of the Impressionist movement who became Edouard Manet's sister-in-law. She appeared frequently in his paintings, for example in his *Le Balcon* (1869, *The Balcony*). She excelled in paintings of domestic interior scenes, as did the American expatriate painter Mary Cassatt (1844–1926), many of whose paintings depict calm scenes of mothers with their young children. More on the margins of the Impressionist group was Edgar Degas (1834–1917). He used pastel paints and played with light and shadow in a manner well in keeping with Impressionism, but pursued very distinctive themes. Quite a number of his works can be grouped into such categories as the traditional one of nudes (bathers, frequently), but also ballet dancers and horses depicted at the racetrack. Like Caillebotte, Degas was a man of some wealth who acquired a large art collection of his own.

Painters of the 1880s in France began to be referred to as "Postimpressionists." They built on the advances of the Impressionists, but often pursued radical directions of their own in highly personal styles that anticipated the later movement known as Expressionism. Certainly there has been no more famous example that Vincent Van Gogh (1853–1890), the Dutch-born painter whose greatest works captured the dazzling light of his Provençal French location of Arles. A brilliantly talented artist tormented by the madness that he was able to channel into intensities of paint and shocking color, it cannot but seem clichéd to repeat the fact that he died unrecognized and impoverished. But now that his name appears regularly in news to note a new record price for a painting and an entire museum devoted to his work is one of the busiest tourist attractions in Amsterdam, it bears remembering.

Van Gogh's friend Paul Gauguin (1848–1903) found his distinctive style when he moved to Tahiti, just as Van Gogh did by relocating to Provence. Gauguin filled his canvases with the images of the tropical paradise he had discovered, finding unusual colors that were as soft and subtle as Van Gogh's were volatile and overwhelming. Use of pastels and an almost ephemeral, hurried-seeming style makes the paintings of Henri de Toulouse-Lautrec (1864–1901) recognizable. He developed a unique style that served also to document the bohemian life of Montmartre, centered especially on the cabaret known as Le Moulin Rouge. Several of Toulouse-Lautrec's paintings feature Jane Avril, a popular performer at this celebrated night spot.

Affinities seem to exist between ideas and theories circulating in the sciences and related disciplines of the age and the works of some well-known Postimpressionist painters. The strange images that stare out from the canvases of Odilon Redon (1840–1916) seem as if they could be candidates to illustrate the early works of Sigmund Freud on dreams. The dreamlike qualities found in the paintings of Henri Rousseau (see chapter 6) have made him a favorite Modern painter. One of the most technically interesting developments in Postimpressionist painting came with *pointillisme* (pointillism), found especially in the works of Georges Seurat (1859–1891) and Paul Signac (1863–1935). They almost seem to be commenting directly on the debate physicists of the day were having about the nature of light. Some held that light was composed of waves, while others asserted the primacy of particles. Seurat and Signac, in painstakingly filling their canvases with tiny glowing dots of paint, seem to be casting their votes with those who argued for particles. The influence of this kind of fascination with detail can be seen in the interior patterns (wallpaper, curtains, dresses) explored lovingly by the painters Édouard Vuillard (1868–1940) and Pierre Bonnard (1867–1947).

The pace of avant-garde artistic movements seemed to accelerate after 1890 or so, as new technological breakthroughs (sound recording, cinema) and more urban development made for even more possibilities in communication and publicity, fueling the expectation that the modernizing process of European culture was irreversible. That sense of the Modern was well established by the last years of the century. The special cultural ambience of the years from 1885, roughly, to 1914 is the subject of the next chapter.

Suggestions for Further Reading

Clark, T. J. *Image of the People: Gustave Courbet and the 1848 Revolution.* Princeton: Princeton University Press, 1982.

Clark, T. J. *The Painting of Modern Life: Paris in the Art of Manet and His Followers.* Revised Edition. Princeton: Princeton University Press, 1999.

Culler, Jonathan. *Flaubert: The Uses of Uncertainty.* Ithaca: Cornell University Press, 1974.

Ferguson, Priscilla Parkhurst. *Paris in Revolution: Writing the Nineteenth-Century City.* Berkeley: University of California Press, 1994.

Fowlie, Wallace. *Climate of Violence: The French Literary Tradition from Baudelaire to the Present.* New York: Macmillan, 1967.

Fried, Michael. *Manet's Modernism, or, The Face of Painting in the 1860s.* Chicago: University of Chicago Press, 1996.

Gullickson, Gay L. *Unruly Women of Paris: Images of the Commune.* Ithaca: Cornell University Press, 1996.

Hollier, Denis, ed. *A New History of French Literature.* Cambridge, MA: Harvard University Press, 1989.

LaCapra, Dominick. *"Madame Bovary" on Trial.* Ithaca: Cornell University Press, 1982.

Lerner, Warren. *A History of Socialism and Communism in Modern Times: Theorists, Activists, and Humanists.* Englewood Cliffs, NJ: Prentice-Hall, 1982.

McLellan, David. *Karl Marx.* New York: Penguin Books, 1978.

McLellan, David. *Marxism After Marx: An Introduction.* Boston: Houghton Mifflin, 1981.

Matsuda, Matt K. *The Memory of the Modern.* New York: Oxford University Press, 1996.

Ollman, Bertell. *Alienation: Marx's Conception of Man in Capitalist Society.* Second Edition. Cambridge: Cambridge University Press, 1976.

Ross, Kristin. *The Emergence of Social Space: Rimbaud and the Paris Commune.* Minneapolis: University of Minnesota Press, 1988.

Vincent, K. Steven. *Pierre-Joseph Proudhon and the Rise of French Republican Socialism.* New York: Oxford University Press, 1984.

Chapter 6

Fin-de-siècle European Culture,
1885 to 1914

The phrase "fin-de-siècle," literally "end of century," was of French coinage, applied in the late nineteenth century to a bohemian, "decadent" style or pose struck by certain artists and aesthetes. It implied a mood of cynicism and world-weary resignation, and even willful self-indulgent hedonism in the face of impending doom. Through the distorting lens of historical hindsight, the phrase has come to be applied to an entire period of cultural history; roughly the last two or three decades of a time of high-spirited frivolity and complacency definitively shattered by the carnage of the great war of 1914 to 1918.

But there was much more to the period the French also liked to call *la belle Epoque* (very loosely translated as "the good old days") than this. Like all historical periods, it was far more complex and contradictory than the stereotypical picture implied by the labels assigned it by the periodization of historians. For all the confidence and material complacency many Europeans displayed, there were deep worries and vexing anxieties. But let us remember that this does not mean that even the most inveterate saber-rattlers anticipated the scale of destructiveness, devastation, and disillusionment that would come after 1914. People living through historical periods, even when they recognize them as such, do not view themselves merely as actors in a prologue to a dramatic new age to come.

Late Nineteenth-Century
Socialism and Anarchism

The late nineteenth century was a period in which political reaction, as in the ongoing repudiation of the Paris Commune of 1871, expressed itself simultaneously with the impressive growth of socialist parties, as membership in trade unions swelled and workers accelerated their demands for a better life. The largest and most successful socialist party, the German Social Democratic Party (known by its German initials of SPD), paradoxically defended what its leaders August Bebel (1840–1913) and Karl Kautsky (1854–1938) viewed as orthodox Marxist theory while pursuing a politically opportunistic policy of accommodating itself to bourgeois politics, even for a time forming an alliance of convenience with the "Iron Chancellor," Otto von Bismarck.

While most workers placed their hopes in political parties intent on electoral gains in major legislative bodies, some embraced violence as a means of dramatizing their plight. Anarchist theorists in such countries as Russia and France preached a "propaganda of the deed" and were responsible for a number of political assassinations during the period from 1880 or so to 1914, for example the assassination of Tsar Alexander II in 1881. Bourgeois France trembled at the bravado of the anarchist assassin François-Claudius Koenigstein (1859–1892), a.k.a. "Ravachol," who went defiantly to the guillotine in 1892, the object of a combination of popular adulation, morbid fascination, and dread.

A figure like Ravachol seemed to embody the theories of the Breton theorist Georges Sorel (1847–1922), whose *Reflections on Violence* set forth a theory of political action based on violent acts that themselves were viewed as revivifying the society in which they occurred. This idea, epitomized in the famous remark by a French commentator who responded to Ravachol's acts by saying that it did not matter what the consequences of a violent act were if the gesture was "beautiful" ("*si le geste soit beau*"), was to have a lasting appeal to political and artistic movements down through the mid-twentieth century.

The Spectacle of Urban Culture

The tyranny of majority opinion applies as well to the reputation enjoyed by historical periods, and thus the decades prior to the Great War continue to be known for the material prosperity of a bourgeois-dominated nascent consumer society. It was to this sector that writers and artists addressed their works, while at the same time these supposed arbiters of elevated taste increasingly indulged themselves in the popular pursuits of the mass culture of spectacle and entertainment that horrified intellectuals decried as nothing more than bread and circuses.

The city of Vienna exemplified these contradictory tendencies quite strikingly. As capital of the Hapsburg Austro-Hungarian empire, it was a center of militarism and reactionary (i.e., staunchly monarchist, Roman Catholic, and anti-Semitic) politics. During the 1890s, Viennese city politics became aggressively anti-Semitic, to the considerable alarm of its Jewish citizenry, a significant number of whom occupied positions of real prominence. Sigmund Freud (1856–1939) would become the most famous example.

With its spectacular architecture and dramatic circular street plan, Vienna had become an inviting arena for artistic expression and performance. The cultural tone remained lowbrow, however, epitomized by the popular waltzes of Johann Strauss Jr. (1825–1899). Meanwhile, Freud was at work on his early books that would establish the field of psychoanalysis, the poet Hugo von Hofmannsthal (1874–1929) was applying French Symbolist aesthetics to poetry in the German language, the writer Arthur Schnitzler (1862–1931) was exploring in fiction the psychosexual territory being mapped out by Freud's theories, and painters such as Gustav Klimt (1862–1918) and Egon Schiele (1890–1918) were producing canvases many found disturbing for their blatant sexual frankness.

Vienna and such other major cities as Paris, London, and Berlin were powerful commercial centers for banking and retail business, and large urban populations of the day had greater access to leisure and to the necessary disposable income to indulge themselves. Paris in particular, with its wide boulevards and its large department stores (*grands magasins*), offered one of the most spectacular settings for the practice of the growing new religion of consumerism. This was a new age of mass entertainments and newspapers, such as the London tabloids and the Paris papers with their gossipy *faits-divers* (literally "diverse facts") filled with stories about personalities great and small, kept the public aware of the diversions and distractions of the urban scene. In Paris these included not only the cabarets, music halls, and boulevard theaters, but such wildly popular attractions as visits to the city morgue to view the unfortunates on display and tours of the famous sewer system, considered a model of engineering and a triumph of public health.

Cinema, invented simultaneously in the United States by Edison and in France by the Lumière Brothers, would prove to be the innovation with the most profound and long-lasting effect on modern mass culture. The first screenings of the brief films produced by the Lumières were wildly popular, and of course it was not long before the guardians of official culture began to weigh in against the new medium. After all, photography itself was still receiving only grudging acceptance as a legitimate art form in most quarters. The influential philosopher Henri

Bergson was among those who took it upon himself to denounce this new form of entertainment.

Leading artists and intellectuals felt themselves to be increasingly alienated from bourgeois tastes and popular entertainment, continuing a trend that began in earnest during the Romantic era and that reached a memorable pitch by midcentury in the bitter language of Gustave Flaubert's denunciations of the "stupidity" (*"la bêtise"*) of the stereotypical bourgeois. Romantics had also been known for embracing the use of alcohol and narcotic drugs, and many of the artists of the late nineteenth century shared this tendency. This was a great age, so to speak, of drug abuse. The absurdly potent drink known as absinthe, distilled from fermented wormwood, was as addictive and destructive for users of this time as English gin had been a century earlier. Edgar Degas's 1876 painting *Au café* (*At the Café,* but better known as *L'absinthe*), in which a woman sits stupefied in front of her glass of the sickly greenish liquid, commented powerfully on its effects.

In addition to alcohol, hashish and other narcotic substances remained a lure for many creative souls. Such behavior may have allied artists more with the lower classes than with the bourgeoisie, but all classes were susceptible to addiction. Very little was understood about addiction, and physicians routinely recommended very powerful narcotics. Sigmund Freud believed briefly in the curative powers of cocaine, a belief he abandoned when he realized he had become addicted. Unlike Freud, most users took little time to study the properties of the substances they craved. The abhorrence of the bourgeois public expressed by many aesthetes was due in no small part to the shock of self-recognition felt by those who shared more than they liked to admit with members of the social stratum they scorned.

Friedrich Nietzsche

No thinker produced by the late nineteenth century excoriated the sensibilities of the bourgeoisie more aggressively or expressed more withering scorn for the moral tone they set for society than Friedrich Nietzsche (1844–1900), a tormented, visionary German philosopher whose ideas gained a far more attentive reception in the twentieth century than they ever did in his lifetime. The son of a father who was one of a long line of Lutheran pastors, Nietzsche's philological studies inclined his sympathies toward pagan antiquity, specifically very early Athenian culture, and he blasted his own age as one founded on hypocrisy, paying lip service to an enfeebled Christian morality that preached resignation and subservience—in short, what Nietzsche disdained as a "slave morality."

Nietzsche wrote with greater intensity (suffering all the while from excruciating migraine headaches) and with more deliberate stylistic innovation than any philosopher of his century. Indeed, his propensity to favor aesthetically interesting style over systematic, expository argument made the reception of his work even more difficult than his controversial ideas might have suggested. His first book (1872), *The Birth of Tragedy,* argued for a reinterpretation of Greek culture in favor of the anarchic, "Dionysian" energies embodied in the ancient religious festivals that evolved into Athenian tragedy, as opposed to the rational "Apollonian" emphasis customarily accorded the "Golden Age" of Athenian culture commonly celebrated as the foundation of Western civilization.

In a series of unprecedented texts marked by deliberately fragmented, aphoristic style published throughout the next decade or so, including *The Genealogy of Morals, Beyond Good and Evil,* and the mock biblical *Thus Spoke Zarathustra,* Nietzsche unraveled a highly nuanced, at times wildly contradictory thread of an argument about the central drama of the modern age, to whit that "God is dead," because we have killed "him" in our hearts. Therefore it is incumbent on each person to "become what you are," ideally to become the "overman" (*übermensch*), a being not constrained by the limits imposed by bourgeois morality. En route, he offered a baffling series of observations about everything from gender difference to aesthetics and the mystery of creativity. The complicated stylistics in which Nietzsche's arguments are embedded have meant that issues of careful textual editing and translation have been crucial in determining how his work is to be approached.

This is an especially urgent consideration since his earliest reputation was as an apostle of brute strength and of the claims of a "master race." This is how his concept of the "overman" was first understood, and the unfortunate result was that, from the writings of Sorel through the selective uses made of his ideas by followers of Mussolini and Hitler, Nietzsche was interpreted as a proto-fascist, someone who rationalized violence against those, racially or otherwise, considered inferior. This legacy had much to do with the influence of his very bigoted older sister, Elisabeth. She cared for him from the time of his mental collapse in 1889 until his death in 1900, serving as his (de facto) literary executor. Working from disparate fragments left after his death, she compiled the book *The Will to Power,* which seemed to argue for a "master race" neo-Darwinian kind of philosophy and that echoed her own anti-Semitic views. There is bitter irony here, since Nietzsche had broken off his great friendship with the eminent German composer Richard Wagner due to the latter's racist, anti-Semitic views.

Joseph Conrad and the Ethics of Cultural Domination

European literature at the turn of the twentieth century began to show the effects of the various debates having to do with the supposed inevitability of the domination of one people or one race by another. The way had been prepared for these ideas by the misapplication of Darwinian ideas to the cultural sphere, as well as by the rise of new human sciences such as anthropology, tied as it was to the European colonial project. (See chapter 3.) Most modernist writers inspired by Nietzschean ideas (including the distorted impression left by *The Will to Power*) would come to prominence after World War I, but one pioneer of literary Modernism whose fiction comments very much on the colonial enterprise was Joseph Conrad (1857–1924).

Conrad's is a remarkable story, for he emigrated to England from his native Poland at the age of nineteen, knowing but a few words of English and then went on to become one of its greatest prose masters. His own adventures as a seaman in the Far East influenced such novels as *Almayer's Folly* (1895), *Lord Jim* (1900), and *Typhoon* (1903). He later wrote novels that dramatized the violence of colonial domination and the conflict between idealism and opportunistic greed, as in *Nostromo*, set in South America.

Later novels, including *The Secret Agent* (1907), set in Europe, and *Under Western Eyes* (1911) and *Victory* (1915) continued to explore themes of morality, conspiracy, and violence, but nowhere did Conrad dissect the brutality of colonial domination as vividly as in his 1902 novella *Heart of Darkness*, inspired by his own disillusioning experiences in the Congo. Narrated through the eyes of the world-weary Marlow, this tale of the bloody depredations of the ruthless Kurtz is all the more effective for the dispassionate way the tale is presented. In most of his books, Conrad is content to be a storyteller, not revealing much about his politics. But, like Balzac exposing the inconsistencies and social ills of early nineteenth-century France despite his own monarchist leanings, Conrad's understated approach is that much more powerful. His is a literary vision that is ever more compelling as one looks back over a century of unprecedented violence and atrocities.

Stéphane Mallarmé and Symbolism

As literary Modernism emerged, one notable way to express the scorn intellectuals felt for the bourgeoisie was to produce writing that refused all concessions to readers' tastes and literary expectations, something that could certainly be said of Nietzsche's style(s). The artist dramatized his sense of isolation and disdain for fashion by giving free rein to experimentation, even at the risk of intelligibility. It would be enough to be appreciated by a "happy few" readers. This phrase was associated with Stéphane Mallarmé (1842–1898), the Symbolist poet known to only a select circle of fellow aesthetes (but that circle included the painters Edouard Manet and James MacNeill Whistler) who posthumously exerted an enormous influence over literature, including criticism and theory, throughout the twentieth century.

Symbolism had begun in French poetry with Baudelaire and was carried forward by Rimbaud and Verlaine. In Symbolist doctrine, the reader of a literary work should expect to encounter a complicated set of phenomena, expressive both of the associative state experienced by its author and of the inherently complex character of literary language, which especially produces symbols freighted with the sometimes unfathomable psychological residue of their creation. The reader should be prepared to surrender to a no less complicated set of reactions.

Mallarmé's achievement was to pursue this aesthetic with a visionary emphasis on the determining power of written language. The role he gave language, more specifically the written marks on the page, was so great that it implied discarding altogether the referential function of literature. In a founding gesture that came to apply to all genres of Modernist art, Mallarmé crafted poems that were "about" poetry; writing about writing. Many of his later works resembled a kind of word sculpture, with unusual typography and unpredictable configurations of words. Exaggerated attention to the poem's physical appearance was most fully realized in his visionary long poem *Un coup de dés* ("A Roll of the Dice"), in which the boldface type of the title words of the poem skip down the page like dice rolling across a tabletop.

Mallarmé propounded his aesthetic theories about poetry, art, and writing at regular Tuesday evening gatherings at his Paris apartment. In attendance were painters, musicians, writers, and critics. His conversation had a mesmerizing effect on the members of his little circle, as the younger symbolist poet Paul Valéry (1871–1945) attested in particular. He commented that Mallarmé, intoning softly as he leaned against his mantel, cigarette in hand, spoke as if he personally had invented language.

Symbolism spread beyond France. The German writer Stefan George gathered a circle of young aesthetes about him, much as Mallarmé had in Paris. And Hugo von Hoffmansthal spread the Symbolist gospel in Vienna. Arguably the greatest of all Symbolists was Rainer Maria Rilke (1875–1926), a native of Austria who worked many years in Paris as the sculptor Auguste Rodin's secretary. In a life cut short by tuberculosis and the hardships of military service in the Great War, Rilke produced some of the most beautiful poems in the English language.

Symbolist writings promoted the view that art could offer a kind of secular salvation in a world devoid of religious mysteries or an escape from cheap and mundane aspects of life. In the case especially of a writer like Mallarmé, it seemed to represent the ultimate in artistic retreat from social or political concerns. But even Mallarmé, as recent studies have shown, made pronouncements from time to time on the events of the day. During the last years of his life, a political scandal developed in France that was to have profound consequences for France and eventually for all of Europe. This was the famous "Dreyfus affair." It so preoccupied opinion for a decade or more that virtually no one could remain neutral in the face of what came to be known simply as *"l'affaire."*

The Dreyfus Affair

Volumes have been written about this case, and we can but briefly summarize its broad outlines here. Alfred Dreyfus (1859–1935) was a career military officer who was court-martialed and found guilty in 1894 of selling military secrets to Germany. In a humiliating ceremony, he was stripped of his rank and discharged as a traitor. Almost immediately after he was sent, under a sentence of hard labor, to the South American fortress prison of Devil's Island (off the coast of French Guiana), doubts surfaced regarding the conviction. But even when another officer emerged as the real culprit, the army, backed by the government, made it clear it would rather keep an innocent man incarcerated than admit to a cover-up. The more anti-Semitic among them even reasoned that Jews in general were "guilty," even if Dreyfus himself was not.

Enough doubt existed by 1898 for Major Esterhazy, who had surfaced in the minds of many Dreyfus supporters (and for Colonel Picquart in the Army Office of Counter-Intelligence) as the more probable suspect, to be subjected to court martial for the very crime of which Dreyfus had been convicted. His swift acquittal, despite compelling evidence, prompted novelist Émile Zola (1840–1902) to compose a fierce letter denouncing the military and government cover-up in the case. The letter, which appeared as the entire front page of a pro-Dreyfus newspaper called *L'aurore,* came to be known as *J'accuse!,* since each paragraph began "I accuse . . ." Zola's attack intensified the national debate, and he temporarily fled to exile in England after his own conviction.

The debate was especially rancorous due to the virulent anti-Semitism of anti-Dreyfusard opinion. That Alfred Dreyfus was a Jew became an issue as early as 1894, as anti-Semites argued that his treason was typical; that Jews were loyal to their "race" first, to France second. Such expressions stupefied the Dreyfus family and their friends and supporters, for they were typical of assimilated French Jews. They certainly regarded themselves as French. Prominent figures, including writers like Zola and Anatole France (1844–1924), took up positions on both sides of the debate as French opinion, as well as that of interested observers abroad, became alarmingly polarized. A famous political cartoon of the day depicted a family dinner that begins with the admonition of the head of the family that at all costs the group should avoid talking about the Dreyfus case. The following illustration shows a wild melee, with the caption "They talked about it."

Recent scholarship emphasizing gender has even called attention to the use of sexual stereotyping in political cartoons surrounding the case. For example, the right-wing anti-Dreyfus press frequently ran cartoons that portrayed pro-Dreyfus men as effeminate, even shown in drag. The none-too-subtle message was that their political sympathies called their manhood into question. The visual savagery was matched by vitriolic writing—from both journalistic camps—that often led to duels. This was an age much preoccupied with "honor," especially imagined slights to masculine honor. For many, that was precisely the question raised by the alleged treason. For anti-Semites, Jews were by definition dishonorable. Theodor Herzl (1860–1904), a Viennese journalist, covered the second Dreyfus trial, and his disillusionment at the hideous spectacle of anti-Jewish hysteria influenced his founding of Zionism, the effort to encourage European Jews to move to Palestine.

Meanwhile Dreyfus, a broken man due to his harsh imprisonment, agreed to accept a presidential pardon, offered not long after a second trial had resulted in a repeat of his first conviction. Finally, in 1906, he was cleared of all charges, given his back pay, and promoted to colonel. He served one additional year in the army. He lived quietly until 1935, but it was not until 1998, the centenary year of Zola's famous letter, that the French government fully admitted its errors and those of its military. Although the Dreyfus matter was resolved in time for its namesake to enjoy happier circumstances, the poisonous rhetoric of bigotry fueled new political movements in France and throughout Europe that would bear dangerous fruit decades later. In France, reactionary writers Charles Maurras (1868–1952) and Maurice Barrès (1862–1923), the latter associated for a time with Symbolism and other highly experimental literary movements, founded the proto-fascist party Action Française, which stood for such French "traditional values" as monarchism and Catholicism. They wrapped themselves not so much in the tricolor as in the standard of Joan of Arc.

The Artistic Avant-Garde Before 1914

Even though some prominent writers had played public roles in the Dreyfus affair, for many others, especially for a younger generation interested in new aesthetic directions, the whole business dramatized the sordid character of political life, a life from which the serious artist should hold aloof. The two decades, roughly, preceding the outbreak of World War I, were the heyday of the avant-garde in European artistic circles, and, for the most part, those involved were as eager to detach themselves from bourgeois politics and culture as they were to break with their elders in various artistic fields.

Especially in the visual arts, wave upon wave of avant-garde movements upheld the banner of Modernism, each intending to be more modern than the last. As the name implies, avant-garde artists formed the front line of assault against the retrenched forces of aesthetic convention and complacency of taste. An uncomprehending public barely had time to adjust to the latest artistic heresy before a new "ism" announced itself, as when "Postimpressionism" superceded Impressionism by the 1890s. Just as in the relation of the term "Postmodern" to Modern, this was "post-" not in the sense of negation, but as in building on the gains of the earlier movement. Where Impressionist painters had sought to capture the first fleeting impression or visual effect of a scene, Postimpressionists subjected that moment of sudden realization to relentless geometric analysis, as in the "Pointillist" canvases of Georges Seurat (1859–1891) and Paul Signac (1863–1935).

This effort had led Postimpressionists to the choice of often bizarre, unconventional colors, and subsequently the group of French artists known as les fauves (or "wild beasts") produced canvases aflame with bold oranges, sizzling pinks, and vibrant purples. The young Henri Matisse (1869–1954) was the best-known member of the group. They pursued color as an end in itself. Similarly, Paul Cézanne (1839–1906) explored, in both landscapes and still lifes, the multiple planes and surfaces presented by the objects of his painterly gaze. The result was a style of representation in which objects seemed forever in the act of composing themselves, of coming into a kind of focus.

Cézanne in turn was an enormous influence on Cubism, associated primarily with the French painter Georges Braque (1882–1963) and the Spanish painter Pablo Picasso (1881–1973), who took up residence in Paris. Their canvases, sculptures, and other works increasingly dissected represented subjects into lines, planes, and a variety of geometric sections, often displaying more than one side of a three-dimensional object at once, as in a woman's face in semiprofile. Associated with Cubist painters were poets, such as Max Jacob (1876–1944) and Guillaume Apollinaire (1880–1918). The latter, an important figure for young unconventional writers in prewar Paris as well as during the war, created poems using bizarre typography that amounted to a kind of literary Cubism. He called his shaped poems *calligrammes.*

The circle of artists around Picasso and Apollinaire defined a generational shift in the history of bohemian Paris. Originally concentrated in the North Paris district of Montmartre, early in the twentieth century they moved south to Montparnasse, which they helped to redefine as an artistic quarter. They supported adventurous literary reviews and frequented cafés and cabarets that featured the emerging new music that we know today as jazz. These tastes would continue with subsequent literary and artistic avant-gardes throughout the early decades of the new century.

The Italian Futurists shared many affinities with the Cubists, but were even more aggressively Modernist. Taking their cue from their chief theorist and spokesman Filippo Marinetti (1876–1944), they celebrated the wonders of new machines, treating technological innovation as utopian. In paintings and sculptures, the artists Giacomo Balla (1871–1958), Umberto Boccioni (1882–1916), and Gino Severini (1883–1966) dramatically portrayed the dynamism of mechanical forms. This was in keeping with the views of Marinetti, who disdained traditional motifs in art, pointedly expressing scorn for such a painter as Amadeo Modigliani (1884–1920), who reveled in new explorations of the artistic convention of the female nude. In one of his "Futurist Manifestos" Marinetti declared that the billowing exhaust of a moving automobile was more beautiful than that venerable sculpture that anchors one wing of the Louvre Museum, the piece known as *The Winged Victory of Samothrace.*

The literary side of Futurism expressed itself in the formation of new magazines and reviews in major Italian cities, such as *Leonardo* and *La Voce,* both operating in Florence. These were the creations of a new generation of writers, including Giovanni Papini (1881–1956) and Giuseppe Prezzolini (1882–1982), who looked to Paris as a beacon of avant-garde culture. They embraced the futurists to some extent, but also adhered to the Symbolist aesthetic associated in Italy with the celebrated writer Gabrielle d'Annunzio (1863–1938). His aristocratic bearing and disdain for popular taste would eventually evolve into fascism and fervent support for Benito Mussolini. This also was the path such Futurists as Marinetti followed.

Referring to specific artists as members of avant-gardes can be highly misleading. It is not as if they marched in lock-step under the standard of their particular "ism." Often those with the greatest influence, especially on rebellious younger artists, were isolated figures aloof from any one circle. Such a memorable iconoclast was the outrageous French playwright and all-around provocateur Alfred Jarry (1873–1907). If anything, he was known even more for his personal conduct than for his writings, and that may well be accepted as a principle of avant-garde identity: the life as its own work of art.

In 1896, Jarry, a virtually unknown Paris writer transplanted from Laval in Brittany, brought to the stage his obscure play *Ubu roi* (*King Ubu*). The title character "Ubu" was identified as the King of Poland, and the play was more or less an adaptation of the plot of Shakespeare's *Macbeth*. Ubu appeared as an impossibly bloated pear-shaped figure (which for French culture called to mind the cartoonist Daumier's caricature of the July Monarch Louis-Philippe, known derisively as *"le poire"*—"the pear"), speaking in a high-pitched, grating, machinelike voice. Moreover, his speech mangled even the most commonplace words. In a move that so scandalized the audience that the play had to be interrupted due to several minutes of ensuing pandemonium, the first word of the play, solemnly intoned by Ubu, was *"merdre !"* Not only was this an unacceptable word (*merde* = "shit") for the theater-going public of the day, but Jarry had inserted an extra "r," compounding the impropriety through misuse of the sacred French language.

Jarry gained instant notoriety and went on to write several more "Ubu" plays. But he became known more for his antics: for the pet owl he kept, and for his habit of sitting in cafés drinking absinthe (he became a severe alcoholic), which he sometimes colored with ink. When things got too quiet, he would fire a loaded pistol into the air. Even more outrageous was his speech and appearance, which came to resemble that of his character Ubu. Jarry's one additional activity was his improbable project for a "College of Pataphysics" to promulgate the field of knowledge "pataphysics," which he had invented (and that presumably only he could fathom).

The overworked cliché "ahead of his time" is nevertheless appropriate for this one-of-a-kind literary personality who died in wretched poverty and obscurity. Later the Surrealists would champion him, and the decade of the 1960s saw several new productions of his most famous play around the world. Later generations of French or Francophile writers, just for fun, formed a "College of Pataphysics." The Beatles mentioned "pataphysics" in a song on their album *Abbey Road,* and in the mid-1970s an unconventional rock band from Cleveland, Ohio, emerged calling itself "Pere Ubu," with a lead singer whose shrieking suggested the famous Ubu voice. By the late 1980s some American newspapers began running the offbeat comic strip "Zippy the Pinhead," whose protagonist has the "Ubuesque" look. The cartoonist himself made clear his debt to Alfred Jarry by illustrating a recent paperback book about him.

A far less volatile example of an isolated artist more or less adopted by the early twentieth-century avant-garde was the self-taught painter Henri Rousseau (1844–1910). He was known as Le Douanier Rousseau, for he made his living as a French customs official. In 1886 he began to exhibit his paintings in the Salon des Indépendants (the annual exhibition for innovative artists that began in 1884), immediately attracting the attention of younger artists searching for new approaches. Rousseau often worked on a large scale, filling his canvases with the lush foliage of his imagined tropical scenes, as in *La Charmeuse des serpents* (1907, *The Snake Charmer*) or *Le Rêve* (1910, *The Dream*), or the calm vast sky of *The Sleeping Gypsy* (1897). The dreamlike atmosphere of that and other Rousseau paintings made him a great favorite of the Surrealists.

Most people were not all that concerned with the antics of artists, however intentionally shocking they might have been. However, the unconventional sexual behavior of artists, long a distinguishing characteristic of bohemian types, occasionally provoked the wrath of the bourgeois public. Especially in the period under consideration here, this aspect of bohemian culture awakened morbid anxieties already directed toward particular kinds of sexual behavior, especially sexual freedom for women and homosexuality.

Sexuality and "the New Woman"

Avant-garde artists formed a reputation for relaxed sexual morals, but on close examination their behavior proves to have been far from "anything goes." No less than the rest of their fellow bourgeois did they adhere to a double standard where women's sexual expression was concerned. Men expected to be able to pursue multiple sexual relationships, but not women, most contradictorily. Limits were placed on women artists sexually, just as they were expected to play a lesser, supporting role in the artistic groups of which they were members.

As examples, consider the sculptors Camille Claudel (French, 1864–1943) and Clara Westhoff (German, 1878–1954), each of whom at different times associated herself with the famous sculptor Auguste Rodin (1840–1917). In Westhoff's case, this came about through her marriage to Rainer Maria Rilke. In Claudel's, the identification with Rodin was stronger and more direct. They became lovers. As in Westhoff's case, Rodin admired and encouraged her sculpture, but he may have gone further still, taking credit for works she actually produced. As had been true for centuries, a woman artist working in a male artist's *atelier* might end up with the kind of anonymity art museum curators designate by the phrase "School of . . ."

In many other social spheres, especially in urban locations, what late Victorians called "the New Woman" was emerging, gradually gaining access to male professions, demanding suffrage, and behaving with greater candor and social audacity. Such a woman became an object of dread and morbid curiosity, as can be glimpsed in artistic and literary expression of the age, as well as in popular culture. An example of the former is in the paintings of the Viennese artists Gustav Klimt, where provocative female subjects meet the viewer's gaze with bold defiance. We might also cite the tragic heroines of Henrik Ibsen's (1828–1906) plays. Their unhappy circumstances imply a withering critique of middle-class marriage. In the realm of popular literature, Bram Stoker's (1847–1912) 1899 novel *Dracula* presents female figures, those transformed into vampires by their contact with the title character, as voracious sexual predators spelling doom for the hapless men in their path.

Stoker's novel about mysterious Transylvania was written in London, and it betrays the sexual anxieties of the late 1890s in England. There and elsewhere in Europe, this was a time of the rapid spread of syphilis, which people then regarded with the kind of fatalistic dread that the AIDS epidemic would produce a century later. The hypocritical behavior of promiscuous men—hypocritical because of their insistence on chaste and monogamous marital partners—was clearly the chief reason for this epidemic, but women, or more particularly "the New Woman," became the scapegoats. A promiscuous woman was equated with a prostitute, and prostitutes were seen as socially necessary dangers. Émile

Zola portrayed a prominent courtesan in his novel *Nana,* in which the title character succumbs horribly to the ravages of syphilis.

An additional anxiety about the so-called New Woman was her lack of shame; her lack of concern about social approval and opinions about her behavior, whether heterosexual or homosexual. Especially in the case of homosexuality, which people of the time often referred to discreetly as "inversion," it was considered essential that the behavior express itself in the most furtive, closeted manner. As a result of the growing social power and legal influence of the medical and psychiatric professions, with their penchant for detailed clinical taxonomies, specific acts such as "sodomy" were newly criminalized in many European countries late in the nineteenth century. In England the most famous victim of these aggressive new statutes was the flamboyant playwright and novelist Oscar Wilde (1854–1900).

Wilde's literary notoriety stemmed not only from his authorship of the very successful novel *The Picture of Dorian Gray* and his delightful comedy-of-manners plays, but also from his association with a short-lived avant-garde literary magazine called *The Yellow Book.* The controversial illustrator Aubrey Beardsley (1872–1898) contributed to this review, and he and Wilde together epitomized what was known in literary circles on both sides of the English Channel as "decadence." Beardsley, with his sexually audacious engravings, expressed the sexual libertinism of contemporary bohemianism, and Wilde, with his resplendent sartorial style, embodied the "dandyism" that decades before had been associated with Baudelaire in France. But it was Wilde's out-of-the-closet sexual preference that attracted the greatest notoriety. His behavior was on a real collision course with a newly punitive legal opposition to homosexuality. Although married and the father of children, Wilde made no attempt to hide his relationship with a male lover. He was convicted and sent off to jail in 1898. The experience destroyed his physical and emotional health, and he died in exile in Paris in 1900.

Women were similarly expected to keep any sexual behavior that fell outside the bounds of heterosexual conjugal relations private. One very striking example of a highly intelligent woman, considered influential in her time, who shocked many through her personal daring was the Russian-born Lou Andréas-Salomé (1861–1937). A lifelong, prolific writer, she was born to a family of German-speaking Jews and spent much of her life in points west, in Switzerland, Germany, and Austria. She was married to her husband for forty-five years although the marriage was never consummated. At the age of thirty-five she met the troubled young poet Rilke and they became lovers. Previously she had spurned a proposal of marriage from no less a genius than Friedrich Nietzsche. Much later in life (1928) she would publish a critical study of Rilke's work.

As a writer, Salomé's interests were quite diverse. She published works of formal literary scholarship, such as *Henrik Ibsen's Female Characters* (first published in German, in Berlin, in 1892), in which she signaled the strong interest in female psychology and sexuality that would be engaged by her subsequent encounter with psychoanalysis. She wrote one of the first sympathetic treatments of Nietzsche's philosophy, *Friedrich Nietzsche in seinem Werken* (1894, *Friedrich Nietzsche in His Works*). She shared somewhat Nietzsche's skeptical view of religion, a subject she explored in several essays written from the late 1880s through the middle of the decade following. Her intellectual exchanges with the profoundly influential Jewish thinker Martin Buber (1878–1965) led to her book *Die Erotik* (1910, *The Erotic*). In it she explored both women's erotic and spiritual longings.

With this combination of interests, it is not surprising that Salomé embraced psychoanalysis shortly thereafter. Her greatest intellectual friendship was with Sigmund Freud. He analyzed her and they maintained a warm friendship after the analysis ended. She became an analyst herself, and Freud credited her with several important insights, especially those having to do with feminine sexuality. Salomé was the very embodiment of the kind of woman, acting freely on her own sexual impulses, so feared by the mainstream culture of the day. It is in fact fitting that she embraced psychoanalysis, which owed its origins to the "problem" posed by what had been seen as a uniquely feminine disorder: "hysteria."

Sigmund Freud, Hysteria, and Psychoanalysis

Recent feminist criticism and scholarship has focused in detail on nineteenth-century literary episodes involving characters whose symptoms are viewed by husbands, parents, or others as problems demanding medical treatment. The psychiatric profession of the day had a limited terminology to apply to the disorders they sought to treat, and they tended to make very heavy use of the few they had. One of these, certainly, was "hysteria." Although it was believed to be a uniquely female malady, what was it, exactly? Even though in common usage "hysterical" suggests loud, frantic, even violent actions, patients deemed "hysterical" in the 1880s and 1890s were more often painfully reticent, even catatonic. If they were married women, their unresponsiveness to their husbands was the source of pressure brought to bear on doctors to correct the problem.

Jean-Martin Charcot (1825–1893), of the Salpêtrière Clinic in Paris, was considered the medical professional most successful at treating hysterical patients, and the young Viennese doctor Sigmund Freud (1856–1939) considered himself fortunate to be able to study with Charcot from 1886 to 1887 thanks to a fellowship. As a medical resident in Vienna, Freud had begun seeing female patients whose symptoms baffled him as well as his senior colleagues. Charcot had established a reputation for treating hysterical symptoms using hypnosis, and Freud was eager to learn this technique. Ultimately, however, Freud retained little of lasting value from his time at Salpêtrière. Charcot may have been able to make hysterical symptoms disappear while his patients were under hypnosis, but the symptoms persisted once the spell was over.

Back in Vienna, working with an older doctor named Josef Breuer (1842–1925), Freud gradually abandoned the practice of hypnosis and experimented with other techniques. He moved from interviewing (even interrogating) patients to placing chairs so that doctor and patient faced somewhat away from each other, finding that patients were less intimidated by him this way and talked more freely. Eventually he hit upon the use of the analytic couch, with the patient as relaxed as possible and speaking by "free association" about whatever came to mind (the cardinal rule of the analytic session). As Freud himself was happy to acknowledge, it was his patients who led him to what came to be called psychoanalysis or "the talking cure."

In the early years of his psychoanalytic practice, Freud produced some remarkably diverse writings. In their very diversity they make it difficult to define or situate psychoanalysis exactly. Beginning first in collaboration with Breuer, there were the case studies, a kind of biography (albeit anonymous) that charted the heroic struggles of people suffering profound unhappiness to understand themselves more fully as a means of gaining a greater degree of control over their lives. "Anna O.," "Little Hans," and "The Wolf Man" are as vivid as any fictional characters, and they appeal to readers in that way. This very feature made Freud worry that any claim psychoanalysis might have to be "scientific" was thus undermined.

In addition, Freud used self-analysis as the path toward describing the complicated work of the unconscious through dreams. Many consider the book published in 1900 as *Die Traumdeutung* (*The Interpretation of Dreams;* the German has the advantage of emphasizing the ongoing productions of meaning rather than a kind of static analysis) to be Freud's greatest achievement and one of the landmark books of the last century. Freud distinguished between the literal, or "manifest," content of a dream and its less apparent, or "latent," meanings. One of his most famous formulations in the book was that a dream is a "fulfillment of a wish." This was an insight he applied to many of the things patients unwittingly revealed during analytic sessions.

Another genre for Freud was the more formal exposition of psychoanalytic theory, and several of his most significant theoretical texts were published in the period before 1914, the period during which he formed a psychoanalytic movement whose principal figures included Carl Jung (1875–1961), Alfred Adler (1870–1937), Ernest Jones (1879–1958), Sandor Ferenczi (1873–1933), Karen Horney (1885–1952), Helene Deutsch (1900–1984), and Otto Rank (1884–1939). By far his most controversial work was the *Three Essays on the Theory of Sexuality* (1905), in which Freud defined human sexuality as a lifelong process, quite at odds with prevailing idealized notions of childhood innocence, for example. He also argued against absolute definitions of masculinity, femininity, heterosexuality, or homosexuality. He showed these to be approximate terms and, furthermore, dismissed the idea of "perversion," arguing instead that there is no "natural" object of desire or means of sexual expression.

Like so many other great theorists, however, Freud showed another side in these essays that helps to explain why fierce interpretive debates persist to this day over what we might want to call the "sexual politics" of psychoanalysis. In the third essay, "The Transformations of Puberty," Freud takes up the question of how boys and girls negotiate their different paths of adult sexuality. He argues that girls abandon clitoral stimulation and resign themselves to a "vaginal" emphasis befitting the procreative role. Among other things, he appears to argue that the sexual drive is in and of itself "masculine." Passages like these seem to be in keeping with the notorious and much-misunderstood Freudian concept of "penis envy" and provide ammunition for those who wish to argue that Freudian theory is hostile to women, and particularly to lesbians (or any women not entering into sexual activity for procreative purposes).

Curiously, though, since Freud (like Darwin and Marx) returned later in life to his earlier writings and made significant modifications in them, it is possible to derive two very different readings from this single controversial essay. For example, the same section of "The Transformations of Puberty" that contains this ironclad formula for the attainment of adult feminine sexuality includes a footnote added in 1915 that offers a very open-ended view of the possible developmental paths available sexually to human beings. Freud's later insertion of material that contradicts a key part of his earlier argument helps to explain why there have been "Freudian feminists" as well as anti-Freud feminists. Each camp can find textual support for its particular claims about Freud and psychoanalysis.

Equally controversial for many have been Freud's "metapsychological" writings, in which he sought to apply theories that emerged from analytic practice to broad social and cultural topics. The first such work, *Totem and Taboo,* appeared in 1913. It is a work of mythography (Freud was a passionate collector of Egyptian and Greek antiquities, which often included statuary depictions of mythological characters), and in it Freud describes a primal myth whereby the sons killed and cannibalized their father and tribal chieftain in order to copulate with the mother. This was of course an application of Freud's controversial oedipal theory to the shadowy regions of mythological past from which the Oedipus story emerged in the first place. Freud hypothesized that the sons compensated for the overwhelming guilt they suffered as a result of their deeds by instituting moral laws, including the incest taboo. Freud's implicitly skeptical view of the claims of religion can be seen here, and it is no accident that opposition to Freud often has been strongest in religious quarters.

Despite the fact that the adjective "scientific" was one Freud would have welcomed, it has become a commonplace of European intellectual history to characterize this period as one of a turn toward "the irrational," expressing displeasure with the hubristic claims of science and, most particularly, of Positivism. The reality is more complicated than that, however. Freud was not alone in his approval of the scientific enterprise. He stood for a considerable expansion of its boundaries, much as Marx and Engels had wished to establish historical materialism as science.

Philosophies of Consciousness and the Imagination

Similarly, the German philosopher/historian Wilhelm Dilthey (1833–1911) argued for a new approach to knowledge organized around "sciences of the mind." (*Geisteswissenschaften:* no one English translation can be satisfactory, since the German *Wissenschaft* can mean both "knowledge" and "science," while *Geist,* also depending on context, can refer to "mind" or "spirit"), with "Hermeneutics," or the would-be science of interpretation, as the principal methodology. In Italy, Benedetto Croce (1866–1952) also combined philosophical and historical interests to seek to overcome the sterility of positivism and an attendant overly factual emphasis in historical study. Croce, through his challenging reinterpretations of Vico, Hegel, and Marx, articulated an iconoclastic idealism that influenced the entire generation of young Italian intellectuals that came of age before World War I, even when, as in the case of the Futurists, their response was to argue against it.

But by far one of the most charismatic and influential thinkers who led the rejection of Positivism, and by extension its crudely Cartesian foundation, was Henri Bergson (1859–1941). As a philosopher, he pondered the claims of physical materialism in the face of human mental experience of time and memory. In his books *Matter and Memory* (1896) and *Creative Evolution* (1907) he gave serious attention to the claims of modern science but also emphasized dimensions of human experience, notably the imagination and unconscious life, that do not lend themselves to materialist analysis, searching all the while for ways to bridge the seeming gap across the twin categories of Cartesian thought. Bergson gave fullest expression to his belief in some profound human essence that defies rational dissection in *Creative Evolution*'s concept of *l'élan vital,* or the life force he posited as the impenetrable reality of all organic matter. These ideas found a willing audience in Bergson's well-attended lectures at the Collège de France in Paris.

Their considerable appeal may help to explain why the French were much slower to embrace Freudian ideas than were other Europeans. In a way, Bergson's ideas about human creativity and imaginative experience were a complement to those offered by the influential American philosopher William James (1842–1910) in his *Principles of Psychology,* particularly his concept of the "stream of consciousness" within which we experience ideas and sensations. This phrase would later be applied to any number of modern artists, and the young aesthetes in Bergson's lecture audiences were no less inclined to resonate to his ideas about memory and the creative experience.

The New Physics

The suspicious view of science that lay behind the enthusiastic reception of Bergson's ideas was, paradoxically, based on stereotypical notions of intellectual posturing and claims of epistemological certainty that were beginning to give way, especially in the area of physics. During the second half of the nineteenth century, following the direction established by Michael Faraday (1791–1857) and James Clerk Maxwell (1831–1879), physicists were preoccupied with electromagnetism and with debating whether light was composed of waves or particles, or both. These subjects were beginning to erode the dominance of the Newtonian paradigm, with its absolute concepts of time, space, and indivisible atoms.

In 1885 the physicist A. A. Michelson (1852–1931) and the chemist E. W. Morley (1838–1923) conducted a famous experiment designed to prove the existence of an "ether" through which particles of light move. When they failed to do so, questions multiplied about Newtonian explanations. Not long thereafter, J. J. Thompson (1856–1940) and Ernest Rutherford (1871–1937) discovered that the supposedly indivisible atom was composed of a nucleus with electrons and other particles moving about it. As Max Planck (1858–1947), Niels Bohr (1885–1962), and others built on this research, the field of quantum physics was born. Quantum physics established that energy within atoms exists in discrete packages called "quanta." It was apparent that physicists' ability to predict the location or behavior of subatomic particles was severely limited, something that would be theorized much later by Werner Heisenberg (1901–1976) as the "uncertainty principle."

The most revolutionary rethinking of all of those puzzles afflicting contemporary physics was being carried out in Switzerland by a minor patent clerk named Albert Einstein (1879–1955). Not yet a professional physicist, he embarked upon a series of thought experiments that he formulated in 1905 as a theory of "special relativity" and then broadened ten years later into his theory of "general relativity." The term "relativity" here refers to time and space, the twin Newtonian absolutes. Einstein argued that under extreme circumstances, as when moving objects approach the speed of light, they increase in mass, alter the space around them, and, depending on the point from which they are observed, change the nature of time itself. Einstein summed this up with his famous equation $E = mc^2$ (energy = mass times the speed of light squared).

It would take decades before the far-reaching implications of Einstein's bold hypotheses would become clear. By 1913 he had turned to quantum physics, along with Planck and others. Even though the general public took little notice of the groundbreaking investigations going on in physics, however, it is quite striking how these challenges to the way reality was perceived had their parallels in the arts, including such popular entertainment as cinema. In painting, the pointillist canvases of Seurat and Signac, with their divided particles of light, Cézanne's studies in shifting perspectives, and the Russian painter Wassily Kandinsky's (1866–1944) blotchy shapes and smears all seemed to continue the fascination with particles, waves, and orbiting electrons.

New Directions in Music

The experimental music of the era seems also to challenge age-old perceptions and responses to sound. Composers had long drawn inspiration from literary sources and historical events, but those of the late nineteenth century in particular had turned to very imaginative, experimental writing for their pieces. Claude Debussy (1863–1918) created music that was the equivalent of Impressionism as well as Symbolism, basing one of his most popular works on Mallarmé's poem *Prélude à l'après-midi d'un faune.* The Viennese composer Richard Strauss (1864–1949) created a stirring "tone poem" based on Nietzsche's *Also Sprach Zarathustra* that equaled its literary model in apocalyptic tone. Debussy's pupil Maurice Ravel (1875–1937) refined the Symbolist tradition further, often moving close to jazz influences.

Other new composers experimented with new tonal scales, as in the twelve-tone system introduced by Arnold Schönberg (1874–1951), challenging the audience's ears to adapt to new ways of listening. The spirit of randomness being implied by the new physics and being pursued in avant-garde writing and the visual arts was embraced by the music of the eccentric French composer Erik Satie (1866–1925), whose humorous pieces poked fun at the pretensions of the high classical tradition. Satie declared his music was "not to be listened to," but merely to decorate or provide atmosphere.

As for popular tastes, urban audiences flocked to boulevard theaters and music halls to enjoy lighthearted fare that was often ribald in content. By war's eve in 1914, strains of American Dixieland or jazz were beginning to be heard in European cities and would quickly increase in popularity. This was also a great period for renewed interest in folk music. As modern nations centralized their state apparatuses and educational systems, regional languages and dialects began to be threatened. In response, folk music societies organized to preserve and disseminate the ballads and dance tunes of rural areas and remote regions.

In the British Isles, late Victorian England had undergone a wave of nostalgic enthusiasm for folk forms. The writer William Morris helped create the "Arts and Crafts" movement, which embraced traditional styles and influenced especially the domestic, decorative arts. In a complementary effort, folk music enthusiasts collected traditional songs from Scotland, Wales, and the north of England. In Ireland, nationalist sentiments embraced the Gaelic language, and the poet William Butler Yeats (1865–1939) drew on traditional lyrical forms for inspiration. Lady Gregory (1852–1932) and he founded the Abbey Theatre in

Dublin, where their plays and those by John M. Synge (1871–1909) provided a rallying point for the Irish cause.

Clearly, the period before World War I was one of enormous ferment and diversity, whatever may be said about its social and political stability relative to the disarray created by the war. One very ambitious and controversial spectacle occurring in Paris in 1913 may serve as an appropriate finale to this epoch. The émigré Russian composer Igor Stravinsky (1882–1971) and the Russian ballet impresario Serge Diaghilev (1872–1929), founder of the Ballets Russes staged an elaborate production of *Le Sacré du printemps* (*The Rites of Spring*), combining Stravinsky's challenging new music with the equally challenging choreography that featured the sensational dancer Vaslav Nijinsky (1889–1950), who revolutionized dance by breaking with the formalism of classical ballet, replacing soaring vertical movements with more earthbound (and earthy) ones.

Like the Wagnerians before them, whose influence in France had been felt by Debussy and many others, Stravinsky and Diaghilev sought an overwhelming, total aesthetic experience. In 1917 they would expand this idea further with a performance called *Parade* that featured not only dance and Stravinsky's music, but sets and costumes designed by Pablo Picasso and a libretto by the young writer Jean Cocteau (1889–1963). The opening performance of *Le Sacré du printemps* immediately entered into legend for the scandal it created. Audience members did not understand the music and appeared to find the pelvic gyrations of Nijinsky's faun deeply offensive. Their catcalls, whistles, and other shrill protestations were reminiscent of the response to Jarry's *Ubu roi* years earlier.

Whatever immediate disappointment Diaghilev and Stravinsky may have felt, Cocteau was later to observe that the event went off as planned. In other words it was meant to jar the audience, to astonish them with a demonstration of uncompromisingly modern art. At the close of a turbulent and shocking century, it is nearly impossible to avoid the temptation to see the event as a harbinger of things to come.

Suggestions for Further Reading

Adamson, Walter L. *Avant-Garde Florence: From Modernism to Fascism*. Cambridge, MA: Harvard University Press, 1993.

Berenson, Edward, *The Trial of Madame Caillaux*. Berkeley: University of California Press, 1992.

Bernheimer, Charles, and Claire Kahane, eds. *In Dora's Case: Freud-Hysteria-Feminism*. New York: Columbia University Press, 1985.

Gay, Peter. *Freud: A Life for Our Time.* New York: Norton, 1988.

Nehamas, Alexander. *Nietzsche: Life as Literature.* Cambridge, MA: Harvard University Press, 1985.

Pletsch, Carl. *Young Nietzsche: Becoming a Genius.* New York: The Free Press, 1991.

Rearick, Charles. *Pleasures of the Belle Époque: Entertainment and Festivities in Turn-of-the-Century France.* New Haven: Yale University Press, 1985.

Schorske, Carl E. *Fin-de-Siècle Vienna: Politics and Culture.* New York: Vintage Books, 1981.

Schwartz, Vanessa. *Spectacular Realities: Early Mass Culture in Fin-de-siècle Paris.* Berkeley: University of California Press, 1999.

Seigel, Jerrold E. *Bohemian Paris: Culture, Politics, and the Boundaries of Bourgeois Life, 1830–1930.* New York: Penguin Books, 1987.

Shattuck, Roger. *The Banquet Years: The Origins of the Avant-Garde in France, 1885 to World War I.* Revised Edition. New York: Vintage Books, 1968.

Showalter, Elaine. *Sexual Anarchy: Gender and Culture at the Fin de Siècle.* New York: Viking, 1990.

Sonn, Richard D. *Anarchism and Cultural Politics in Fin-de-siècle France.* Lincoln: University of Nebraska Press, 1989.

Chapter 7

The Great War, the Avant-Garde, and Literary Modernism, 1914 to 1939

It is difficult not to conclude that the Great War of 1914 to 1918 set in motion many of the violent forces and much of the cultural despair that bedeviled the remainder of the twentieth century. The war shattered the confident ideals of an entire generation, many of whom in their disillusioned state would succumb to the lure of the apocalyptic politics of fascism. Of course the war, and the lethal Spanish flu epidemic of 1918 that carried away even more victims than had the weapons of war, decimated the youthful population of Europe. Egon Schiele and his young family were among the influenza casualties.

No one death is necessarily more tragic than another, but histories of the modern arts have made us very conscious of the talented young men whose lives were cut short by the war's carnage. These famously included the English poets Rupert Brooke (1887–1915) and Wilfred Owen (1893–1918). Umberto Boccioni (1882–1916), the Italian Futurist artist, was killed in combat. The mystically inclined, patriotic French poet Charles Péguy (1873–1914) perished in the Marne very early in the war, and the influential Polish-born French poet Guillaume Apollinaire died in 1918 as a result of his war wounds. Those writers fortunate enough to survive the war showed through later works how much it haunted them. One of the most eloquent in this regard was the English poet Siegfried Sassoon (1886–1967). But by far the most influential indictment of the monstrous bloodshed came from a German war veteran, Erich Maria Remarque (1898–1970). His *Im Westen nichts neues* (translated as *All Quiet on the Western Front*) was by far one of the best-selling books of the 1920s and 1930s, and the successful American film based on it exposed even wider audiences to its pacifist message.

From the Trenches to the Avant-Garde

Disillusionment with the war did not have to wait for postwar exposés. Desertion from all armies involved began to be common before the war was even half over. By 1916 a number of young deserters and conscientious objectors had made their way to the neutral haven of Switzerland. Artists among them especially began to "discover" themselves as a subculture in Zürich in 1916. This city already included among its exiles the Russian Bolshevik leader V. I. Lenin, and the expatriate Irish writer James Joyce was also established there, at work on his ambitious novel *Ulysses*.

In a small side street in the heart of Zürich, Hugo Ball (1886–1927) and Emmy Hennings (1885–1948) opened a bohemian gathering spot they called the Cabaret Voltaire, a name selected for the tolerant internationalist outlook it suggested. Ball, a poet, was a deserter from the German army. Jennings was an artist who specialized in creating fanciful hand puppets. Soon after the cabaret opened in February 1916, an unusually talented group of artists and writers, several of whom would become major figures in modern art, became its habitués. From Germany came Hans (Jean) Arp (1887–1966) and his wife, Sophie Taeuber-Arp (1887–1943). He was a sculptor, and they both shared a fascination with the Cubist-inspired art of collage. Also "German," in the same conflicted sense as Arp (who came to prefer the Gallic "Jean"), was the painter and sculptor Max Ernst (1891–1976). As a resident of Alsace, seized by Prussia in the 1870 victory over France, he was drafted into the German army but soon deserted.

Several highly experimental poets, including the Romanian expatriate Tristan Tzara (1896–1963) and Richard Huelsenbeck (1892–1974) of Germany, also participated in the activities of the Cabaret Voltaire, which began to include bizarre poetry performances such as "simultaneous poems," which three or more poets would recite loudly in their respective languages (the same poem in multiple translations); a deliberate internationalist cacophony. Tzara had the inspired idea to cut words out of newspapers and mix them up in a hat. An improvised "poem" would consist of reading the word aloud in the order in which they were drawn from the hat. This procedure had its visual equivalent in Arp's collage work. He would cut up pieces of colored paper and toss them into the air, then gluing them onto a background just as they happened to fall. He considered this making art "according to the laws of chance."

These artists brought together ideas and techniques being explored by the various avant-garde movements of the day, such as Cubism with its use of collage. Cubist artists such as Pablo Picasso had been among the first Europeans to embrace American-style jazz music, this taste in turn being related to a great fascination with African forms. At the Cabaret Voltaire, Romanian artist Marcel Janco (1895–1984) exhibited his distinctive masks inspired by African ceremonial objects, and performances began to include them. Hugo Ball, dressed in a metallic-looking cardboard costume so that he looked like walking Cubist art, presided over increasingly raucous gatherings. Jazz music was played, or sometimes a kind of noise music (*bruitisme*) using found objects. Italian Futurists had similarly experimented with "found sound" and noise music.

In the midst of the mad ferment of the Cabaret Voltaire, Tzara, Ball and others came up with an appropriate name to signal their childlike sense of playful spontaneity as well as their deliberate break with the art of the past. That word was "Dada," and they both embraced and mocked it, deliberately baffling later art historians by producing conflicting accounts of the word's discovery. The ultimate irony is that Dada became merely a specific chapter in the history of modern art, for the expressed intention of the Dadaists was "anti-Art." They wished not to be taken seriously, except as opponents of "Art" as it had functioned within Western bourgeois society, where more often than not the artist had been but the plaything of the wealthy bourgeois.

The Zürich Dadaists were close in playful spirit to the expatriate French painter Marcel Duchamp (1887–1968), who spent the war years in New York City, where his explicitly Cubist painting *Nu descendant un escalier* (*Nude Descending a Staircase*) had been a *succès de scandale* at the groundbreaking Armory Show in 1913. During the following years Duchamp, known as much for his fierce love of the game of chess as for his art, experimented with a new kind of art object he called "ready-mades." These included a simple hardware store snow shovel he titled *In Advance of the Broken Arm,* a porcelain urinal called *Fountain,* and a reproduction of Leonardo da Vinci's *Mona Lisa* with the addition of a penciled-in mustache and Van Dyck beard. This Duchamp mischievously dubbed *L.H.O.O.Q.,* letters that in French pronunciation sound like *"Elle a chaud au cul"*—"She has a hot ass." In subsequent years Duchamp, the American painter and photographer Man Ray (1890–1976), and others who came to be referred to as New York Dadaists maintained close ties with the artists of the Cabaret Voltaire, helping to set the stage, especially in Paris, of Surrealism.

With the war's end, Dadaists dispersed to other European locations. Hugo Ball dropped out of the art world altogether and embraced mystical religion. Richard Huelsenbeck became a physician, eventually making his way to New York City. Other veterans of the Cabaret Voltaire kindled the flames of Dada briefly in other European capitals, most notably Paris and Berlin. The Paris Dadaists, including Tzara and Ernst, gradually turned toward the more programmatic movement of Surrealism, dispensing with the avowed anti-art stance of Dada. But Berlin was another story. The Berlin Dadaists found themselves in a volatile political environment at the outset of Germany's doomed post-war Weimar Republic, and they moved in a very leftward political direction, seeking common cause with proletarian political groups.

Principal figures included George Grosz (1893–1959) and John Heartfield (1891–1968), artists known for savage caricature and what can only be described as "German self-hatred." This they exemplified by changing their names. Grosz had been "Gross" originally. He intended to soften the pronunciation, rendering it less obviously Teutonic, by changing the final letter. Heartfield took this much further, for he had been born Helmut Herzfelde. "John Heartfield" was quite a departure from that very German name. His brother Wieland Herzfelde (1896–1988), a poet associated with Berlin Dada, retained his birth name.

Grosz was skilled in the art of caricature, with bankers, professional army officers, and all overfed complacent bourgeois types as his special targets. He filled his drawings and paintings with their grotesque images. John Heartfield pioneered in the genre of photomontage—creating politically explosive collages out of bits of photographs. He dabbled as well in film. Before Hitler's rise to power in 1933 he directed his visual barbs at the Nazis.

Berlin Dadaists excelled in inflammatory provocation. In 1920 they held a Dada "fair" at a Berlin gallery at which they passed out leaflets bearing the slogan *"Kunst ist Scheisse"* ("Art is shit"). Gallery-goers entered a room dominated by a large object suspended from the ceiling and calculated to offend: a life-size effigy of an Imperial German Army officer with the head of a pig. But Heartfield and his group were not content merely to scandalize the bourgeoisie. They attempted to forge alliances with workers and radical parties that sought to speak in the name of the proletariat. This, after all, was the period immediately following the Bolshevik Revolution, and all European politics was defined in one way or another by responses to this epochal event. There had even been a period beginning after the war's end when Bolshevik-style uprisings had been attempted in Germany, Poland, and Hungary. The short-lived "Spartacist" uprising was crushed in Berlin in 1918, and its leaders Rosa Luxemburg (1871–1919) and Karl Liebknecht (1871–1919) murdered.

These bloody beginnings left Germany's Weimar Republic beset by disaffection from the Right, which wanted to complete the process of destroying the unions and all left-wing parties, and from the Left, which stood for repudiation of Germany's militaristic past. Under John Heartfield's direction, the Berlin Dada group founded its own little magazine with the aim of bridging the gulf between avant-garde artists and German workers. But actual workers no doubt remained quite baffled by the bizarre activities of the Dadaists, and the magazine's whimsical title probably added to their befuddlement: *Jedermann sein eigner Fussball* ("Every Man His Own Football"). The editors sponsored a festive parade designed to bring workers and artists together, and used the occasion to distribute complimentary copies of the magazine. A number of workers joined the parade and partook of the general hilarity, but no lasting political gains resulted from the event.

The would-be radical political engagement of the Berlin Dadaists strikes a dissenting chord given the general tone of cultural responses to the Great War. More typically intellectuals of the 1920s pursued either escapist routes, like the expatriate American "Lost Generation" in Paris in the 1920s (such young writers as Ernest Hemingway and F. Scott Fitzgerald, calling on Gertrude Stein and rubbing elbows with the likes of Pablo Picasso), or gave way to deepening despair and cultural pessimism. Such a turn can be detected in many of the most important works Sigmund Freud wrote in the late stages of his career.

New Developments in Psychoanalysis

The book that most signaled a major shift in Freud's thought was *Beyond the Pleasure Principle,* published in 1922. In it he introduced a new idea, that not only did human beings seek to maximize pleasure, but a "death drive" (*Todestrieb*) within all organic matter impelled human beings toward self-destruction and annihilation. The concept of the death drive originated with Sabina Spielrein, a Russian psychoanalyst who had been analyzed by Freud's former colleague Carl Jung and who became Freud's friend after her analysis ended (by which point Freud and Jung were no longer on friendly terms). Freud's receptivity toward this dark new theme certainly owed something to the disillusioning experience of the war, which ended with the defeat of the Austro-Hungarian forces in which Freud's own sons had served. Moreover, Freud's beloved daughter Sophie fell victim to influenza. His description of her young son at play provides the memorable scenario upon which Freud builds his disturbing new theory.

Later during the same decade Freud again took up the threads of the "metapsychological" analysis he had begun in 1913 with *Totem and Taboo*. In *The Future of an Illusion* (1927) he argued that religious beliefs derive from infantile feelings of helplessness and awe having to do with one's parents, so that concepts of God are so much misrecognition and projection of these primal fears. Like a latter-day Voltaire—although one who had shed even that author's minimal deist beliefs—Freud lamented the obstacles to human progress and happiness brought about through deference to an imagined supernatural realm. In *Civilization and Its Discontents* (1929) Freud drew on his psychoanalytic theory to portray civilization as a coercive force that plunges human beings into grim resignation at best and profound unhappiness at worst by denying the gratification of our most primitive libidinal drives (including that which impels us toward violent acts).

During these last two decades of his life (he died in 1939), Freud was plagued by illness and ended his life by having to flee his home once Vienna was under Nazi occupation, but he enjoyed a greater than ever reputation. He saw to corrected editions of his voluminous writings, presided over the international institution psychoanalysis had become, and gave a number of well-attended lectures, two volumes of which were collected for publication. Occupying some niche between his published case studies and his more intricate theoretical works, the lectures offer specific refinements of the terminology Freud had devised to describe the various agencies of the unconscious, and often include some of his more provocative or enigmatic comments, including several on the topic of feminine sexuality.

Well before these last years of Freud's life, dissenting voices had emerged within the immediate circles around the founder of psychoanalysis. Melanie Klein, Karen Horney, Helene Deutsch, and Ernest Jones (Freud's biographer) had all objected to deterministic aspects of Freud's theories of feminine sexuality, and Melanie Klein (1882–1960) came to reject his emphasis on the oedipal stage of childhood. Instead, she focused on the primary objects (especially the Mother) found in the child's environment during the first year of life, and went on to found the "object relations" school of psychoanalytic theory. Other dissenters from Freud included Wilhelm Reich, whose radical politics were met with disapproval by the International Psychoanalytic Association, while his sexual theories (especially concerning the importance of orgasms) managed to get him drummed out of the Austrian Communist Party.

But the most celebrated and influential of all former Freudians was Carl Gustav Jung, the Swiss analyst whom Freud had regarded with a fatherly affection until their irrevocable break in 1913. Jung, from a Swiss Pietist background, ultimately objected to Freud's atheism and strong sexual emphasis. Building on Freud's study of dreams, Jung went on to elaborate an extensive, scholarly analysis of the symbols found in especially powerful, compelling dream images. Whereas Freud had shown less interest in the specific content of dreams and more in the unconscious processes at work in them, Jung, as his many followers since have done, searched dream narratives for evidence of enduring symbols he called "archetypes," which he went on to argue drew their power from their membership in a universal storehouse of archetypes Jung called "the collective unconscious." This powerful concept has inspired generations of ethnographers, folklorists, mythographers, and literary critics, among other specialists, to develop comparative analyses of cultural mythic symbols found around the globe, often drawing striking parallels among legends, myths, and religious beliefs.

While this kind of emphasis lent itself to broadly humanitarian fraternal feelings, the insistence on certain powerful archetypes has at times played into less benign hands. For example, Jung's concepts of the masculine and feminine sides of human nature, which he expressed by the terms "animus" and "anima," found an echo in some Nazi circles, where rigid stereotypes of masculinity and femininity were promoted at the expense of feminists and homosexuals, among others. Cultural historians in recent years also have objected that Jungian theory is thoroughly ahistorical and cannot account for specific uses made of stories and legends in particular historical periods. Nonetheless, Jung's influence has been enormous, at least rivaling that of Freud by the late twentieth century. During the 1920s prominent people eagerly sought him out, just as many had Freud. James Joyce sent his daughter to be analyzed by Jung.

The Heyday of Literary Modernism

Whether they inclined toward Jung or Freud, or toward such earlier theorists of human psychology as William James or Henri Bergson, writers of the 1920s and 1930s gave free rein to complicated, sometimes baffling but often lyrically stunning explorations of their inner states. This often made for writing that followed not only the "stream of consciousness" of which James had spoken, but the labyrinthine passages of the unconscious where dream fragments, sensations, and fantasies proceed in no fixed order. The writers who pursued this quest for "inner space" represent a further step away from the obligation felt by earlier generations of artists to represent the social or natural world.

Both preceding and following the war, "Expressionism" had been the name applied to writing and especially visual art that represented the powerful emotional or psychological states of the artists, although the realm of the unconscious often received less emphasis than the artist's conscious mental state. Dreams nevertheless played a role, as in the plays of August Strindberg (1849–1912), the tormented Swedish writer who built on the naturalist theater of Henrik Ibsen (1828–1906), of George Bernard Shaw (1856–1950) in England, and of Anton Chekhov (1860–1904) in Russia. In Germany the earliest fictions of Thomas Mann (1875–1955) and Hermann Hesse (1877–1962) can be called Expressionist, and the painter Max Beckmann (1884–1950), like his Austrian counterpart Oskar Kokoschka (1886–1980), produced canvases vibrant with the emotionalism of their creator. Paul Klee (1879–1940) was an iconoclastic, mystical Swiss painter whose canvases contain hauntingly simple childlike images. The Russian-born modern master of abstraction Wassily Kandinsky (1866–1944) went through an early Expressionist phase, during his involvement with the German "Blaue Reiter" group of artists. A neo-Romantic quality in paintings dramatized the profound feeling of the artists who produced them, something certainly anticipated by the Postimpressionist art of Vincent Van Gogh.

For the novelists and poets now associated with the high point of literary Modernism, inheriting a Symbolist linguistic credo and embracing the unavoidably recondite material of the creative unconscious, the ruins of the postwar world around them seemed to necessitate the journey within, even if that journey often led to a psychological no-man's land.

The voyage within developed in stages. For some of the most important writers of the early 1920s, the social world still provided ample subject matter, even if perceived and reported through the lens of intense introspection. Marcel Proust (1871–1922) is the defining example for French fiction. After becoming known in his young years as something of a social climber and man about town, Proust, plagued with severe asthma and often quite ill, more or less confined himself to his bed after his beloved mother's death in 1905 and remained there for the most part, working assiduously on his epic novel *A la recherche du temps perdu* (literally *In Search of Lost Time* but more often translated as *Remembrance of Things Past*). It runs to four long volumes in the standard French edition but consists of seven shorter books that can be read separately.

On one level, Proust's novel is a lament for a vanished social world, especially the seemingly carefree world of the French haute bourgeoisie in the period leading up to 1914. The young narrator "Marcel" gradually discovers love, social mores (including the extremely conflicted views of homosexuality found among the sophisticated elites), and the vocation of an artist through a series of characters portrayed quite vividly in these pages, some of the richest in all of French prose. But a much more profound aspect of this partly autobiographical work is its discussion of memory, the memory the writer hopes to be able to call upon to reconstruct the lost world and to redeem "lost time" through the means of literary creation. As he recounts several episodes in which "Marcel" is overwhelmed by the sudden uprush of long-dormant memories, Proust distinguishes between willed, conscious memory (which cannot help but fail us) and the involuntary memory awakened by random encounters with smells, tastes, sounds, and other sensations. This latter type of memory, inspired by the Symbolist concept of *synaesthesia,* thanks to the pivotal episodes in which its operation is described in Proust's novel, has since come to be called "Proustian" memory.

André Gide (1869–1951) was a French novelist who shared many of Proust's concerns, including the need to recover the bygone world of Belle Epoque Paris. His *Les Faux-Monnayeurs* (1925, *The Counterfeiters*) contained vivid portrayals of the histrionics of such fin-de-siècle figures as the unforgettable Alfred Jarry. Gide was eager to explore new stylistic directions that freed writers from the intimidating examples of the novelistic masters of the previous century. He is famous for his exasperated quip, when asked to name the greatest French writer, *"Victor Hugo, hélas!"* ("Alas, Victor Hugo.") By this he meant that younger writers had to fight against the sense that nothing new could be accomplished that could rival the accomplishments of such a master, especially one who so towered over the French cultural landscape. Gide's later fiction, offered in a distinctively lyrical style, did point the way to newer models of writing. His *L'immoraliste* (1902, *The Immoralist*) introduced the kind of rootless antihero that would become such a staple of fiction after mid-century. Like Proust a homosexual, Gide dealt much more directly in this book with his protagonists's sexual preference than Proust had, even if by later out-of-the-closet standards his approach remains rather oblique.

Sexual audacity and vivid descriptive prose marked by a strong neo-Romantic sensibility were the hallmarks of the novels of the French writer Sidonie-Gabrielle Colette (1873–1954), known to an admiring if occasionally scandalized public simply as "Colette." After an adventurous early life that included a stint as a Paris music-hall performer, Colette threw herself into writing. Although she wrote throughout her life and became most widely known as the author of *Gigi* (1944), which was adapted for the popular 1958 film, the decade of the 1920s was the period of her most important literary achievement with the novels *Chéri* (1920), *La Fin de Chéri* (1926, *The Last of Chéri*), and *Le Blé en herbe* (1923, *The Ripening Seed*). Love affairs and the discovery of love by young people are the central themes of these books. Colette went on to write characteristically frank memoirs—for example, *Mes Appresentis-sages* (1936, *My Apprenticeships*)—and, especially through widely reproduced portraits by several of France's leading photographers, to become an iconic figure of twentieth-century French culture.

Lyricism in prose, in some cases a legacy of the prose poems of such Symbolist writers as Rimbaud, Mallarmé, and Valéry, combined with deep psychological introspection in some of the greatest fictional achievements of writers during the 1920s. The German writer Hermann Hesse's (1877–1962) books *Demian* (1919), *Siddhartha* (1922), *Steppenwolf* (1927), and *Narcissus and Goldmund* (1930), among many others, captured the profound disillusionment of the postwar generation of German youth. This sensibility, tempered with elements of neoromanticism and nightmarish glimpses of new forms of cultural alienation, made him a writer whose books continued to appeal to youthful readers later in the century (which in turn sometimes produced a negative backlash of critical opinion).

Two great English novelists of the period whose fiction takes us within the often emotionally turbulent and complicated psyches of their principal characters were D. H. Lawrence (1885–1930) and Virginia Woolf (1882–1941). In both cases they represent a recognizable social milieu, but the accent falls always on the haunted interior of their subjects' consciousness (which of course includes the unconscious). The class formation of these two writers could hardly have been more divergent. Lawrence was the frail, sickly, sensitive product of a Lancashire coal-mining family. His great *Bildungsroman Sons and Lovers* (1913) portrays the excruciating discomfort of growing up with an artistic temperament in such a coarse, seemingly doomed environment. Yet while Lawrence through this and other novels (e.g., *The Rainbow,* 1915; *Women in Love,* 1916; *Aaron's Rod,* 1922; *The Plumed Serpent,* 1926; and *Lady Chatterley's Lover,* 1928) clearly expressed the determination to embrace a life of beauty and aesthetic refinement, he also sought to compensate for his own physical frailty by extolling the virtues of characters who exhibit the violent iconoclasm evoked by the more excessive passages of Nietzsche. This kind of fascination with brute violence attended by the implication that bourgeois democratic society is "effeminate" was called more and more into question with the rise of fascism.

Where Lawrence's artistry had to contend with a frail body, the exceptional brilliance of Virginia Woolf's writing emerged through increasingly debilitating struggles with a tormented mind. (She suffered from an extreme case of manic-depression.) She lost this battle in 1941 when she took her own life, but not before producing a voluminous body of writing that included novels, diaries, letters, criticism, and occasional essays. Born Virginia Stephen, Woolf was the product of a privileged, highly conspicuous late Victorian family. She married the writer Leonard Woolf (1880–1969), and together in London they anchored the formidable group of aesthetes and scholars known as the Bloomsbury Group. Through their circle the Woolfs supported a number of activities in the arts. They also established their own press, The Hogarth Press, which very notably brought out the *Standard Edition* of Freud's works in English translation.

Many of Virginia Woolf's novels, like Lawrence's, were partly autobiographical, and like him she also provided recognizable historical and social settings that capture certain essences of early twentieth-century English life. Yet far more than he, she moved increasingly toward a flowing, spiraling prose style that plunged ever more deeply into the psychic recesses of her characters, what she called "the wedge-shaped core of darkness." Her greatest work of the 1920s shows both tendencies at work. *Mrs. Dalloway* (1925) narrates the events of a single day in London, where Clarissa Dalloway, a pillar of high society, busies herself with preparations for her elegant party. All the while, through the memories, regrets, and longings of several characters—especially the title character—the reader enters an interior world of human emotion that is far more profound and powerful than any of the surface occurrences noted at the chronological level of narrative.

Woolf's next novel, the elegiac *To the Lighthouse* (1927), represented a more powerful surge of "stream of consciousness," as the author cathartically confronted the complicated emotional legacy of her childhood. *To the Lighthouse* contains one of the most powerful portrayals in all literature of a mother-daughter relationship. Woolf was concerned with all aspects of relationships between women, including the erotic dimension. Although very much committed to her relationship with her husband, Leonard, her most passionate bond was the one she experienced with the writer Victoria Sackville-West (1889–1962).

Virginia Woolf continued to explore the themes she dealt with so masterfully in *Mrs. Dalloway* and *To the Lighthouse* all the way through to her last novel, *Between the Acts* (1940). After completing each one, she was subjected to ever-more-intense bouts of the manic-depressive disorder she suffered. Her nonfiction covers a wide range of topics, literary and otherwise. Literary themes dominate in the two collections she published under the title *The Common Reader* (1925). Her strong feminist beliefs received eloquent expression in *A Room of One's Own* (1929) and *Three Guineas* (1933). Probably no writer in English has exerted a more powerful influence over the course of twentieth-century feminist thought than Virginia Woolf, and she remains unmatched for the psychological acuity she was able to express in her novels.

Woolf's Bloomsbury circle included the novelist E. M. Forster (1879–1970), and he shared some of her important characteristics as a writer, including her introspection and her attention to the psychological intricacies and obstacles that complicate human interpersonal relationships. Like Woolf, he was also a prolific writer of literary essays and criticism. And finally, as with Woolf, his homosexuality was a very important part of his makeup as a writer, although the one novel he devoted to the subject, *Maurice,* was not published until the year after his death, despite having been completed in 1914.

Inspired in part by the domestic conflicts he observed between his own parents, several of Forster's novels, including *A Room With a View* (1908) and *Howard's End* (1910), focus on the disappointments in human relationships caused in part by inhibitions and the distances people set between themselves. Forster explored this to great effect in his novel *A Passage to India* (1924), where the psychological tangles human beings ensnare themselves in are played out against the backdrop of colonial India, a country the author had visited twice. As in the works of Conrad that probed the motivations of people operating in colonial settings, Forster's book is made all the more compelling through the portrayal of characters deluded by their own ideas and defeated by their own best intentions, even when those intentions give evidence of an admirable generosity of spirit and tolerance of cultural difference.

By far the most ambitiously experimental novelist of the early twentieth century in English was the Irish expatriate writer James Joyce (1882–1941). Perhaps the word "English" should be qualified, for the dauntingly polyglot Joyce increasingly moved toward a prose style that played and punned with words along multiple linguistic registers. His earliest books, *Dubliners* (1906) and *A Portrait of the Artist as a Young Man* (1912), portray the Dublin of his upbringing and, in the latter book, lays bare the rage of youthful rebellion against a stifling, controlling Irish Catholic family felt by the future writer Stephen Daedalus, the novel's "artist as a young man."

The book was Joyce's farewell to Ireland, and he was to spend the rest of his life in exile in France and Switzerland. Dublin continued to haunt his creative imagination, however, and figures most prominently in his breakthrough novel *Ulysses*. This book, published in Paris in 1922, pointed the way to a whole new world—one we have come to call "Joycean"—for this particular literary genre. In a modern reworking of Homer's *Odyssey*, Joyce takes the reader on a meandering journey through Dublin, Ireland, during the course of one twenty-four-hour period. It happens to be June 16, 1904. Our "guide" is the tumultuous mental world of one Leopold Bloom, who meets with friends, including the young writer Stephen of Joyce's earlier novel, shops for food, attends to certain bodily functions whose details are part of the narrative, and worries about the infidelities of his wife, Molly, whose surging monologue brings *Ulysses* to its memorable close.

The frank discussion of the body's longings and most intimate routines and procedures kept *Ulysses* at the center of legal proceedings in Europe as well as in the United States, where it was the subject of a landmark obscenity case in 1933 (decided in favor of the book). It was also, from the start, one of the world's most difficult books to read and understand. Joyce seemed to cast his lot with the Mallarméan stance as an author for the "happy few" willing to invest enough time to meet the heavy demands the text exacts of them. That celebrated difficulty has spawned any number of critical guides and exegeses, all of which have made it easily one the most formally examined literary works in the Western tradition and have placed Joyce on a par with Shakespeare and Dante in this regard.

Joyce's next and final work, *Finnegans Wake* (1939), surpassed even its predecessor by light-years in complexity, with its multilingual prose pastiche and arcane allusions to three Italian writers: Dante, the sixteenth-century heretic Giordano Bruno, and the almost forgotten eighteenth-century philosopher Giambattista Vico. It is a rollicking tempest of a book, where earthy, slapstick humor and scholarly erudition merge into some new and unprecedented discourse. Moreover, time itself strays from its conventional linear pattern in a book where the last word of the text is "The," coiling back around to the opening "riverrun."

If Joyce was the Irish writer who defied the literary public, the poet William Butler Yeats (1865–1939), who wrote many of his greatest poems during the decades between the world wars, basked in the adulation especially of Irish compatriots. He embraced the very culture Joyce had fled and, becoming a member of the Irish Senate in his last years, was an important symbol of the new nation. (Independence from Great Britain came in 1922.) As a younger poet, Yeats had articulated a fervent Irish nationalism, demonstrating a fascination with ancient legends and lore, including a love of the Gaelic language. But as a poet he drew on sources beyond Ireland, more generally from the Symbolist aesthetic that defined much of European poetry of his generation.

In his remarkable prose work *A Vision* (1909), Yeats elaborated an intricate, obscure cosmology and artistic credo, complete with private symbols whose interrelationships came to define some of his more difficult poems. This mystical esotericism was reminiscent of William Blake, whose literary reputation Yeats did much to rescue from oblivion. Yeats's formulation of a private cosmology bore some kinship with his admiration for the ideas of Nietzsche, and the apocalyptic tone and aristocratic aloofness of that philosopher's texts (e.g., *Zarathustra*) has its echoes in some of Yeats's more difficult poems. One of the most admired later poems, "The Second Coming," alludes to the obscure theories of *A Vision* and expresses a dark foreboding of the clouds darkening over Europe in the late 1930s, epitomized by the final lines about a "rude beast" detected "slouching towards Bethlehem to be born."

This combination of esoteric symbolism and Nietzschean doomsaying has led some critics to accuse Yeats of flirtation with fascism. In terms of disillusionment with bourgeois politics and morbid dread of mass culture, there may be some truth in this. But it is probably safe to say that Yeats leaned no more toward fascism than many of his artistic contemporaries, and his embrace of the Irish struggle against Britain may even suggest political kinship with the more "Left" postcolonial movements of liberation that came to the fore during the last half of the twentieth century.

Politics, technology, and the alienation produced by twentieth-century life shaped the literary creations of Aldous Huxley (1894–1963), scion of a famous and controversial English family (his grandfather was T. H. Huxley). Such early works as *Antic Hay* (1923) and *Point Counter Point* (1928) satirized contemporary English society, but Huxley was to make a dramatic departure with a groundbreaking and wildly successful novel published in 1932. This was the dystopic work *Brave New World*, which portrays a future society of defeated souls dominated by technocrats and psychological manipulation. Few twentieth-century novels commented as persuasively on the totalitarian horrors of the age. Along with the continued popularity of *Brave New World*, Huxley's later works increased his influence for the generations following World War

II, especially during the 1960s. These included *The Devils of Loudon* (1952), Huxley's historical investigation of bizarre episodes involving a seventeenth-century convent, and *The Doors of Perception* (1954), an account of the author's experiments with hallucinogenic drugs.

In France during the 1920s, Paul Valéry (1871–1945) stepped into the role of Symbolist poet and aesthetician created by his mentor Stéphane Mallarmé, though Valéry would enjoy much more prominence and recognition during his life than had Mallarmé. In 1925 Valéry was elected to the august Académie Française. Like his predecessor, Valéry was an all-around man of letters and in addition to his poems produced writings on philosophy, art, and notably theater. His musings on the latter topic were published under the title *Monsieur Teste*. His greatest poetic achievement was the calm, contemplative poem, rife with allusions to Western philosophy, *"Le Cimitière marin"* ("The Cemetery by the Sea"), published in 1922.

Other great Symbolist European contemporaries in poetry retreated much more into private realms, in some cases living lives hampered by debilitating illness or marked by considerable obscurity. Although in failing health in his difficult last years, Rainer Maria Rilke produced his most profound and haunting poetry in his *Duino Elegies*. The tone of these poems is one of brooding resignation, with the enduring truth of artistic creation as the only redemptive hope that can be glimpsed. Rilke's poems remain remarkable achievements in the German language, for he brought his Francophilic tendencies to bear so that German took on some of the lighter touches of Romance languages. It was the kind of effort Nietzsche, with his love of the Italian language, had been able to achieve for German prose. Rilke spent his last days in a Swiss sanatorium. Like Joyce, he lies buried in Switzerland, where his tombstone is inscribed with his brief, disturbing poem "Rose, oh reiner Widerspruch" ("Rose, oh Pure Contradiction").

Introspective poetic exploration reached extreme lengths in the iconoclastic achievements of Fernando Pessoa (1888–1935). His poems have become the most admired in twentieth-century Portugal, but he toiled in almost complete obscurity, earning his living as a minor office clerk in Lisbon. If he was self-effacing in his daily life, he called the self even more radically into question in the following way. Modern poets have certainly done much to undermine the large role, developed by Romantics, of the authorial self or subject, but no one has gone as far in this regard as Pessoa. He dislodged the poetic persona by multiplying it. He published his poems under several different names, which he called "heteronyms." To an impressive degree, the poems shift in tone, style, and imagery from "author" to "author." An Anglophone, Pessoa also wrote a number of poems in English.

Elsewhere on the Iberian peninsula, Pessoa's contemporary Federico García Lorca (1898–1936) provides a contrasting example of a poet very much acclaimed in his lifetime. His was a flamboyant personality, and he lived his life in the thick of public events, traveling widely and eventually falling victim to Generalissimo Francisco Franco's fascist Falange militia in the first months of the Spanish Civil War. *Poeta en Nueva York* (*Poet in New York*) was his best-known collection of poems; poems that celebrate the dynamism of that great modern city where he spent several months in 1929 at Columbia University. But although the stance and sentiments of Lorca's poetry were modern, he drew formally on traditional songs of his native Andalusia. His were not the modernist poetics of Symbolism, for example.

For Western Europe, Lorca's populist leanings were the exception rather than the rule for this period of history. Aloof, quasi-aristocratic disdain for the vulgar masses is more typical, especially for those poets working in the consciously difficult, post-Mallarméan tradition. The American-born, naturalized English poet T. S. Eliot (1888–1965) epitomizes these tendencies, and his groundbreaking poems, like those of his American poetic mentor Ezra Pound (1885–1972), have been among the most influential of the century. He enjoyed a long reign at the top of the modern English poetic canon.

In 1922, the same year in which Joyce published *Ulysses,* Eliot published "The Waste Land," a poem that captured like no other the mood of ominous dread suffusing the hectic urban atmosphere that increasingly defined European civilization as the twentieth century advanced. Like Pound, who reportedly pared down the original version of the long poem by half, Eliot displayed his considerable erudition through each section of his master-work. The poem bristles with quotes and paraphrases not only from such poets as Baudelaire, but from such sacred texts as the Hindu Upanishads. Eliot was supplying the equivalent for poetry of the heavy learning Joyce brought to his fiction. But Eliot went him one better: He supplied footnotes!

Much like the "fugitive" poets of the American Deep South, Eliot's distaste for the banal, impersonal character of modern culture led him to embrace an almost feudal vision of culture. While qualitatively different from the anti-Modernism of fascism, it was no less reactionary. Personally, Eliot found solace more and more in Anglican religious observance. The careful, elegant structure of *The Four Quartets* (1943), his last major collection of poems, builds steadily toward a peaceful mood of religious consolation. Eliot tried his hand successfully at several literary genres. He wrote plays, critical essays, and the light verse of his much-loved *Old Possum's Book of Practical Cats* (1936). He was not always the imperious, crisp, and correct person his appearance and carefully mannered accent indicated.

Eliot's "The Waste Land" and Yeats's "The Second Coming" have often been compared for the tone of foreboding that warn of horrors to come as the twentieth century unfolds. Some additional examples from prose fiction should be cited. Perhaps fittingly, they all come from the German language. The name of one of these is commonly used in adjectival form to refer to the alienating, impersonal nature of modern institutions and societies. That word is "Kafkaesque," and the writer was of course Franz Kafka (1883–1924).

Very little of his work was known until after his death. *Der Prozess* (*The Trial*), his most famous novel, was published the following year, in 1925. It is the maddening story of one Joseph K., a man who has been arrested and who faces trial, only he can learn neither why he has been arrested nor the name of his offense. A person facing punishment without out understanding the reason is a favorite Kafka theme, rendered horrifically in his story "In the Penal Colony." Kafka showed his readers a world devoid of reassurance or even logic one can comprehend, except perhaps at the moment of death. A lonely, persecuted office worker, this was much the way the author experienced his own society. As a Jew and a member of the minority German-speaking community in Prague, Czechoslovakia, Kafka was doubly an outsider. The desperate attempt to be understood and accorded sympathy by the majority culture found powerful expression in the story "Metamporphosis," in which the protagonist Gregor Samsa wakes one day to discover that he has been transformed into a giant hideous beetle.

Few writers have suggested more ominously than Kafka that human beings are increasingly not "at home" in modern society. Some have suggested that a newly diminished, psychologically shriveled kind of person is being created by the brutal forces of modernity. The German novelist Robert Musil (1880–1942) suggested as much in the very title of his ambitious long work, *Der Mensch ohne Eigenschaften* (*The Man Without Qualities*). Musil's novel has been compared both to Joyce's *Ulysses,* for its detailed cultural references, and to Proust's *A la recherche du temps perdu* for its introspective psychology.

But in many ways perhaps the most sweeping indictment of contemporary civilization by a German author came from Thomas Mann (1875–1955) in his great allegorical novel *Der Zauberberg* (*The Magic*

Mountain), published in 1924. Mann's literary reputation had been established well before 1914 with his early novel *Buddenbrooks* (1901) and his compelling novella of aesthetic decadence *Tod in Venedig* (1912, *Death in Venice*). When he received the Nobel Prize in Literature in 1929, he was recognized not for *The Magic Mountain* but for his earlier work.

Subsequent critical opinion has placed the huge novel of 1924 in a much more prominent position. The title refers to the location of a Swiss sanatorium that Hans Castorp, the youthful protagonist, has entered. The astonishing encounters and experiences he has there add up to a disillusioned survey of modern civilization much like Eliot's "The Waste Land." Mann's novel is another of those interwar literary works that in retrospect seems a harbinger of the devastation to come in another catastrophic war, and indeed Mann was one of the most prominent of a whole generation of German intellectuals who were able to escape Hitler's Germany for refuge in the United States, where the author lived from 1933 to 1952.

Suggestions for Further Reading

Eksteins, Modris. *Rites of Spring: The Great War and the Birth of the Modern Age.* New York: Anchor Books, 1990.

Fussell, Paul. *The Great War and Modern Memory.* New York: Oxford University Press, 1975.

Gay, Peter. *Weimar Culture: The Outsider as Insider.* New York: Harper & Row, 1968.

Kern, Stephen. *The Culture of Time and Space, 1880–1918.* Cambridge, MA: Harvard University Press, 1983.

Lee, Hermione. *Virginia Woolf.* New York: Knopf, 1997.

Norris, Margot. *Beasts of the Modern Imagination: Darwin, Nietzsche, Kafka, Ernst, and Lawrence.* Baltimore: Johns Hopkins University Press, 1985.

Rubin, William S. *Dada and Surrealist Art.* New York: Abrams, 1968.

Wohl, Robert. *The Generation of 1914.* Cambridge, MA: Harvard University Press, 1979.

Chapter 8

Philosophy, Politics, and
Culture in Crisis, 1914 to 1945

Novelists and poets brooding on all that afflicted modern civilization had their counterparts in philosophy and related fields. The German philosopher/historian Oswald Spengler (1880–1936) sounded an ominous death knell with his multivolume work *The Decline of the West,* published soon after World War I. Spengler likened civilizations to organic beings and therefore inescapably finite in duration. As his title suggests, he judged Western civilization to be entering its senescence. A less pessimistic, if no less alarmist, tract was *The Revolt of the Masses* (1929), by José Ortega y Gasset (1883–1955), the leading member of the generation of Spanish intellectuals that followed the influential Miguel de Unamuno (1864–1936), whose *The Tragic Sense of Life* (1913) had summed up the prewar mood of Spain's intellectual elite. Breaking with the discussion of social class found throughout modern writing, Ortega argued for an elitism of taste and aesthetic refinement that could overcome what he saw as the pervasively degrading influence of mass culture. While a carefully constructed, thoughtful book, the argument of *Revolt of the Masses* was but a newer version of the essential view Matthew Arnold had expressed decades earlier in *Culture and Anarchy.* Now, however, it entered the volatile climate of emergent fascism. Fascist politicians were no less contemptuous of the masses whose allegiance they cynically manipulated, yet antidemocratic intellectuals played right into their hands, usually unwittingly.

Meanwhile, philosophy for the most part continued its steady retreat from the sociopolitical world. In England, following Bertrand Russell (1872–1970) and George Moore (1873–1958), the movement known as Logical Positivism pursued an antimetaphysical line of thought, ever more preoccupied with elegantly constructed arguments and mathe-matically precise proofs. Ludwig Wittgenstein (1889–1951) was an Austrian philosopher who befriended Russell as his student at Cam-bridge University and, after bitter wartime military service for the los-ing Austro-Hungarian cause, returned to spend most of his later years in Cambridge.

Wittgenstein, fond of language games and cerebral challenges of all kinds, was a brilliant and difficult philosopher whose treatise *Tractatus Logico-Philosophicus* (1922), with its use of symbolic notation, is notori-ously complicated and daunting for most readers. Remarkably, he com-pleted the initial draft of the manuscript in the trenches as an Austrian soldier in 1916. His *Philosophical Investigations,* culled in part from his students' notes and published posthumously in 1953, was more accessi-ble. Wittgenstein emphasized the determining power and real limits that language imposes on knowledge and argued that, because of inescapable properties of language, the world in large part defies our attempts to philosophize about it.

During most of his life, Wittgenstein's work was known to but a small circle of people. More celebrated in their time, yet destined even more to exert enormous influence on philosophy in later decades, were the two major thinkers associated with Phenomenology. Edmund Husserl (1859–1938), who was born in Vienna but moved on to teach in Ger-man universities until Nazi policy turned him and other Jews out in 1933, inaugurated this movement, which redefined the object of phi-losophy as the careful examination of the effects on human conscious-ness of the phenomena we encounter in what Husserl called the "life-world." Thus Husserl emphasized perception rather than a priori concepts in the mind.

Husserl's student Martin Heidegger (1889–1976) built on the work of the mentor he repudiated when he himself embraced Nazi ideology. Like Nietzsche, whose major reinterpreter he became, Heidegger stud-ied ancient Greek thought in detail and came to believe that virtually all of Western metaphysics followed from a serious misunderstanding of what the Greeks meant by "being." His exploration of the linguistic nu-ances of being is at the heart of his masterwork *Sein und Zeit (Being and Time,* 1927). Heidegger's preoccupation with language set the stage for much of late twentieth-century philosophy, and his concept of human beings as being inexplicably hurled, or "thrown" *(geworfen)* into exis-tence became the foundation of the Existentialist movement of the 1940s. His personal response to twentieth-century existence was to em-brace the anti-Modernism of the Nazi Party. As rector of the University of Freiburg in the Black Forest region of Germany, he became famous for the Swabian peasant garb he preferred.

But retreat from modernity or espousal of fascist ideology were not the only paths taken by German philosophers of the interwar years. In Frankfurt during the 1920s a group of philosophers and critics sympathetic to the Bolshevik Revolution and dismayed by the defeat of revolutionary movements in Germany and elsewhere in Europe founded the Institut für Sozialforschung (Institute for Social Research). Led by philosophers Max Horkheimer (1895–1973) and Theodor W. Adorno (1903–1969), this group of intellectuals sought to look deeply within bourgeois culture to understand its resistance to radical politics. Their methodology was a hybrid of Marxism and Freudian psychoanalysis, increasingly associated with Erich Fromm (1900–1980) and Herbert Marcuse (1898–1979) after Hitler's rise to power sent the group into American exile. From that vantage point, Horkheimer and Adorno, the latter a gifted amateur classical pianist, made the mass "culture industry" the major object of their "Critical Theory" and also participated in a group study, designed to explain German support for Hitler, called *The Authoritarian Personality*. Horkheimer and Adorno returned to Germany after World War II, but Marcuse stayed in the United States for the rest of his life, as did Leo Löwenthal (1900–1993), a sociologist and founding member of the Frankfurt School who wrote studies of media and popular culture.

A brilliant, cultivated critic associated briefly with the Frankfurt School whose influence on literary theory and criticism grew much greater by the century's end was Walter Benjamin (1892–1940). Benjamin was a very complicated man with interests both in Marxism and esoteric Judaism and both high culture and popular culture. He wrote ingeniously about the role of photography in modern culture and argued that the "aura" of artworks had been eroded in the era of "mechanical reproduction." Benjamin's Marxist historical materialism, tinged with elements of gnostic Judaism, shaped his aphoristic "Theses on the Philosophy of History." (1950; written 1940) His work on Baroque German drama engaged him in dialogue with the radical playwright Bertolt Brecht.

A Francophile who wrote a number of his essays in French, Benjamin emigrated to France in 1933, where he carried out an ambitious program of research on Parisian culture in the ages of the July Monarchy and the Second Empire. Benjamin saw the decades from 1830 to 1870 as the time of the emergence of modern consumer culture, and he designated Paris as "the capital of the Nineteenth Century." He deeply loved such French writers as Baudelaire and Proust, but his embrace of French culture also prevented his timely escape from the Nazi advance. After France fell in 1940 he made his way south into the Pyrenees. When detained temporarily by guards at the Spanish border, he panicked and committed suicide by swallowing cyanide.

Surrealism

The years Benjamin spent in Paris were the heyday of French Surrealism. The Surrealists had emerged in 1924 from the ranks of Parisian Dada, but unlike the "anti-art" Dada, theirs was a more programmatic movement, as made apparent by the formal expression of their spokesman's André Breton's *Manifestos*. Breton (1896–1966) was a poet of a decidedly theoretical bent. The politics he urged on Surrealists was vaguely Marxist, and he expressed keen interest in Freud's theories of the unconscious. This emphasis in turn led him to proclaim a literary genealogy for Surrealists that included such maverick nineteenth-century writers as Lautréamont and Rimbaud, writers who explored the landscapes of dreams. Surrealist writers also upheld the renegade example of the forbidden tradition in French writing inaugurated by the Marquis de Sade. Breton's example of deliberately transgressive writing was of enormous interest to Georges Bataille and Maurice Blanchot, writers loosely associated with Surrealism whose work would become much better known in later decades.

Fellow French poets Robert Desnos (1900–1945), Louis Aragon (1897–1982), Philippe Soupault (1897–1990), Paul Éluard (1895–1952), and Benjamin Péret (1899–1959) certainly shared these enthusiasms, but the most stunning works that celebrated or invoked the dreaming state were paintings and films. The flamboyant Spanish artist Salvador Dali (1904–1989) created highly arresting scenes, using a combination of realistic imagery and distorted, anamorphic perspective. *The Persistence of Memory* (1931), the desertlike scene featuring Dali's famous limp watch, is one of the most notable examples of his early Surrealist technique. Former Dadaist Max Ernst worked often on a very large scale in his canvases, but his most thoroughly oneiric images came in his collage series *La Semaine de bonté,* whose ironic title (*The Week of Goodness*) belied the fact that the assemblages of vintage illustrations and engravings in Ernst's pictures frequently portrayed acts of great violence and rendered scenes of terror and dread.

Two Belgian painters, René Magritte (1898–1967) and Paul Delvaux (1897–1994), created some of the most haunting canvases. Magritte's method seems to have been to lure the implied viewer into a state of complacency by using draftsmanlike realistic representation but then altering one crucial element in the painting, thereby launching the viewer into a dreaming state through odd juxtapositions or other anomalies. An example is his *L'empire des lumières* (*The Empire of Lights*), where we see a tranquil evening street scene, only to realize that the sky above is lit brilliantly as if at noon. Another is *La chambre d'écoute* (*The Listening Chamber*), where an impossibly gigantic Granny Smith apple swells to fill the entire space within a room. Magritte also played games with language, pictorial and otherwise, that called the act of representation itself into question, as in his canvas *Ceci n'est pas une pipe* (*This is Not a Pipe*). These very words appear as a caption for a perfectly rendered meerschaum. The viewer is confounded, but may also reflect that, indeed, it is not a pipe. It is a picture of a pipe.

Delvaux's paintings invariably featured statuesque (and statue-esque, as in immobile) women staring fixedly as if under hypnosis. The atmosphere he depicts is calm, but not without a touch of the menace that haunts the canvases of the Italian Surrealist Giorgio de Chirico (1888–1978), where deserted streets and cityscapes punctuated by the occasional passing locomotive far in the background suggest impending doom. One of Delvaux's most unsettling works in this regard is *Les Phases de la lune* (*Phases of the Moon*), in which two soberly dressed professional men, perhaps scientists, examine a seated voluptuous woman, nude except for a huge red bow tied around her breasts. In the background, a parade of other female nudes is led by another group of formally attired men.

Mysterious women also populated the often enormous canvases of the painter—sometimes associated with the Surrealists—Balthasar Klossowski, known as Balthus (1908–2001). Typically they were very young women, barely pubescent, and his portrayal of such models often garnered criticism. The French painter (whose immediate family of Polish origins had settled in Paris by 1903), increasingly famous in his later years, invariably expressed surprise at this judgment, calling attention instead to the enigmatic expressions of models seemingly lost in unfathomable reveries. Balthus's mother Baladine was a lover of Rilke's, and the poet encouraged the young painter. During a life that spanned most of the twentieth century, Balthus was a fixture in international artistic circles, and, like Salvador Dali, he befriended many entertainers and socialites.

The representation of women by Delvaux, Balthus, and other male artists has been at the center of feminist reevaluation of Surrealist art in recent years. Critics have called attention to the dismembered dolls that imply actual female bodies in the photography of Hans Bellmer (1902–1975) and have remarked on the tendency of Surrealists, like other self-styled avant-garde artists, to appear progressive and forward-looking in many areas while remaining quite misogynistic. Feminist scholarship has also focused renewed attention on women artists in the movement, such as Meret Oppenheim (1913–1985), whose sculptures and assemblages were every bit as disturbing and in keeping with Breton's theories as the paintings of Magritte or Dali. Her legendary fur-lined teacup with saucer was the sensation of the 1936 Dada/Surrealism exhibition at New York's Museum of Modern Art.

Surrealists embraced the newer arts of photography and cinema. The American artist Man Ray, active with Marcel Duchamp in New York Dada circles during the previous decade, established himself in Paris during the 1920s. He was accomplished both as a photographer and as a painter. In photography, he invented a technique he called the "Rayograph," whereby common household objects were placed directly on photographic paper. When the paper was exposed to light, the resulting "camera-less" photographs conveyed an air of mystery much in keeping with the Surrealist aesthetic. (See chapter 13.)

The most famous Surrealist film was *Un chien andalou* (*An Andalusian Dog*), the collaboration of the Spaniard Luis Buñuel and Salvador Dali. Its memorable imagery included the infamous scene in which a human eyeball appears to be sliced in half by a razor. Equally odd but somewhat more benign were some of the sequences in the short film *Entr'acte* (1924) by René Clair, climaxed by a camel pulling a hearse endlessly around the base of the Eiffel Tower. Marcel Duchamp and Man Ray were featured in another scene in which they are absorbed in a rooftop chess game that comes to an abrupt end when a huge wave washes over them.

By turns whimsical and serious, forged in relation to the main political and theoretical currents of twentieth-century culture, Surrealism remained one of the most influential movements of contemporary art, and the term "surreal" as synonym for "bizarre" or "strange" entered everyday speech for good.

Intellectuals and the
Political Challenges of the 1930s

Like some Dadaists before them, some Surrealists had dabbled in Marxism, but they had no real contact with workers—not even Aragon and his Russian-born wife, the novelist Elsa Triolet (1896–1970), or poet

Paul Éluard, staunch members of the notoriously doctrinaire French Communist Party. But by the decade of the 1930s, as the success of fascism created a growing sense of urgency for parties of the Left, the need for artists and intellectuals to find common cause with the proletariat found expression both in theory and practice. The Nazis were showing themselves to be particularly adept at manipulating cultural symbols and creating propaganda through traditional print media and also the popular new medium of film. Accordingly, intellectuals on the Left turned much more of their attention to the cultural realm.

In marked contrast with the Frankfurt School theorists, whose avowedly radical politics did not include a sympathetic view of nonelite culture, a breakthrough in Marxist theory beyond the impasse felt by radical bourgeois intellectuals who desired proletarian revolution but disapproved of proletarian forms of cultural expression came in the work of Antonio Gramsci. Gramsci (1891–1937) was one of the founders of the Italian Communist Party. Born to a large poor family in the coal-mining region near Turin, Italy, Gramsci was cursed with a sickly, disfigured (hunchback) body that had to withstand many years in Mussolini's prisons. He died while still a prisoner.

His large collection of prison writings, the *Quaderni del carcere* (*Prison Notebooks*), published after his death, contain his most influential observations about politics and culture. Gramsci's great achievement as a Marxist theorist was to refine and improve the theory of ideology first introduced in *The German Ideology* (1845) by Marx and Engels. That book contained the famous claim that the ruling ideas of any age have invariably been the ideas of its ruling class. Later Marxist theorists, and especially Soviet ideologists, continued to suggest that the dominant social class automatically enjoyed the ability to promote its ideas and values, at times ascribing an absolute determining power to this advantageous social position.

Instead, Gramsci delineated a more complicated sociocultural realm wherein the dominant class sought determinedly—but never with complete or absolute success—to instill its ideas in the subordinate (Gramsci's term was "subaltern") class(es). The key term he employed, borrowed from military and diplomatic analysis, was "hegemony." As he defined it, hegemony stood for the ongoing attempts of the ruling class to convince the subaltern classes of its right to rule. This endless project exerts itself through all social and political spheres—the government, education, family, the arts—what Gramsci termed "civil society."

Crucial to Gramsci's thought was the insistence that hegemony can never be an absolute or complete process. There will always be sectors of civil society resistant to or not completely penetrated by hegemony. This makes dissent or opposition possible—in other words, "counter-hegemony." In *The Prison Notebooks* Gramsci also insisted on an expanded definition of "intellectual." Anyone, he argued, potentially can be an intellectual, but only a limited number of people are called upon to occupy such a role. This view, combined with Gramsci's nuanced view of hegemony (in contrast to an absolute deterministic "ideology" imposed by the ruling class), would lead later generations of Marxist intellectuals, including historians, to search for examples of peasants or workers who, often surprisingly in periods marked by low literacy rates, took the opportunity to express and sometimes act on heretical, radical opinions. It would also encourage stronger appreciation of the "counterhegemonic" potential within folk culture and even of the uses the "subalterns" sometimes make of the mass cultural forms Frankfurt School theorists had assumed automatically to be indoctrinating and stultifying.

Socialist parties and trade unions during the 1930s needed increasingly to mobilize against both the devastating effects of the Great Depression and the growing threat of fascism. Particularly in the latter half of the decade, the time of the Popular Front in France and Spain and the Spanish Civil War (1936–1939), workers used cultural activities such as music and theater to alert a broad popular audience, and a number of artists and intellectuals made common cause with them. When Franco's Falange forces rose up against the Spanish Republic in 1936, an international army of volunteers headed to Spain to rally to the republic's defense. Many internationally prominent writers, including the American Ernest Hemingway (1899–1961), George Orwell (1903–1950) of England, André Malraux (1901–1976) of France, and Arthur Koestler (1905–1983; Hungarian-born, naturalized English citizen), joined in the battle for the doomed Spanish Republic and wrote novels and memoirs based on their experiences.

Culture and Entertainment in the Era of the Popular Front

This was the era of Popular Front politics in Western European countries, as fascist powers flexed their military muscle and the Spanish conflict showed itself more and more to be a dress rehearsal for the coming world war. The sense of great danger was fueled in part by Soviet propaganda, as Stalin consolidated his power in the Soviet Union by staging show trials in which his Bolshevik rivals confessed not only to being allies of

Stalin's nemesis Leon Trotsky, but also agents of Nazi Germany. Prime Minister Léon Blum's Front populaire coalition in France was perhaps the best example of this attempt to unite all antifascist parties—not only socialists or communists—against the menace from the Right. Partly in response to the perceived skill of the Nazis in disseminating their propaganda through cultural activities, working-class organizations in European countries concentrated much of their activity on cultural work, everything from educational improvement to theatrical performances.

Radical, consciously politicized theater had already been an important means of involving workers and Left bourgeois intellectuals with one another. Before 1933 the most striking developments were those in Berlin, where theater producer Erwin Piscator (1893–1966) and playwright Bertolt Brecht (1898–1956) both embraced what they called "Epic Theater," a means of jolting complacent audiences into radical political engagement. Their methods of achieving this were quite different: Piscator drew on such politically minded nineteenth-century playwrights as Friedrich Schiller and Georg Büchner to stage modern versions of their plays that would serve to dramatize contemporary social injustices. Brecht was no less didactic, but sought to bring audiences to similar insights through deliberate distancing in his theater.

In such historical plays as *Mother Courage* and *Galileo,* as well as in *The Threepenny Opera,* his famous comic opera collaboration with composer Kurt Weill (1900–1950), Brecht sought through deliberate distancing, both in the play's language and its staging, to create what he called the "alienation effect" *(Entfremdungseffekt)* that would lead the public to a more profound slow realization of the cruel contradictions of their society. The point was not to achieve immediate identification with what was presented on stage, but to distance the audience in a way that would "defamiliarize" them with the social reality they took for granted. Brecht meant for the process to be a slow, reflective one, with startling realizations detonating some time after in the consciousness of audience members.

In England, the Communist wing of the Labour movement launched what was called the "Worker's Theatre Movement," which lasted from 1926 to 1936, ending at approximately the time that the Popular Front was formed. Once that occurred, Communists set aside their political differences with other parties. Worker's Theatre groups presented their own plays in productions typically using modest halls and bare stages. Plays exposed the injustices of capitalist society at home in England as well as elsewhere in the empire. Conditions in India were of special interest.

Of more far-reaching consequence in England was the Workers Education Association (WEA), which developed more or less under Labour

Party auspices as early as the 1880s, encouraged by such late Victorian social critics as William Morris and John Ruskin. Affiliates of the WEA met
in locations throughout the country. At the height of the Depression, as
many as 90,000 took part in their classes and discussions. The participation of workers would inaugurate an intellectual tradition rather unique
to England, where elite academic institutions exercised less of a monopoly on intellectual activity than might be the case in other countries.

Efforts by workers and their sympathizers to involve themselves in
cultural and educational pursuits were earnest and determined, but
could not match the power of a growing mass cultural industry with access to radio, cinema, and phonograph records. The "stars" presented
through these media and appearing at sold-out venues in major theaters
and music halls increasingly overwhelmed entertainers working locally
and without the backing of major promoters.

France during the years prior to World War II offers some striking
examples of entertainers trading skillfully on their working-class roots
and exercising a comradely appeal to a mass of admirers who could feel
that these indeed were "folks like us" even as they sought deliberately
escapist entertainment. Maurice Chevalier (1888–1972) and his female
counterpart Jeanne Marie Bourgeois (1873–1956), a.k.a. Mistinguett,
were singers who became screen stars as well. In these years when
French people knew in spite of themselves of the troubles that lay
ahead, Chevalier projected an ever-sunny upbeat attitude to which his
fans wanted desperately to cling. Mistinguett gained a warm place in the
hearts of Parisians especially as a humble "kid from Belleville," a rough-
and-tumble working class district of eastern Paris also the neighborhood claimed by Edith Piaf (1915–1963), who became an even bigger
singing star, especially after World War II.

These last years before 1939 were the heyday of jazzy big-band
"swing" music, developed in the United States by band leaders such as
Duke Ellington (1899–1974), Count Basie (1904–1984), Louis Armstrong (1901–1971), Benny Goodman (1909–1986), Tommy Dorsey
(1905–1956), and Glenn Miller (1904–1944, a Canadian). Young fans
especially delighted in strenuous dancing to this music, as in the popular jitterbug. These sounds and steps were as popular in Paris and London (and even, although underground after 1933, in Berlin) as they
were in New York or Chicago. Radio broadcasts created the following
and guaranteed the large-scale sale of phonograph records that followed. In the summer of 1939 it may have been true that "the lights
were going out all over Europe," but the younger generation that would
be called upon to sacrifice itself was getting in its last-minute fling.

Fascist Cultural Control and the War Years

Fascist regimes sought relentlessly to control all modes of cultural expression and to suppress such unwelcome elements as jazz, by their definition the savage product of an inferior race. Such control was difficult to achieve in an absolute sense. In Nazi Germany, where vocal groups as far back the early Weimar period had gained popularity by emulating African American styles, young people continued to gather in secret to dance to the forbidden records. In place of suspect popular culture deriving from foreign elements, Nazis worked vigorously to inculcate, and even to invent, a *völkisch* culture that celebrated Aryan racial essence. With the exception of Wagnerian opera, which both complemented Nazi racial ideology and exemplified the kind of *Gesamtkunstwerk* (total work of art) achieved in the spectacular party rally at Nuremberg in 1936 (under the direction of architect Albert Speer and famously filmed by Leni Riefenstahl), little of modern elite cultural expression served to encourage this end. Non-Jewish composers such as Beethoven also were embraced.

A mass exodus of German writers, scientists, and other important cultural figures had followed the Nazi accession to power in 1933. Some writers who remained until the end of the Third Reich constituted an underground "inner emigration," but most often the few notable artists who managed to endure the Nazi period did so in isolation. The Dada artist Hannah Höch (1889–1978) was one such remarkable example, living on in Berlin until the bitter end. She could have no public profile under a regime that opposed itself implacably to "modern art," as seen in the officially sponsored 1937 exhibition of forbidden "degenerate" art (*entartete Kunst*), where works by some of the most celebrated of twentieth-century artists were displayed as examples of all that was alien to Aryan culture. (Many items ended up in the private collections of such high-ranking Nazi officials as Hermann Goering.) Some of the intellectual figures who had been receptive initially to the Nazis but later formed misgivings found themselves reduced to chagrined silence as the Third Reich wore on. The novelist Gottfried Benn (1886–1956) was an example. An opposite case was Ernst Jünger (1895–1998), whose fiction glorifying the sacrifice of German troops in the Great War evolved into pro-Nazi views that continued unabated through World War II. And the eminent philosopher Martin Heidegger remained utterly unrepentant of his embrace of Hitler.

The Nazis were not anti-Modernist in all fields. Architecture and cinema were notable exceptions. Albert Speer, under Hitler's wing, proposed bold plans for grand buildings, parks, and city squares, although it must be acknowledged that most Nazi architectural style was bombastic and tending toward the kind of Kitsch exemplified by the hyperrealistic maudlin sentimentality of officially sanctioned painting. The Nazis also appreciated and exploited the propagandistic advantages of cinema, by definition a modern enterprise, and produced any number of films presenting heroes and heroines who embodied approved racial characteristics or that depicted the unsavory characteristics of treacherous Jews. Purging German culture (and by extension all of Western civilization) of Jewish elements was always the overriding goal.

However much the Nazi agenda may have been repudiated since 1945, and however much we may acknowledge the oppositional voices of such important exemplars of aesthetic modernism as the émigré artists who found temporary refuge in the United States, the Nazi era certainly wreaked lasting damage on German cultural traditions. The grand scale on which its ambitions operated, with its horrific counterpart in the "Final Solution," has guaranteed this. Although not quite as thoroughgoing as the Nazi program for cultural hegemony, efforts under Benito Mussolini's fascist regime in Italy and Francisco Franco's Falangist dictatorship in Spain were quite similar in style as well as intent.

Italian fascism gained political power long before Nazism, but once Hitler established his regime Mussolini's Italy largely followed the German lead in its regulation of the cultural sphere. Anti-Semitic laws were enacted in 1938, much later than in Nazi Germany, and deportation of Jews did not become routine until after direct German occupation of Italy began in 1943. From the very beginning Mussolini's black-shirted followers attempted to evoke the glories of ancient Rome (the very word "fascism" deriving from the *fasces,* or bundles of sticks lashed to ax heads, carried by Roman legions), and in particular Mussolini made the redesign of Rome along fascist lines a central project. Except for this distinctively Italian feature of fascist cultural politics, regulation of culture followed patterns very similar to those seen in Nazi Germany, as in the attempt to eradicate all foreign or "un-Italian" aspects.

Historians have noted geographical differences in the Italian fascist approach to cultural policy, with a relatively greater embrace of urban Modernism in the North but a deliberate strategy of playing on the anti-urban prejudices of the South. Since urban culture was cosmopolitan and thus tainted by alien (i.e., especially Jewish) elements, the regime fostered a deliberately rural cultural emphasis (the Roman redesign remaining an exception) that manifested itself especially in the encouragement of highly sentimental popular songs that drew on traditional peasant styles. Such anti-Modernism was linked as well to strong xenophobic opposition to jazz music, for racist reasons similar to those found in Nazi Germany. Laws adopted in 1939 regulated song lyrics and prohibited the sale of jazz and other American records, in keeping with an announced policy of "Italianization."

After 1939, in part to distract the populace from the grim realities of Italy's worsening military fortunes, the regime strongly encouraged the sentimental comedies that dominated Italian cinema of the day. These films, which featured exaggeratedly masculine and feminine stars, included the early work of Vittorio De Sica (1902–1974). The first great film to appear after Mussolini's fall was Roberto Rossellini's (1906–1977) *Roma città aperta* (*Open City*). Its story begins with the German occupation in September 1943 and shows that Mussolini's domination of Roman culture was never absolute. Rossellini sympathetically portrays a deeply rooted working-class culture that resisted the official fascist model.

All in all, the Italian fascist stance regarding Modernism was even more contradictory in some ways than that found in Nazi Germany. For all the sentimentalizing of rural stereotypes, modern technology and by implication urban industrial culture retained positive connotations. In this respect, it is worth bearing in mind the background of Italian Futurism and the manifestos of Marinetti, who himself later joined the fascist movement. The glorification of sport and physical fitness, although not unique to Italian fascism, also played a modernizing role, particularly in such northern areas as Genoa, where it appealed especially to the younger generation.

Spain under Francisco Franco's regime presents the picture of a much more resolutely anti-Modern version of fascism. The Generalissimo had been glad to benefit from the up-to-date military hardware supplied by the Axis powers during the Civil War of 1936 to 1939, but in all other areas he stood for a reactionary essentialist view of Spanish culture staunchly resisting all modern impulses. The experience of that war had stiffened Franco's resolve in this regard. The Republic had been the very embodiment of progressive modern ideals, and Republican troops had vigorously pursued literacy campaigns and similar policies designed to address the appalling backwardness of rural life. Emancipation of women had also been a Republican ideal, and the term "feminist" had become current. In Franco's view, this was thoroughly alien to Spanish culture.

Franco's regime defined all Modernist culture as narrowly "elite" and skillfully exploited anti-intellectual attitudes combined with strong reassertion of the Catholic faith. Falangist propaganda manipulated the masses through stereotypical folk images in officially sanctioned sport and cinema. The ultimate goal was national unification, in turn linked to hostility toward minority cultures and languages. Mussolini had also banned minority languages, dismissively termed "dialects," but Franco made such prohibitions a real hallmark of his regime. The laws banning regional languages were adopted piecemeal during the Civil War, as Franco's forces subdued one Loyalist stronghold after another. Galician was banned in 1937, Basque the following year, and finally Catalan in 1939, Catalonia being the last bastion of the anti-Franco effort. The fierceness of Franco's ban on the public use of these languages manifests itself today in the violence with which both Catalan and (especially) Basque separatists pursue their political objectives.

Like his counterparts in Italy and Germany, Franco exercised total control of the press, attacked modern forms of commercial popular music, and embraced heroic styles of architecture in order to inspire the nation, seeking especially a uniquely Spanish style. Meanwhile he encouraged the symbolic use of the most traditional elements of Spanish culture. More often than not, this involved the history of Roman Catholicism in Spain. The sixteenth-century mystic St. Theresa of Avila was promoted as a pious rallying symbol for the nation and an implicit criticism of modern "feminist" values. Franco's fervent religiosity was in marked contrast to the atheism of Hitler and Mussolini, even though they both were willing to make use of religious institutions when it suited their purposes.

Franco's determination to control Spanish culture assigned the cultural sphere a greater prominence than that accorded it in most other societies, including democratic ones, and it served utterly to isolate intellectual and artistic elites, leaving no position from which they could express opposition or articulate an alternative vision. Franco's regulation of culture would begin to relax in his regime's later years, but it was virtually uncontested during the decade of the 1940s. In great part, this was because the public rituals and practices of fascism, making use as they did of distinctive folk forms, were themselves aesthetically satisfying at some level, marginalizing the aesthetes who stood for a cosmopolitan Modernism. Each of the fascist regimes succeeded to varying degrees in a kind of "aestheticization" of politics, and increasingly cultural critics argue that this has been an enduring legacy of fascist cultural politics.

The German refugees from the Frankfurt School Max Horkheimer and T. W. Adorno, who spent their years of exile in California, explored this phenomenon in a groundbreaking book called *Dialectic of Enlight-*

enment (1944). Their ostensible object was the examination of Nazi cultural policy, showing the myriad ways Hitler's regime was able to exercise political power and mass indoctrination through manipulating cultural forms. An added and very troubling dimension of their work was the suggestion that similar kinds of ideological intervention and thus regimentation and control of public opinion operate increasingly in supposedly democratic advanced capitalist societies, using consumer culture rather than political institutions avowedly established for propaganda purposes.

France during World War II provides a complex, fascinating, and troubling example of culture under fascist domination. After 1940 France was under direct German military occupation in the north and east, while a collaborationist regime under the aged World War I hero Philippe Pétain was set up in the south and west, with its headquarters in the town of Vichy. France's swift, stunning defeat by Hitler's forces plunged the country into profound despair, but intellectuals and others long sympathetic to fascist ideology began to put forward the argument that France must accommodate itself to what they predicted to be a long period of Nazi German hegemony on the European continent. Many had been members of the reactionary French party Action française, formed by militarists, anti-Semites, and fervent Catholics soon after the conclusion of the Dreyfus affair. In recent years the number of prominent people associated with the Vichy regime or sympathetic to its goals has been shown to have been much greater than the French have cared to admit.

Writers such as Pierre Drieu la Rochelle (1893–1945), a combat veteran of World War I, the brilliant modern novelist Louis-Ferdinand Céline (1894–1961), and the film critic Robert Brassilach (1909–1945) openly expressed their pleasure in the prospect of French literature and French culture generally purged of Jewish influences, and embraced the Vichy ideological triumvirate of "work, family, country." Céline, whose real name was Louis-Ferdinand Destouches, was a physician and had been a writer sympathetic to the Left, and was considered a master at capturing the street argot of the less fortunate classes in such daringly innovative novels as *Voyage au bout de la nuit* (1932, *Journey to the End of the Night*) and *Mort à crédit* (1936, *Death on the Installment Plan*). After he became disillusioned with the Soviet Union, however, he shifted far to the right and began to write virulent anti-Semitic diatribes.

When the Liberation came in 1944, Céline went into hiding in Denmark and was eventually imprisoned there for a year while France sought his extradition. He finally returned in 1951 after being granted amnesty and resumed both his medical practice and his writing career. Drieu la Rochelle committed suicide. Only Robert Brasillach suffered execution (by firing squad), which is now viewed as owing more to his homosexuality and his vicious critical writings than to his collaborationism. But this punishment and others less severe helped give rise to the cultural myth that most French people had sympathized with the Resistance, even if they had not aided it openly. This comfortable delusion began to give way through the influence of a courageous 1969 documentary film by the director Marcel Ophüls called *Le Chagrin et la pitié* (*The Sorrow and the Pity*), which used interviews to reveal the depth and degree of support for Vichy, especially by prominent intellectuals and politicians. The work of exposing the real collaborationist past of such people has been difficult since many took such pains to conceal their own histories. An important example from the history of Nazi-occupied Belgium was the influential critic Paul de Man, who later rose to considerable prominence after emigrating to the United States. Only after his death in 1983 did the story of his anti-Semitic literary criticism (written for a Brussels newspaper in 1941 to 1942) come to light.

To be sure, some prominent writers dedicated themselves to the Resistance and, in some cases, paid with their lives. This was true of Simone Weil (1909–1943), a Jewish-born mystically inclined Catholic convert whose journals (*Cahiers*) contain profound ethical discussions and spiritual probings. Her combination of strong faith and intellectual doubt, reminiscent of her seventeenth-century predecessor Blaise Pascal, can be seen in her book *Attente de Dieu* (*Waiting for God*). Weil's intellectual legacy has been very much linked to her status as a martyr of the Resistance. Another celebrated intellectual who was at risk both as a Jew and as a participant in the Resistance was Marc Bloch (1886–1944). With Lucien Febvre (1878–1956) he had founded the influential historical journal *Annales* in 1929. This journal, where historians published work informed by highly interdisciplinary social science methodology, has remained the single most influential European journal of historical scholarship. Bloch was captured by the Gestapo in 1944 and sentenced to death. As a prisoner awaiting execution he wrote his influential credo as a historian *Le Métier de l'historien* (*The Historian's Craft*).

But by far the most celebrated French writer associated with the Resistance was Jean-Paul Sartre (1905–1980). His reputation was to soar in the immediate post-1945 years, and he long played a Victor Hugoesque role in French culture as intellectual oracle or national conscience. Sartre was a versatile "man of letters" whose writings prior to 1939 had consisted primarily of novels and critical essays. During World War II he

turned his attention more to dramatic works, some of which were produced as plays while he was incarcerated in a German prisoner-of-war
camp. By the war's end his energies were exerted most in the direction
of philosophy, marked especially by his 1943 opus *L'être et le néant* (*Being
and Nothingness*). This intellectual tour de force, forged in dialogue with
Husserl and Heidegger, served to launch the influential postwar movement known as Existentialism. (See chapter 10.) One of Sartre's most
important arguments was that the intellectual ought to be involved (*en-
gagé*) with the political and moral challenges of his time, and his example as a member of the Resistance seemed to put theory into practice.
In recent years scholars have debated the actual degree of Sartre's own
commitment to and risk in the French Resistance.

A writer much less heralded for his assistance to the French Resistance was, like Sartre, to gain substantial recognition in the years just
after the war. This was Samuel Beckett (1906–1989), the Irish-born
writer whose writings of the 1930s and early 1940s (*Murphy,* 1938;
Watt, 1953—written 1942–1944; *More Pricks Than Kicks,* 1934) bore
much of the stamp of his friend and mentor James Joyce. After leaving
Ireland he had lived in London for a time and spent much of the decade
of the 1930s in France. By the French defeat of 1940 he had set up permanent residence in Paris and had married a French woman. Since he
was little known during the war years, he had been able to serve as a
courier for the Resistance, successfully escaping detection. As retiring
and shy as Sartre was gregarious and outgoing, Beckett was never willing to speak to interviewers about his activity. By the end of the war,
he began to show his allegiance to France in another quite profound
way, for he set himself the challenge to write directly in his adopted language. The plays and novels that won him fame by the early 1950s were
the first he had written in French. (See chapter 11.)

Certainly not all writers or artists of the war years involved themselves
directly in politics or in resistance to occupation. The European painters
who emigrated to New York formed the nucleus of the so-called New
York School of artists who created the new nonrepresentational style
that came to be called Abstract Expressionism. In England, where surviving Hitler's "blitz" of 1940 to 1941 became a recurring motif in postwar narratives, both literary and cinematic, one notable literary figure,
T. S. Eliot, moved farther away from the contemplation of the contemporary social and political crisis. Expressing his deepening religious de-
votion, he crafted his major poetic work *The Four Quartets* (1943), tightly
structured around themes of time, memory, and the consolation of re-
demption. A thoroughgoing Modernist in terms of literary form, Eliot's

response to the appalling conditions of twentieth-century life was advocacy of the Anglican church, the traditional literary canon, and the pastoral village life of a vanishing England. As the horrific Second World War came to an end, Europeans were torn between faith in progress to come and nostalgia for a time that could never return. These conflicting impulses would define much of the culture of the next decades.

Suggestions for Further Reading

Adamson, Walter L. *Hegemony and Revolution: A Study of Antonio Gramsci's Political and Cultural Theory.* Berkeley: University of California Press, 1980.

Buck-Morss, Susan. *The Dialectics of Seeing: Walter Benjamin and the Arcades Project.* Cambridge, MA: MIT Press, 1989.

Caws, Mary Ann. *The Surrealist Look: An Erotics of Encounter.* Cambridge, MA: MIT Press, 1997.

Gershman, Herbert S. *The Surrealist Revolution in France.* Ann Arbor: University of Michigan Press, 1969.

Harvey, Robert. *Search for a Father: Sartre, Paternity, and the Question of Ethics.* Ann Arbor: University of Michigan Press, 1991.

Jay, Martin. *The Dialectical Imagination: A History of the Frankfurt School and the Institute of Social Research, 1923–1950.* Berkeley: University of California Press, 1996.

Kaes, Anton et al., eds. *The Weimar Republic Sourcebook.* Berkeley: University of California Press, 1994.

Kaplan, Alice *The Collaborator: The Trial and Execution of Robert Brassilach.* Chicago: University of Chicago Press, 2000.

Kaplan, Alice. *Reproductions of Banality: Fascism, Literature, and French Intellectual Life.* Minneapolis: University of Minnesota Press, 1986.

Miller, Tyrus. *Late Modernism: Politics, Fiction, and the Arts Between the World Wars.* Berkeley: University of California Press, 1999.

Rearick, Charles. *The French in Love and War: Popular Culture in the Era of the World Wars.* New Haven: Yale University Press, 1997.

Suleiman, Susan R. *Subversive Intent: Gender, Politics, and the Avant-Garde.* Cambridge, MA: Harvard University Press, 1990.

Chapter 9

Popular Media and Modern Culture,
ca. 1930 to 1980

Long before the 1930s, "mass" culture (i.e., a generalized market-based array of distractions and entertainments) was developing in Europe. At least as early as 1867, Matthew Arnold had raised troubling questions about it in his book *Culture and Anarchy*. In a book that seeks to examine modern European culture through the end of the twentieth century, we begin this chapter somewhat late in the game, although at a time when improvements in technology (e.g., motion pictures, including the first with sound, increasingly sophisticated sound recording, wireless radio) and transportation were expanding the possibilities for cultural dissemination. Despite the Great Depression, the 1930s would be a time when the "entertainment industry" increasingly moved to the fore of economic life and began to shape patterns of consumption that would be stalled only temporarily by the war of 1939 to 1945. The power of media such as radio and cinema to reach a vast number of people on a scale unapproached by print material was just beginning to be exercised.

As labor agitation gradually succeeded in reducing the number of hours workers worked, increased leisure time and growing affordability of books, newspapers, magazines, radios, and cinema and theater tickets made entertainment loom ever larger in the lives of most people. The appearance of radio sets in average households meant that access to the latest music or drama was no longer limited to residents of large urban centers. Authorities both secular and ecclesiastical frequently expressed concern over possibly deleterious social and cultural effects of mass consumption of the new entertainment, while from the Left came efforts, most pronounced during the Depression years, to put workers in the producing, not just consuming, role of cultural activity.

In recent years the study of popular culture has received more and more attention, first as a separate topic but increasingly included within a broadened definition of "culture," so that historians and others by the end of the twentieth century have been inclined to examine popular culture or the culture of everyday life along with—interconnected with—the previously protected zones of elite culture: literature, music, and art. All the while, cultural critics have continued long-standing debates about the value as well as the disadvantageous aspects of "pop" culture. Probably too much of this discussion has been marked by the notion of "bread and circuses" that harks back to late Roman times. In this view, the passive "mob" of spectators are fed an unwholesome diet of trivial entertainment to keep them pacified and distracted, thus more easily controlled and manipulated by ruling powers.

Even the relatively sophisticated approach to the study of the "culture industry" introduced by Frankfurt School theorists Horkheimer and Adorno (see chapter 8) clings to this venerable presupposition, one that posits "the people" as docile, passive agents available for manipulation by entertainment moguls—ready to be instructed as to their entertainment preferences. A number of observers have pointed out that allegedly radical intellectuals and unapologetic aristocrats are frequently of like mind in this regard, both assuming that "the people" play no active role in the development of popular tastes or trends.

But one does not need to be dismissive of the agency of the so-called masses to raise important questions about the very notion of popular culture, particularly when considering the recently completed century that saw such dramatic technological developments linked inextricably to the spread of a consumerist pop culture. After all, the etymology of the word "popular" certainly suggests "of" or "from" the people, and in this it shares a kinship with the concept of "folk" culture, a standard term at least since early European Romanticism. But to what extent has an increasingly global, highly concentrated, and technologically advanced mass culture industry reflected anything of a genuinely popular culture? The suspicion of cultural critics, that a profit-driven culture industry produces and constructs what we take to be "popular" culture, dies hard. A similar problem exists with the term "mass" in mass culture. Does "mass" imply "from" the great mass of people, or does it refer to the ambitious, extensive scale on which a consumer economy promotes and disseminates culture?

Both in the early and the later decades of the twentieth century, ample reasons exist for concluding the latter. Little in what has been produced by the corporate-owned Western media has promoted the alternate meaning of mass culture, that is, little that would affirm or promote collective, communal identity or values. One of the principal means of demonstrating this point is to pay attention to just how very much of what is reported in the popular press (and later in other media) has to do with celebrities—their lives, personalities, and activities, ranging from the routine to the spectacular. To a certain extent, this emphasis has served throughout modernity to distract disadvantaged observers from their plight. If they could not be glamorous, wealthy, or famous, at least they could experience these states vicariously by consuming media profiles of the privileged few or "beautiful people." In Victorian England, a worker might fantasize that the suit he purchased with his hard-won earnings might transfer some of the charisma of Prince Albert, whose image the advertisement featured, to him. At least on Sundays, when he donned the suit for his stroll in the park or the trip to his "local," he could imagine himself belonging to the social set the garment seemed to signify.

The Popular Press

The popular media of the twentieth century have fostered ever-greater degrees of celebrity fixation. Television has made for a quantum leap in the tendency whereby one feels more familiar with the personalities who populate media representations than with one's own neighbors, but the tendency was already under way in the popular press early in the century. Increasingly, it has not mattered how someone achieved celebrity status. It was simply enough to occupy the spotlight. Personalities at the center of celebrated criminal trials, even infamous murderers, will do nicely. During the summer of 1914, Parisians were so captivated by the elegant society dame Henriette Caillaux, on trial for the murder of a newspaper editor she believed had defamed her politician husband and, relatedly, her honor, that they had little time to heed the gatherings storm clouds of war. For that matter, newspapers preferred to report on the lurid aspects of the trial than to monitor the complicated diplomatic crisis.

Coverage of celebrity scandals and the deeds of notorious criminals typified the European popular press during the 1930s, and once again gossip-filled reports served to distract readers from forebodings of further troubles, especially in the last years before World War II. Popular French newspapers such as *France-Soir* and *Le Petit Parisien* offered readers stories filled with lurid details especially about monstrous criminals. One of the most sensational stories of the decade, one that later inspired

Jean Genet's play *Les Bonnes* (*The Maids*) and two successful French films in 2000, involved the Papin sisters, who brutally murdered their employers (also sisters) after many years of service. They ended up in a hospital for the criminally insane. In the spring of 1939, the French press so inflamed public opinion regarding the approaching execution of the vicious murderer Eugene Weidmann that authorities, anticipating a record turnout, moved the guillotine to the street outside the prison courtyard to accommodate the large crowd of spectators. (The practice since late in the nineteenth century had been to hold executions within prison walls.) Weidmann's German ancestry was central to the hysteria, especially given world events in 1939. The macabre public display in front of a disorderly crowd led Prime Minister Edouard Daladier to take steps to ensure that henceforward the guillotine would do its work out of public view, inside the prison. (France abolished capital punishment in 1981.)

In England the tabloid press—the *Daily Mail* and the *Daily Mirror*—was the popular counterpart to the staid *Times* and the business-oriented *Daily Telegraph*. Tabloid coverage was given especially to the royal family and the social networks in which its members moved. The morbid preoccupation with these elites has long served as a means to offer vicarious participation in the life of the aristocracy, and of course this has been most profitable to the news merchants. The year 1938 brought a crescendo of obsessive attention to royalty, largely because of the marriage and abdication of Edward VIII. This rather frivolous playboy of a Prince of Wales became king upon the death of George V, but very quickly his involvement with a wealthy American divorcée, Wallis Simpson, produced a crisis. Unable to marry a "commoner," and a divorced one at that, Edward abdicated, shocking the nation with a speech broadcast on radio in which he professed the need to marry his great love rather than continue his duties as king. The throne passed to his brother, who became George VI. England had seen three kings in the same year and had witnessed the beginning of the public examination of the private lives of the royal family, a spotlight whose beams widened steadily throughout the rest of the century.

In the British Isles as elsewhere in the world, the daily press occasionally provided outlets for humor writing, an especially welcome diversion in the troubled years of the late 1930s and the 1940s. For about twenty-five years until his death in 1966, the rather staid, conservative *Irish Times* of Dublin featured the regular columns of the wildly imaginative, outrageously irreverent Flann O'Brien, the principal nom de plume of Brian O'Nolan (1911–1966), a career civil servant and novelist. Devoted to the Gaelic language of traditional Ireland, O'Brien called his column *Cruiskeen Lawn* ("The Little Overflowing Jug"), and signed it Myles na Gopaleen ("Myles of the Little Ponies"). The immensely popular newspaper pieces shared the humor of his darkly comic novels, including *At-Swim-Two-Birds* (1939) and *The Third Policeman* (1967). His best work invites comparison to that of James Joyce and Samuel Beckett. But during his lifetime, he enjoyed far more recognition for his journalism than his fiction. As the century advanced, newspapers, especially after they began to feel the competition from electronic media, sought greater variety and included increasing amounts of material designed to attract the casual, occasional reader. The goal was to have a daily paper that would appeal simultaneously to those who wanted details of the political or economic worlds and those whose aim was escapism and lighthearted fun.

An increasing variety of other forms of popular print media flourished throughout the twentieth century in European culture. Inexpensive paperbacks, pioneered by Penguin Books in England, as well as by such publishers as Goldmann in Germany and Livre de Poche in France, accounted for an ever-larger share of book sales. Escapist fiction (romance, detective, fantasy) proved most popular, but paperback titles included everything from how-to books to specialized scholarly works. Comic books found enthusiasts and enjoyed huge commercial success, especially in continental Western Europe. The French character Astérix and the simply drawn Tintin, the creation of a Belgian artist named Hergé, became familiar cultural icons.

Two of the twentieth-century's most beloved and commercially successful authors of detective fiction began their prolific careers during the years between the two world wars. The English novelist and playwright Agatha Christie (1890–1976) introduced the eccentric Belgian detective Hercule Poirot to the reading public in her very first published novel, *The Mysterious Affair at Styles,* in 1920. Her other most famous character, Miss Jane Marple, debuted in 1930 in *Murder at the Vicarage.* They were to reappear in a long series of novels over several decades. Georges Simenon (1903–1989), Belgian-French master of the *policier,* or detective novel, amassed great personal wealth through the more than two hundred novels he wrote between 1923 and 1933. In all he was to write more than four hundred books and may deserve the label of the century's most prolific author. Jules Maigret, his unflappable Parisian police inspector, was every bit as memorable a literary creation as either of Christie's creations.

Radio and Television

However important the press remained, the newer media of radio and cinema (and, eventually, television) loomed ever larger in the lives of most citizens. By the 1930s, the wireless radio set was a mainstay of the middle-class household. Good reception depended on careful jiggling with the knobs, but gathering around the radio for news and entertainment was an evening ritual often approached with great solemnity. Most of the staples of what would later constitute television programming flourished first on radio: news bulletins, interviews, game shows, comedies, drama, concerts. And increasingly, as Edward VIII's abdication showed, people experienced major events as dramatic radio announcements. This would carry over very significantly into World War II: in the somber tones of correspondents reporting from London, Paris, or Berlin, in the bombast of the aging Marshal Pétain announcing in 1940 that he was making "the gift of his person" to France in setting up the Vichy regime, by contrast in the rallying cry of resistance the then-unknown General Charles de Gaulle made to the French from his London exile, or in the cranky harangues of the brilliant American poet Ezra Pound from Mussolini's Rome.

Radio continued to be enormously influential in the lives of Europeans during the 1950s, for television penetrated European culture much more slowly than it did the United States. Much of what people listened to was tightly controlled by networks under state monopoly, but adventurous spirits could seek out independent if not "pirate" stations, often broadcasting from on board ship just outside territorial waters. One of the most influential such stations was Radio Luxembourg, which broadcast much of the popular music resisted by the BBC during the 1950s. This station exposed an entire generation to adventurous new forms of jazz, rhythm and blues, and early rock 'n' roll.

The devastation of World War II and the painful economic recovery in the decade or so thereafter meant that television was slow to become a cultural force in Europe. Even by the early 1960s, by which time television ownership was enormously widespread in the United States, only a minority of European households had sets. Broadcast time was limited to a few hours nightly, and the tendency of European governments to hold monopolies over the networks restricted the range and variety of programming (although the argument that market forces in the United States create their own kinds of restrictions and limitations should certainly be acknowledged). Until the 1970s, this meant that the use of television for official government reporting and dramatic announcements often overshadowed the entertainment function. Still, a growing number of viewers, whether they watched at home or gathered in pubs and cafés, began to enjoy televised dramas, game shows, and sporting events as did their counterparts across the Atlantic.

After 1970, the freer cultural spirit that pervaded Western Europe had begun to manifest itself in television. In France, the Netherlands, and West Germany, among other places, viewers often got the chance to watch lively interviews and debates featuring controversial intellectual or political figures. One of the dominant programs of the 1970s in France was *Apostrophes,* a program devoted to interviews with notable authors, usually but not always French. The program's host, Bernard Pivot, became a major force in French cultural life. Across the Channel in England, the stuffy image of the BBC was exploded by the innovative comedy program, featuring both skits and animation, called *Monty Python's Flying Circus.* The comedy troupe named Monty Python consisted of six Oxbridge- (both Oxford and Cambridge) educated members, one of them an American expatriate, who combined cerebral wit with good old-fashioned English music hall slapstick. They built on the 1960s' tradition of sardonic, subtle English humor pioneered by Spike Milligan and Peter Sellers (and before that by the popular comedy troupe known as "The Goons," which included Milligan and Sellers), but with the success of their television program and subsequent films, they reached an unprecedentedly wide audience of global dimensions.

Cinema, ca. 1930 to 1945

Of course no medium dominated the twentieth century more than cinema, one whose history is largely coterminous with the century's history. During the late nineteenth century, a variety of ingenious devices meant to suggest or simulate motion preceded the invention of the motion picture camera. These included the magic lantern, the phenakistoscope, panoramas, dioramas, the Zoetrope, and the Praxinoscope. Eadweard Muybridge (1830–1904), a British photographer working in California, made the first photographs of bodies in motion by using a series of cameras in succession. By the 1890s several different inventors, including the American Thomas Edison (1847–1931) and the Lumière Brothers—Auguste (1862–1954) and Louis-Jean (1864–1948)—of France, had introduced versions of the motion picture camera.

From the very earliest days, despite technical limitations, motion pictures were embraced enthusiastically by the public. The first films by the Lumière Brothers, *La Sortie de l'Usine Lumière à Lyon* (1895, *Workers Leaving the Lumière Factory*) and *Arrivée d'un train en gare* (1896, *Train Arriving at La Ciotat*) were instant sensations, and the silent film era was born. During the 1920s silent films became highly sophisticated, as in the German Expressionist works of Robert Wiene (1880?–1938, *The Cabinet of Dr. Caligari*) and F. W. Murnau (1889–1931, *Nosferatu*). Directors in the Soviet Union, most significantly Sergei Eisenstein (1898–1948), had introduced influential new techniques such as montage. In 1927 the pioneer French director Abel Gance (1889–1981) developed, much before its time, the wide-screen process for his epic film *Napoléon*.

The following decade brought the first sound films. Fritz Lang's (1890–1976) *M* (1931) built on the German Expressionist tradition and featured a riveting performance by Peter Lorre. But for the most part, as a result of the Depression and then Hitler's accession to power and Nazi cultural control, Britain was to become the leading European film-producing nation of the decade. The boldest and in many ways most influential director was Alfred Hitchcock (1899–1980), who enjoyed a long career both in England and in Hollywood with his suspenseful films, such as *The Thirty-Nine Steps* (1935) and, in later years, *Vertigo* (1958), *Psycho* (1960), and *The Birds* (1963). In France, Surrealists had created innovative films, especially the two collaborations between two émigré Spanish artists, Salvador Dali and Luis Buñuel (1900–1983): *Le Chien andalou* (1929, *An Andalusian Dog*) and *L'Age d'or* (1930, *The Golden Age*). Buñuel fled his native Spain at the time of the Spanish Civil War and resurfaced as a director in Mexico. But certainly the dominant French director of the period before World War II was Jean Renoir (1894–1979), son of the famous Impressionist painter. His *La Grande Illusion* (1937, *Grand Illusion*), a drama set in World War I, ranks as perhaps the greatest antiwar statement ever seen on the screen. *Les Règles du jeu* (*The Rules of the Game*), released in 1939, offers a grim view of jaded members of the privileged class gathered at a country retreat.

One of the most technically gifted filmmakers of the 1930s was also one forever tainted by her association with Nazi Germany. Leni Riefenstahl (1902–) spent most of her later years trying to rehabilitate her reputation and seeking to minimize her Nazi ties while shifting attention to her work primarily as a still photographer. But she did indeed receive attention and sponsorship from Adolf Hitler, whose regime she commemorated in the stunning *Triumph of the Will* (1935) and *Olympia* (1938). The former provided dramatic footage of the carefully orchestrated (by Hitler's henchman Albert Speer) 1934 Nuremberg Nazi Party rally, while the latter was devoted to the 1936 Berlin Olympic Games, which Hitler made every effort to turn into a propaganda triumph.

Despite the achievements of European cinema before World War II, the American film industry played the dominant role and appealed to audiences in Europe more than their own films, a tendency that would become more and more pronounced in later decades. It was already clear that European directors would not be able to compete with the Hollywood "dream machine." Partly out of necessity, they followed another path, one of much more self-conscious artistry. In American films, the names of the glamorous stars overshadowed those of the directors. Europeans would aim for the opposite emphasis, and this tendency would accelerate after 1945. It should also be noted that Europeans led the way in establishing institutions to create cinematic archives to preserve the achievements of the increasingly important art. Most notable in this regard was the French film museum/library the Cinémathèque Française, founded in 1935.

Cinema, 1945 to 1970

The war brought the legitimate film industry to a halt in Europe, although leaden exercises in obvious propaganda were produced in Hitler's Germany and Mussolini's Italy. Some of first films of note to appear at the war's end also came from Italy. Roberto Rossellini (1906–1977) paid tribute to the Roman proletariat that resisted the direct Nazi occupation of their city, which began in 1943, in *Roma Città operta (Open City)*, released in 1945. He followed in 1946 with *Paisà (Paisan)*. In 1948, Vittorio de Sica's (1901–1974) film *Ladri di biciclette (Bicycle Thieves*, although conventionally translated as *The Bicycle Thief)* opened to huge acclaim. A simple story of a poor family's desperate search for their stolen bicycle, it remains one of the most critically admired films ever. By the 1950s the distinctive films of Federico Fellini (1920–1993) deepened the admiration cinephiles felt for Italian cinema. Such films as *La Strada* (1954, *The Street*), *Le notti di Cabiria* (1957, *Nights of Cabiria*), and *La Dolce vita* (1960, *The Sweet Life*), as well as his films of the 1960s and 1970s, burned lasting images of postwar Italian culture, with its joyous affirmation of life tempered with bitter resignation, into the popular imagination.

If Fellini's films affirmed Itailan gaiety, those of the much-admired Swedish director Ingmar Bergman (1918–), although similarly admired internationally, offered Nordic angst and gloom. They also featured bold use of dream sequences and other indications of unconscious turmoil experienced by their characters. Bergman especially assured his reputation with two 1957 films, *The Seventh Seal* and *Wild Strawberries.* Few European directors contributed more to the mystique of the director as artist and visionary than these two giants of the postwar cinema.

But it was in France that the "cult" of the director most vigorously asserted itself. An entire group of talented directors (*metteurs en scène*), including Claude Chabrol (1930–), Eric Rohmer (1920–), François Truffaut (1932–1984), Alain Resnais (1922–), and Jean-Luc Godard (1930–), began making films in the late 1950s, and by the early 1960s were touted as *la nouvelle vague* ("the New Wave"). Many of them had been associated with a critical journal called *Cahiers du cinéma,* and they stood for the idea of the director as the creative force behind the film, the one whose artistry should be given free rein. The director was the *auteur* without whose vision the film could not come into existence. François Truffaut exerted influence both for his films and for his voluminous writings on cinema, many of which had appeared in *Cahiers.* In them he extolled the directors he considered great, including Alfred Hitchcock. His own films were intensely autobiographical. His 1959 film *Les 400 coups* (*The 400 Blows*), based on his brutal experience of reform school was a sensation at the Cannes Film Festival that year and catapulted him into cinematic fame. A young adolescent actor named Jean-Pierre Léaud, who would star (always as the "Truffaut" character) in a long series of Truffaut films, made his debut in that film.

The works of such directors as Truffaut and Godard came to be identified for some time with the heady years of the 1960s, a time of great cultural ferment in France, as elsewhere. But no film seemed to capture that decade's admixture of ecstasy and dread quite like the Italian director Michelangelo Antonioni's (1912–) 1967 English-language film *Blow-up,* based on a short story by the Argentine writer (then living in Paris) Julio Cortázar (1914–1984). A gripping story of a photographer's accidental discovery of a murder (the clues gradually emerging from successive enlargements of one of his prints—hence the title), Antonioni's film shifted the Parisian setting of Cortázar's story to London, and produced memorable images of that city's underground club scene, the camera dwelling on the distinctive fashions and rock music performances of the day.

European Cinema in the 1970s

The French *nouvelle vague* has been credited with revival of cinema at a time of decline in the face of television's growing popularity. The influence of the cult of the *auteur* made itself felt through the cinematic world, even affecting Hollywood for a time, where such maverick directors as Robert Altman (1925–) gained access to major studios not usually accessible to those outside the mainstream. European films of the late 1960s, as well as some notable American films, had emphasized the era's violent political, social, and sexual turmoil, often using deliberate exaggeration to a kind of neo-Surrealist effect, as in Jean-Luc Godard's 1968 film *Week-end,* where automobile crashes proliferate madly across the French landscape.

The early 1970s in particular constituted a boom period for ambitious films by directors seizing total artistic control of their films. Luis Buñuel was especially active during this period. He had experienced a long hiatus from directing after his early collaborations with Dali, then resurfaced in Mexico in the 1950s, where he made such powerful disturbing films as *Los Olvidados* (1950, *The Young and the Damned)* and *Exterminating Angel* (1962). He returned to France and to French filmmaking with his 1967 film *Belle du Jour,* which launched the career of Catherine Deneuve, one of France's most accomplished film actresses of recent decades. His films of the 1970s mark a return to Surrealism, especially *Le Charme discret de la bourgeoisie* (1972, *The Discreet Charm of the Bourgeoisie),* although the improbable episodes are portrayed in a matter-of-fact style that is closer to the grim painterly aesthetic of Magritte than the bombastic Dali.

Other French films of the period were more politically minded, such as *Z* (1969), by the Greek-born director Constantine Costa-Gavras (1933–). His film portrays the takeover by the Greek military junta, which crushed democratic rights, took large numbers of political prisoners, and routinely practiced torture. *L'état de siège* (1973, *State of Siege)* treats similar themes involving the military dictatorship in the South American country of Uruguay.

Probably no film created a greater political stir in France than the ambitious documentary film *Le Chagrin et la pitié* (1969, *The Sorrow and the Pity),* directed by Marcel Ophüls (1927–), himself the son of Max Ophüls, an important French director of the previous generation. This film, examining the history of the central French city of Clermont-Ferrand under Nazi occupation, assaulted the most cherished French myth about World War II, that most French people had supported the Resistance and had tried to protect Jews from deportation. *Le Chagrin et la pitié* provides overwhelming evidence to the contrary, and inaugurated a painful reexamination of the Vichy era's history that continues in France to the present day. The documentary was intended originally for television, but for many years the French government-controlled television network would not permit its broadcast. The prolific director Louis Malle (1932–1996) devoted *Lacombe, Lucien* (1974) to the subject of Vichy. The film's protagonist and namesake is a poorly educated teenage boy who becomes a Vichy paramilitary thug but also falls in love with a Jewish girl.

The early 1970s were a glorious time for Italian cinema. Many of these films likewise explored the unpleasant topic of Italian history during the period of Mussolini's rule. Bernardo Bertolucci (1941–) was the first of the new generation of Italian directors to devote a film to the fascist era in *Il conformista* (1970, *The Conformist*). He extended his historical range more ambitiously in *Novecento* (1976, *1900*), a five hour epic that follows an Italian family from 1900 to 1945. Another important treatment of the Mussolini years was Vittorio de Sica's *Il giardino dei Finzi Contini* (1970, *The Garden of the Finzi-Continis*), based on a best-selling postwar novel by Giorgio Bassini. In a far splashier manner, Lina Wertmüller (1928–), working as usual with the actor Giancarlo Giannini, offered a compelling portrayal of an anarchist assassin of the fascist period in *Film d'amore e d'anarchia* (1972, *Love and Anarchy*) and presented the horror of Auschwitz through the eyes of an Italian prisoner in *Pasqualino settebellezze* (1974, *Seven Beauties*).

By no means did all Italian films of the period explore the history of fascism. Michelangelo Antonioni made interesting use of the American screen star Jack Nicholson as a desperate journalist at his wits' end in the North African desert in *Professione: Reporter* (1975, *The Passenger*). One of the most controversial films of the decade was *L'ultimo tango a Parigi* (1972, *The Last Tango in Paris*), Bertolucci's frank exploration of self-destructive sexual obsession that featured the reclusive actor Marlon Brando in a compelling and disturbing performance. It was an international achievement, using French and English and filmed by an Italian director. The penultimate scene, where dancing couples compete in a tango contest, touches on an important topic in modern French cultural history, for the popularity of the Argentine tango, first introduced in France late in the nineteenth century, had alarmed many French people. They regarded the dance as shockingly, unacceptably erotic.

But Federico Fellini must certainly be considered the most consistently talented and successful Italian director of the decade. He had triumphed during the previous decade with *Otto e mezzo* (1963, *8 1/2*) and *Giulietta degli spiriti* (1965, *Juliet of the Spirits*), and the films he made especially during the early 1970s were filled with energy, wit, and mem-

orable visual wonders, often accomplished through his penchant for let-
ting the camera linger on faces that can only be described as bizarre,
grotesque, or outlandish. In 1969 he startled the public with his *Fellini-
Satyricon,* based on the ancient Roman work by Petronius. The elaborate sets vividly portrayed a late Roman era of extreme decadence and
degradation. Indirectly, Fellini may have been commenting on Mussolini, who sought always to cloak himself and his political movement
in the mantle of Roman glory. Fellini returned to the subject of his city
in *Fellini-Roma* (1971), presented as something of a documentary, with
much attention to contemporary urban problems and challenges.

The Fellini films with the most lasting appeal, however, are the
overtly autobiographical. *I clowns* (1970, *Clowns*) captures the young
artist's fascination with clowns, especially with the complicated, contradictory messages they convey through their highly stylized performances. The unforgettable opening scene shows a huge circus tent
being inflated, as the camera cuts to the face of an excited young boy
sitting up in bed in his nearby house, listening with anticipation to the
sound of the tent being set up. Elated that the circus has come to his little town, next day he accompanies his parents and, predictably, is frightened out of his wits by the clowns. After this prologue, using the
quasi-documentary approach of *Roma,* Fellini takes the viewer on a
tour of scholarly archives devoted to the clowns' art, and includes
lengthy discussions of the time-honored stereotypes of, for example, the
clown "Auguste" and "the white clowns." The even more autobiographical *Amarcord* (1973, Italian for "I Remember") explored themes
of youthful sexual awakening as well as political awareness and disillusionment, set as it was during the Mussolini era.

Easily one of the most ambitious directors of these years, one whose
uncompromising vision and meticulous methods bear comparison to
someone like Orson Welles in addition to his great European contemporaries, was Stanley Kubrick (1928–1999), the American director who
spent the majority of his career working in his adopted country of England. His greatest achievement remains the futuristic *2001: A Space
Odyssey* (1968), based on the highly regarded science fiction novel by
Arthur C. Clarke. In keeping with its era, this was filmmaking as "mind
expansion." His next film, *A Clockwork Orange* (1971), based on Anthony Burgess's very dystopic novel of an England terrorized by amoral
youthful gangs speaking an argot comprised of several European languages (including most prominently Russian), stirred up a great deal of
controversy. This was due especially to scenes of graphic violence filmed
in a highly artful stylized manner, set to music on a stunning soundtrack

by the electronic keyboardist Walter (who later became Wendy) Carlos, with synthesized renditions of Scarlatti, Purcell, Rossini, and others. *2001* had also made memorable use of music, especially *Also Sprach Zarathustra,* the dramatic tone poem by Richard Strauss.

Perhaps in response to the storm kicked up by *A Clockwork Orange,* Kubrick turned for his next film to a largely forgotten novel by Thackeray, *Barry Lyndon* (1975). Critics and film buffs admired the attention to the period detail of the novel's eighteenth-century setting, but it was a commercial disaster. Kubrick compensated for this by scoring a commercial triumph with *The Shining* (1979), based on the horror novel by the successful American writer Stephen King and featuring a terrifying performance by Jack Nicholson. As for native-born English directors, one who made an enormous splash for his often bombastic cinematic excursions was Ken Russell (1927–). He made the critically acclaimed film *Women in Love* (1969), certainly one of the most successful adaptations ever of a great Modernist novel (by D. H. Lawrence). His next film was *The Devils* (1970), an adaptation of the book *The Devils of Loudon* by Aldous Huxley. The broodingly charismatic actor Oliver Reed starred in this story of demonic possession in a medieval French city. Later Russell films such as *The Music Lovers* (1970), purportedly a biographical account of the composer Tchaikovsky, and *Tommy* (1975), an adaptation of the rock opera by The Who, drowned in excess.

Many of the best films of the decade dealt powerfully with the complexities of love, desire, and family entanglements. Feminism and the gay rights movement worldwide were leading more and more people to understand such topics as "political," that is, containing rituals of power, dominance, disenfranchisement, and longed-for liberation. The 1970s films of Sweden's Ingmar Bergman probed scenarios of marriage, parent-child relationships and other painful kinds of affective webs prefigured by his own tormented childhood. Not surprisingly, films like *Cries and Whispers* (1972), *Face to Face* (1976), and *Autumn Sonata* (1978), which sometimes brutally dissected these phenomena, suggested much of psychoanalytic theory, which itself was enjoying a great resurgence in Europe during the 1970s. (See chapter 11.) But Bergman also drew on the literature of Scandinavian Expressionism, especially the work of the tortured playwright August Strindberg, whose explorations of life as a dream (and a nightmare at that) preceded the Freudian or Jungian versions of that theme. Bergman's films dramatized more than ever the psychoanalytic insight that the unconscious is a kind of cinematic screening room.

Bergman's lead actress in all three films was Liv Ullmann (1938–), a Norwegian actress and writer who would begin directing her own films by the early 1990s. She shared this career trajectory with Jeanne Moreau (1928–), the French star of Truffaut's *Jules et Jim* (1961, *Jules and Jim*). The feminist movement produced great activity on all artistic fronts in the 1970s, and film was no exception. The West German director Margarethe von Trotta (1942–) considered themes of women's liberation in relation to other forms of revolutionary politics in her films, and played an important role in postwar German cinema, especially as it confronted the Nazi era. Her finest achievement in this regard, after working at the theme in several films during the 1970s, was her 1981 film *Die Bleierne Zeit* (*Marianne and Julianne*). It is the story of two sisters, daughters of a stern Lutheran pastor from whom they nevertheless absorbed a passion for social justice. Marianne becomes a violent revolutionary with West Germany's Rote Armee Faktion (Red Army Faction), while Julianne becomes a journalist, outwardly leading a much more conventional life but also filled with admiration for her sister.

In many ways the most fascinating feminist films, and also perhaps the most technically audacious, were those of Chantal Akerman (1950–) of Belgium. She completed nine films during the period 1968 to 1978, including most famously her unsettling 1975 film *Jeanne Dielman, 23, Quai du Commerce, 1080 Bruxelles*. The title refers to the fact that the lead character is a prostitute who works out of her modest home. In this lengthy, somber black-and-white film, we observe Jeanne as she receives "tricks" in her kitchen while her teenage son is away at school, prepares meals, and goes through her other daily routines. The kitchen is the film's central focus, recalling generations of patriarchal adages about a woman's proper place. The most unusual physical feature of the film is that the camera is placed at a height of about five feet (the character's approximate height). As a result, the walls and ceilings of the room loom mightily above the field of vision, as do the adult characters who troop through. This is jolting, and deliberately so, for feminist film criticism of the masculinist gaze that dominates female subjects has pointed out that, among other things, cameras typically have been operated by men, who have a height advantage over women, so that women appear to be dominated as they are viewed from above. In 1978, Akerman released a film about the trials of a young woman filmmaker called *Les Rendez-vous d'Anna*.

Akerman's cinema was a way of applying in practice the claims of feminist theory (see chapter 12), which was all about confronting silences, absurdities, and inconsistencies in Western cultural history. Her work and those of other self-consciously feminist directors of the 1970s prepared the ground for European women directors later in the century.

English feminists were among these pioneering directors. These included Laura Mulvey (1941–) and Peter Wollen (1938–), themselves important writers of cultural theory and criticism, whose influential 1977 film was *Riddles of the Sphinx*. One of the most innovative directors of all was Sally Potter (1949–), who reworked the Puccini opera *La Bohème* in the haunting 1979 film *Thriller*. Potter enjoyed success with films during later decades of the century.

West German artists, including filmmakers, who came of age after 1945 had a similar need to face up to aspects of their culture's recent past that their parents' generation had been most reluctant to acknowledge, perhaps for obvious reasons. Rainer-Werner Fassbinder (1945–1982), Werner Herzog (1942–), Wim Wenders (1945–), Volker Schlöndorf (1939–), and Margarethe von Trotta came to be viewed as the German "New Wave" (Neue Welle) of directors. They endorsed their French namesakes' cult of the *auteur* but turned their attention primarily to breaking the silence that blanketed the immediate German past, although, especially in the case of Herzog, sometimes they ranged over farther reaches of their culture's history.

Through writings, interviews, and a prolific filmography, Fassbinder spearheaded the movement. His combative personality, militant homosexuality (his 1975 film *Faustrecht der Freiheit—Fox and His Friends*—with himself playing the lead role, critiqued the political ambivalence of the gay community), and heavy drug use kept him in the headlines. His films dealt with a wide range of subjects, as was evident from his examination of social class, ethnicity, and generational difference in *Angst essen Seele auf* (1973, *Fear Eats the Soul*), a film about the marriage of a young Moroccan worker and his German wife twenty years his senior. The Fassbinder films that concentrated on the Nazi era or its immediate aftermath attracted the most attention, especially *Die Ehe der Maria Braun* (1978, *The Marriage of Maria Braun*) and *Lili Marleen* (1980). The former featured a powerful performance by Hanna Schygulla (1943–), one of the most gifted European film actresses of her generation. She is featured in a number of his films. Fassbinder's most ambitious effort was *Berlin Alexanderplatz*, based on the novel by Alfred Döblin. It was first broadcast in parts on German television in 1980 before being released to theaters.

The Third Reich was also at the center of two powerfully disturbing films by, respectively, Hans-Jürgen Syberberg (1935–) and Volker Schlöndorff (1939–). Syberberg's film *Hitler, Eine Film aus Deutschland* (1977, *Hitler, A Film of Germany*), directly confronted the taboo subject of Hitler as representative of the German people. Older than the directors associated with the Neue Welle, Syberberg's very title insists that the Third Reich's history cannot be separated from the history of the German nation and its people. In interviews, he spoke of his intention to show "the Hitler in us." Schlöndorff's most celebrated film was *Die Blechtrommel* (1979, *The Tin Drum*), an adaptation of the Günter Grass novel (see chapter 10) that forced the post-1945 generation to confront the Nazi past. The film was at least as controversial as the novel.

Wim Wenders, a cosmopolitan sort who studied film in Paris and has spent much time in the United States, attracted early notice with a film called *Die Angst des Tormanns beim Elfmeter* (1971, *The Goalie's Anxiety at the Penalty Kick*), which offers a look at the bleak existence of those left behind by the postwar "German miracle" economy. Later films displayed urban European culture increasingly influenced by American and other cultural imports. His *Der amerikanische Freund* (1977, *The American Friend*) features the controversial actor Dennis Hopper in the title role, moving through the underworld of Hamburg, the city whose World War II devastation is starkly visible on the screen. Cultural migrations of all kinds increasingly would come to dominate the films of Wenders, who by the 1980s often worked with English-speaking actors.

By far the most visionary—even possessed—of all the German New Wave directors was Werner Herzog (1942–), who embraced a view of cinema as redemptive, able to plunge viewers into a dreamlike state not unlike aspects of the Surrealist aesthetic. Herzog's restless interests ranged widely over German literature and history (including the history of cinema) and eventually would lead him to remote corners of the earth in order to investigate forgotten or overlooked peoples and places. From his earliest films, he was attracted to marginal, freakish subject matter. The entire cast of his *Auch Zwerge haben klein angefangen* (1968, *Even Dwarves Started Small*) consisted of dwarves, and the scenario has them taking over the institution in which they are housed, a radical political act much in keeping with the revolutionary mood of the year in which it was filmed.

Herzog throughout his career also has been known for the extreme lengths, physical and otherwise, to which he will push both himself and his actors, as when he perched his film crew next to the mouth of an active volcano in Guadeloupe that was literally in danger of erupting while they were there (*La soufrière*, 1977). It had been reported that everyone in the town nearest the volcano had departed save one old man, and Herzog and his crew set out to interview him. Herzog worked frequently with Klaus Kinski (1926–1991), a brilliant but notoriously volatile, unstable actor with whom he clashed at times. Kinski starred in

Aguirre, der Zorn Gottes (1972, *Aguirre, the Wrath of God*), a film based on the murderous exploits of a sixteenth-century conquistador in Peru. The treacherous terrain and climate made the work hazardous for the crew and aggravated the tension between Herzog and his star. Kinski also starred in Herzog's remake of Murnau's silent-film vampire classic *Nosferatu* (1978) and *Woyzeck* (1979), based on the Georg Büchner novella about a hapless soldier.

Several of Herzog's films of the 1970s dealt with characters or situations involving extreme mental states, or in one case (the 1977 film *Stroszek*) with a lead character somewhat challenged in his mental capacity. A famous episode from early nineteenth-century German history provided one memorable scenario. Herzog's *Jeder für sich und Gott gegen alle* (1974, *Every Man for Himself and God Against All*) was his version of the story of Kaspar Hauser, the mute, seemingly catatonic young man discovered one day in Nürnberg in 1830 and then mysteriously murdered there precisely three years later, after an interval during which he learned to speak and became an accomplished musician. *Herz aus Glas* (1976, *Heart of Glass*) took Herzog's preoccupation with mysterious mental states even further. This film is, on one level, a story about a village whose glass-making industry and principal means of livelihood is threatened by the death of the craftsman who held the secret for manufacturing the unusual reddish glass. While the townspeople fret, they are harangued by a seemingly mad visionary who dwells just beyond their town. For this film, Herzog learned hypnosis and actually hypnotized the members of the cast—all except the character playing the "madman." The actors move about in a trancelike state. The film's dreamlike character is intensified by Herzog's soundtrack, which uses the instrumental music of a German group called Popol Vuh, who incorporate Indian sitars and Andean music into their compositions. They were used also for the soundtrack of *Aguirre*.

The final collaboration between Herzog and Kinski provides the most extreme example of the director's cinematic zeal. This was the outrageously arduous project *Fitzcarraldo*, which took four years to complete and was finally released in 1982. It was the story of an early twentieth-century Irish entrepreneur Fitzgerald (the title is his name as rendered by Spanish speakers) who has the insanely ambitious dream of establishing an opera house in a remote corner of Peru, near a dangerous part of the Orinico River. Moreover, he wants to bring the great tenor Enrico Caruso there to perform Verdi. Unable to navigate the river at a crucial juncture, he inaugurates the desperate plan of hiring Indian forest dwellers to transport his steamship over a mountain in order to reach his destination. These exertions were actually performed by Herzog's crew and extras and, as in the screenplay, led to accidental deaths and tremendous financial cost. Along the way, actors defected from the project, it was threatened by loss of financial support, Herzog himself became terrifically ill with a tropical disease, and real death threats were exchanged among the film's principals. The rigors of such filming nearly drove all involved mad, but was finally realized although it never achieved enough market success to compensate for its cost.

It is clear, in retrospect, that the period of European history between the end of World War II and the early 1980s or so was rich in cinematic talent. Just to list the names of the directors discussed above is to reinforce the point that this was a great era in the history of modern cinema. But it must also be acknowledged that the ability of the giant Hollywood film industry to influence, even dominate, the tastes of the filmgoing public remained far greater than all the European production companies put together. For that matter, by late in the century India had by far the largest film industry, although consumption of its products was limited largely to the subcontinent and the Indian diaspora. Of course, that encompasses approximately one-sixth of the world's population. American companies were unsurpassed when it came to distributing their products around the globe, and 1970s directors such as Steven Spielberg or George Lucas dwarfed their European counterparts when it came to box office. But the Fellinis and Truffauts and Bergmans of the film world set the aesthetic standard by which directors everywhere measured themselves, and helped to shape and redefine the vocabulary of film.

Popular Music

Many in the generations coming of age after 1945 defined themselves perhaps more by their musical than their cinematic preferences. The young people whose generation sacrificed most in the war had found big-band "swing" music and the energetic dancing it inspired a welcome respite from the horrors of their time. (See chapter 8.) This may have been the first generation of young people in the twentieth century to feel bound to one another through their era's music. Just as after the previous world war, when African American GIs remaining as expatriates in France helped introduce the public there to such artists as Sidney Bechet and Louis Armstrong, the late 1940s and early 1950s saw frequent appearances in European locations by leading jazz artists of the day. Many of them, frustrated by the entrenched "Jim Crow" society that persisted in the American South even after yet another generation of African Americans had served their country, chose the expatriate life in such cities as Paris, Stockholm, and Amsterdam. Through their presence, Europeans were exposed to new styles, such as be-bop, and, later in the 1950s, to so-called cool jazz. Performers including Dexter Gordon (1923–1990), Champion Jack Dupree (1910–1992), and Eric Dolphy (1928–1964) made their homes in Europe, and, through their frequent European tours, the great artists of the period, such as Billie Holiday (1915–1959), Charlie Parker (1920–1955), Thelonious Monk (1917–1982), Bud Powell (1924–1966), Charles Mingus (1922–1979), John Coltrane (1926–1967), and Miles Davis (1926–1991), found a following in Europe.

Jazz was by no means to everyone's taste, although its influence could be found in genres of music native to Europe. The great jazz guitarist Django Reinhardt (1910–1953) was a Gypsy, a member of the nomadic group long feared, despised, and persecuted throughout Europe. Yet admiration for him often led to the acknowledgment of the importance of Gypsy music. Many Europeans admired their equivalent of the mainstream pop "crooners" one found in the United States around 1950. In France, the long tradition of *cafés-concerts* that had produced such wartime stars as Edith Piaf and Maurice Chevalier (see chapter 8) remained strong. By the 1950s it had produced a style of music called *chanson* (literally "song"). Performers in this genre wedded pop sensibility to French folk traditions, often accompanying themselves on acoustic guitar or singing against simple background provided by accordion or piano. The mood created was often one of nostalgia for a lost, or least threatened, French national character. Piaf remained an essential influence, and other singers paid her the supreme compliment of performing her songs. Some, such as Charles Aznavour (1924–), held close to a jazz aesthetic while others, such as Françoise Hardy (1944–), Belgian singer/songwriter Jacques Brel (1928–1979), Leo Ferré (1916–1993), and the often-ribald Georges Brassens (1921–1981), based their songs on folk sources. The *chanson* field continued to evolve in later years through singers who reached out to embrace other musical genres, creating interesting hybrids with rock 'n' roll or reggae. A leader in this regard was the notoriously dissolute Serge Gainsbourg (1928–1991), esteemed by his devoted fans and a reliable source of tabloid gossip.

The late 1950s were a time of rich musical ferment in England. Fondness for American jazz persisted, but moved from the swing and be-bop emphasis of the period immediately following World War II into a movement that became known as traditional, shortened to "trad jazz." Trad jazz artists favored older styles of New Orleans music, especially "Dixieland." As in the United States during the 1950s "Beat" era, jazz aficionados mingled with bohemian artists and writers in London clubs. Also by the late 1950s, American rock 'n' roll had invaded the British Isles, and in some cases performers known only marginally in the United States, such as Gene Vincent (1935–1971) and Eddie Cochran (1938–1960), became huge stars in the British Isles. Other would-be popular musicians held somewhat aloof from rock 'n' roll, or at least from what they perceived to be some of its more trivial or adolescent manifestations. Some of them sought involvement in more traditional musical genres. Corresponding somewhat to the early "folk music" boom in the United States (ca. 1959 to 1962), folk-based music in England was known as skiffle. Often fast-paced and even resembling in structure more frenetic forms of rock 'n' roll such as rockabilly, skiffle groups adhered to a strict formula for instrumentation, featuring acoustic guitar, drums, and a homemade washtub bass.

Some musicians involved themselves both with skiffle and rock 'n' roll music. John Lennon (1940–1980)was one the best-known examples. He formed a skiffle-based band known as The Quarrymen before he went on to be a founding member of The Beatles. Whether they inclined toward acoustic or electric guitars, however, young English musicians of this period tended to represent the social stratum most marginalized by the stagnant postwar British economy. Their counterparts in the more privileged classes were university-bound, but they were for the most part on the "vocational" track. (A notable exception was Mick Jagger (1943–) of The Rolling Stones, who enrolled in the London School of Economics.) In terms of education, typically this meant that the most to which they could aspire was enrollment in an art school, a uniquely British institution that combined vocational training with courses in the fine arts, often taught by émigré faculty in close touch with the European avant-garde.

As an art student in the early 1960s, Peter Townshend (1945–), later the lead guitarist for The Who, was inspired by a lecture given at his school by Gustav Metzger (1926–), a German-born artist living in England. Metzger practiced "auto-destructive" art, and was inspired by such earlier figures in the avant-garde tradition as the Italian musician, painter, and writer Alberto Savinio (1891–1952)—brother of Giorgio de Chirico—who, after emigrating to Paris, became notorious for his performances at the piano, onto which he poured blood before demolishing the instrument for his finale. Townshend's penchant for smashing his guitars on stage was very likely inspired by Metzger. Many of the most obviously art-conscious British pop musicians of the later 1960s and 1970s, for example the members of Pink Floyd, shared Townshend's educational background, including exposure to the European avant-garde.

Many of these same art school students cultivated a deep enthusiasm for traditional American blues and rhythm and blues music, and they held on to these early roots of rock 'n' roll even as their American contemporaries had lost sight of them. Van Morrison (1945–), leader of a blues-based mid-1960s rock band called Them, refers often in his songs to growing up in grim working-class Belfast, Northern Island, where he and his bandmates responded eagerly to early blues singers like Blind Lemon Jefferson (1897–1929) and Leadbelly (Huddie Ledbetter, 1885?–1949). The story goes that Brian Jones (1942–1969) and Keith Richards (1943–) of The Rolling Stones met when they both noticed each other traveling on the London "Tube," each carrying records by Muddy Waters (McKinley Morganfield, 1915–1983), Howlin' Wolf (Chester Burnett, 1910–1976), Chuck Berry (1926–), and Bo Diddley (Ellas McDaniel, 1928–), the best-known artists on Chicago's Chess label.

The fact that several legendary American blues musicians toured Europe in the early 1960s fueled even more of this interest in the music. One of the most influential was the singer and harmonica virtuoso Sonny Boy Williamson (Rice Miller, 1899–1965), who toured England late in his life, playing at one point with The Animals and, during his last tour (1965), with The Yardbirds. Both of these 1960s English rock bands began by performing blues standards. Several of the best-known British rock stars served musical apprenticeships with singers and band leaders who were blues enthusiasts. Alexis Korner (1928–1984) was such a singer, and Mick Jagger was one of his discoveries. John Mayall (1933–) was also a longtime bandleader, whose group The Bluesbreakers was a proving ground for a long list, most famously Eric Clapton (1945–), of musicians who would play leading roles in British rock music.

Use of blues influences continued all through the 1960s and into the early 1970s. The band Ten Years After, Savoy Brown, and an early version of the group Fleetwood Mac—led by John Mayall's Bluesbreakers alumnus Peter Green, (1946–)—were among the more successful examples (although far removed from the huge commercial success after 1969 of the blues-inspired band Led Zeppelin, often considered the progenitors of "heavy metal" music). However, many of the British bands that came to prominence during the 1960s drew on sources other than the blues. Nearly all of them, including The Beatles, were impressed by the "soul music" sounds of such important

American centers of black music as Detroit, Memphis, and Philadelphia. The Kinks, the first band to use deliberately distorted guitar sounds, took inspiration for much of its music from the middlebrow tradition of the English music halls, reworking many of their stock themes in a rock 'n' roll context.

By the late 1960s one important trend under way was a return to the traditional folk music of the British Isles, but reinterpreted with electric guitars and amplified instruments. Fairport Convention and Steeleye Span were two of the most influential such bands. Singers Nick Drake (1948–1974) and John Martyn (1948–) combined folk-inspired music with subtle jazz effects. Successful rock bands like Traffic and Jethro Tull incorporated jazz motifs, while the powerful blues-rock trio Cream brought jazz-style improvisation, with extended "jams," to their version of rock 'n' roll. Still other groups, especially once rock music came to dominate the music business by later in the decade, bridged the gap between pop and classical. The Beatles, the most famous of all British musicians, made occasional use of string orchestras and found their music compared favorably to classical genres. Their most famous rivals for pop music dominance, The Rolling Stones, remained firmly within the rock 'n' roll tradition, particularly emphasizing its roots in the blues.

These two somewhat contrasting groups powerfully dominated late-1960s pop music and together made an enormous impact on global youth culture, affecting everything from fashion, to drug use, to intellectual and even spiritual trends. For lasting global influence, no one matched The Beatles. Their fame and commercial success reached such an enormous level that for many people around the world they symbolized British culture, and seemed to represent a reversal of that nations' declining fortunes. They released a very large number of recordings in a relatively short time (ca. 1961 to 1970) and toured to mass acclaim until 1966, when they abandoned concerts to concentrate on increasingly ambitious studio recordings and on individual projects. The most controversial of all was John Lennon, especially through his partnership with his second wife, Yoko Ono (1933–), an avant-garde artist who had been associated earlier with the Fluxus group. (See chapter 10.) In 1968, The Beatles founded their own business, the Apple Corporation, and began releasing on this new label their own recordings and those by others. This was a first for the music business, but it was doomed by mismanagement and outright theft by the band's business associates. Meanwhile the group that had most dominated popular music during the second half of the decade was headed for breakup. During the late 1960s it seemed that headlines from London were either about antagonisms within The Beatles or about the drug busts and other legal difficulties of the controversial Rolling Stones.

The influence these two bands had on the music world cannot be overestimated. Early in their careers they spawned a legion of would-be successor bands that together were experienced as a "British invasion" particularly of American musical culture, and the ambitious scale on which The Beatles and The Rolling Stones came to operate inspired other bands (e.g., The Who) to emulate them. In addition, the rock music that emerged from Britain reinvigorated what had been perceived as a moribund pop music scene in the United States. After the example particularly of The Beatles, many of the musicians who had turned toward traditional folk forms now embraced electrified instruments and forged a new "folk-rock" sound.

The pivotal figure in this regard was the brilliant American singer/songwriter/musician Bob Dylan (1941–). His "antihero" brand of personal charisma exerted a profound spell over young people in Europe. In France it was noted that he had made reference to such poetic influences as Villon and Rimbaud. In Jean-Luc Godard's 1965 film *Masculin/Féminin,* a character played by Jean-Pierre Léaud repeatedly soliloquizes *"Qui êtes-vous, Robert Zimmerman?"* ("Who are you, Robert Zimmerman?"—Dylan's real name). Dylan befriended members of The Beatles, made two highly publicized tours of the British Isles, and jolted his folk music following by wedding his increasingly complicated lyrical vision to loud strident rock arrangements. Dylan and American-style folk rock then significantly influenced Britain, so that the period from 1965 to 1975 was marked by cross-fertilization of musical ideas between the two cultures. One of the most important examples of such a crosser of national boundaries was the highly original guitar virtuoso Jimi Hendrix (1942–1970). He first toured England as a member of Little Richard's band, but stayed on to form a trio, consisting of himself and an English drummer and bassist, called The Jimi Hendrix Experience. Although short-lived (due to Hendrix's drug overdose death in 1970 at the age of twenty-eight), this was to be one of the most influential musical groups of the late twentieth century.

Like many musicians of the day, Hendrix owed his reputation as much or more to his memorable appearances at huge music festivals than to his recordings. The 1969 Woodstock Festival in upstate New York remains the most famous example, and Hendrix perhaps the musician most associated with it. But festivals were crucial in Europe as well. In 1970 a throng equal in mass to that of Woodstock descended on the Isle of Wight, one of the Channel Islands. The huge lineup of artists performing there included Bob Dylan and The Band. It was Dylan's first public performance in more than two years and was shrouded in the aura of mystery that had become typical of his celebrity. He had declined to perform at the Woodstock Festival, despite (or because) of its location near his own home. The Isle of Wight extravaganza was a one-time affair, but several European pop music festivals became annual events. One of the most important was England's Glastonbury Fair.

But certainly for most people, recorded music was central to their experience and awareness of the day's artists. During the second half of the decade, the long-playing record album came to replace the 45 RPM single as the medium of choice for artists and consumers alike. Before this point, the LP was associated almost exclusively with classical or jazz music. Fans of The Beatles, The Rolling Stones, and Bob Dylan awaited each new album the way admirers of a great novelist might anticipate the next opus. Many British bands carried this idea to considerable, sometimes grandiose lengths. The Who received accolades for their 1969 double-album release *Tommy,* touted as the first "rock opera." Actually, The Kinks had preceded them a year earlier with the nostalgic *Village Green Preservation Society.*

Not all successful bands took themselves so very seriously. Ray Davies (1944–) of The Kinks was an especially good example of a singer using self-deprecating irony. Many English bands employed whimsy and a playful spirit in their music, often emulating the controversial American musician Frank Zappa (1940–1993). Perhaps the best example was a highly influential group called the Bonzo Dog Band. Musically they drew on a wide range of styles, including jazz and early rock 'n' roll. Their songs were more often elaborate comedy skits, in the spirit of The Goons or Monty Python.

By 1970 even classical music buffs had begun to acknowledge that the best contemporary popular composers, especially John Lennon and Paul McCartney (1942–) of The Beatles, bore comparison with the great figures of the Western tradition. In June of 1967 a band called Procol Harum surprised listeners with a highly successful tune called "A Whiter Shade of Pale," with its Bach-like organ lead-in. Some English musicians active in pop groups were conservatory trained or had absorbed deep influences from the twentieth-century musical avant-garde. Among these were the members of the Soft Machine, who took their name from a William Burroughs novel. They structured their compositions much like classical pieces. Typically one would fill an entire side of a long-playing vinyl album. Robert Fripp (1946–), a highly original guitarist who invented new tunings and experimented with a variety of electronic effects, led a band called King Crimson. Its music was a meeting ground of rock, jazz, and classical genres. But no group achieved greater acclaim or struck greater financial gold than the band Pink Floyd. Their early recordings were much in the "psychedelic" vein of the 1966–1967 period, but after 1970 each of their albums was a self-conscious "work," intended to be listened to in its entirety, as one would a symphony or as listeners had learned to do with The Beatles' *Sgt. Pepper's Lonely Hearts Club Band*. Pink Floyd's 1973 album *Dark Side of the Moon* was their most obvious attempt yet to succeed at this level, and it quickly became one of the largest-selling albums ever.

What some were calling "art rock" was very influential on the European continent. In West Germany the bands Tangerine Dream and Can featured highly skilled musicians who gained a strong international following. Brian Eno (1948–), an innovative avant-garde electronic music specialist who had been one of the founding members of a self-consciously arty British band called Roxy Music, often spent time in Berlin recording with like-minded musicians there. Meanwhile the trend of a kind of rock-classical music fusion continued. Two of the most commercially successful English bands along these lines were Yes and Genesis. Yes featured elaborate keyboard work that made obvious reference to the classical repertoire, while Genesis, also made up of very sophisticated musicians, became known for especially grandiose effects in their stage shows, with lead singer Peter Gabriel (1950–) attired in a variety of bizarre costumes. Affectations like these defined what many labeled the "glam rock" movement, featuring singers who cultivated an androgynous look and took a highly theatrical approach to their concerts. David Bowie (1947–), a prolific songwriter whose career has encompassed many different phases, was perhaps the best-known figure associated with this trend.

By the mid-1970s, a strong reaction against the "baroque" excesses of rock music began to stir. Driven by bitter resentment against the economic hardships of low employment and the heavy-handed law enforcement of the Thatcher era, a new generation of working-class youth, many of them from an art school milieu similar to that of their early 1960s predecessors, began to create an angry-sounding, bare essentials kind of rock 'n' roll music called "punk." The punk stance, including music but also personal appearance and fashion, was in strong reaction against the "hippie" culture of the late-1960s early 1970s rock musicians and profoundly against the overblown, heavy production and performance of their music. Punk rockers wore their hair short, sported torn T-shirts and sturdy boots, and performed music that was the delib-

erately violent antithesis of the peace-and-love stance of their predecessors. They also restored to rock 'n' roll the raw energy and excitement
of its earliest exponents.

Punk was not without its antecedents, including such maverick
American performers as The Velvet Underground and The Stooges. In
contrast to the arena-based, heavily produced rock music of the early
1970s, so-called pub rock (music by bands playing in small clubs, sometimes even in pubs) had brought greater intimacy and a rootsy feel back
into rock music. Many pub rockers, such as Dave Edmonds (1944–) of
Wales, Dr. Feelgood, and Ducks Deluxe, harked back to the rockabilly
style that had been so popular in England in the era of Gene Vincent
and Eddie Cochran. Brinsley Schwarz was an influential band that experimented with American-style country and western sounds, and Graham Parker (1950–) and his band The Rumour featured a high-energy
show that borrowed heavily from the rhythm and blues and soul music.
Musicians like these pointed the way to a simpler back-to-basics style.

Punk musicians embraced an unabashed amateurism, and there was a
kind of democratic outlook expressed in the notion that anybody who
learned a few basic guitar chords could start a band. One notable change
was that larger numbers of women began to form bands and to appear
with instruments, whereas female lead singer or backup singers had
been virtually the only roles available to their older sisters, so to speak.
Punk rock performances also demonstrated their disdain for the adulation audiences had shown for rock musicians of an earlier era, and did
much to break down divisions between audience and performer. More
than a few music critics have compared the early punk sensibility to
Dadaism in its zero-degree primal anti-aesthetic stance. Like Dada,
punk's influence eventually spread to other countries, certainly to the
United States, and even to Japan. Continental European bands adopted
the punk style. One of the most successful "punks" on the Continent
was a Belgian singer who called himself Plastic Bertrand.

The band that heralded the punk phenomenon to most of the world
and whose explosion into notoriety in 1977 was most analogous to the
detonation of Dada in 1916 was the quartet known as the Sex Pistols.
The very name encapsulated the mix of sex and violence that had made
A Clockwork Orange shocking. The snarling, spitting, belching lead singer
John Lydon (1956–), known as Johnny Rotten, provided the antiheroic
face and voice that brought them notice. His surly belligerent presence
on stage was met with a response in kind by frenzied audiences whose
behavior, clothing, and gestures associated punk with violence in the
minds of many. All of this was thoroughly calculated. The Sex Pistols

were the creation of an enterprising young promoter named Malcolm McLaren (1946–). He coached the group's members on their appearance and comportment, just as Brian Epstein (1934–1967) had The Beatles or Colonel Tom Parker had Elvis Presley.

Their music was every bit as controversial as their behavior. In early 1977 the BBC refused to play their single "God Save the Queen," a full frontal assault of disrespect and scorn for England's royalty, scoffing at the escapist fantasy the institution provided for a "dreaming" England. Conservative members of Parliament were vociferous in their denunciation, and manager McLaren could not have been more delighted with the publicity. By the time their one and only album, *Never Mind the Bollocks: Here's the Sex Pistols,* was released in December of 1977, the band was on the verge of breakup, and its dissolute heroin-addicted bass player "Sid Vicious" (1957–1979) would die of an overdose the following year. But the album had a profound impact with its simple slashing guitar chords, pounding drums, and songs like the banned "God Save the Queen," the neo-Nietzschean "Antichrist," and "Holidays in the Sun," the powerful opening track that warned of neo-Nazi movements.

The relationship of English punk rock to fascist politics is troublesome, complicated, and contradictory. Neo-Nazi activity in Europe in the late twentieth century was directed against immigrant groups especially, and leaders of these xenophobic movements tended to recruit as members young men (and sometimes women) who were poorly educated, underemployed, and disenfranchised. In the 1960s and 1970s, England had taken in a significant number of immigrants from South Asia and the West Indies. Enoch Powell was a hatemongering politician who had inflamed some citizens against the new immigrants. At least some punk rock enthusiasts shared such views. These included most famously the "skinheads."

A shaved head also was one way to show contempt for the long hair sported by an earlier generation whose brand of rock music punks scorned. Punk "fashion" occasionally included swastika emblems, even a German World War II–era helmet, and certainly the heavy boots used by storm troopers. It remains unclear how much of this was for shock effect alone, for many in the punk movement embraced the music and, by extension, the culture of England's immigrants. Not a few punks loved the reggae music of Jamaican immigrants and, by extension, were attracted to the culture of which it was an expression. The fast-paced dance music called "ska," a style that had preceded the emergence of reggae in the mid-1960s, had enthusiastic followers, especially among groups of working-class young men whose appearance was often identical to that of neo-Nazi skinheads. The skinhead look was never reliable as an indicator of political leanings.

By the late 1970s, as the first waves of punk ebbed away, a number of so-called two-tone bands—bands with both white and black members—emerged, usually playing either straightforward ska music or a hybrid rock/reggae. Examples included The Specials, The Selecter, Bad Manners, and UB 40. The visual effect of short-haired or shaved-head white musicians alongside Jamaican immigrants sporting long dreadlocks was quite stunning, and such bands became a force for opposition to racism in England. They joined with singer Elvis Costello (1954–) in the organization Rock Against Racism. An unusually prolific songwriter, Costello (real name Declan MacManus) made his debut as a punk rocker but went on to have a lengthy career, exploring many different styles of music.

The punk group that enjoyed the greatest commercial success during the late 1970s and early 1980s with a brand of music clearly influenced by Jamaican styles was The Clash, a quartet whose early sound bore some similarities to the raging sound of the Sex Pistols, but who exhibited little of the self-destructive tendencies of those *enfants terribles.* Before disbanding in 1982, they moved steadily in an increasingly radical political direction, always the inclination of lead singer Joe Strummer (1952–). "Guns of Brixton" was an inflammatory call to resistance against police violence, which had been especially flagrant in the London neighborhood of Brixton, where many West Indian immigrants resided. In 1980, The Clash released *Sandinista,* an album whose title was an obvious tribute to the Nicaraguan revolution. Since the band lasted only about five years, this intervention into politics was short-lived. Representative of the West Indian immigrant community that inspired The Clash, Linton Kwesi Johnson (1952–), a Jamaican immigrant poet who began performing in the late 1970s, held to a consistently leftist political stance over a long career. A poet, he intoned his *patois* lines against a strident Jamaican "dub" beat, a form of music with heavily accentuated bass and drum parts. Police violence particularly against blacks was one of his most important topics.

An achievement of punk rock with lasting significance for popular music was the leading role taken by women. All-woman bands, such as The Slits and The Raincoats, enjoyed success at least during the immediate punk era (ca. 1977 to 1979). Politically minded punk bands like The Gang of Four and The Mekons included female members as players as well as singers. Certainly some bands adhered to the old formula of lead female vocalist with supporting male musicians. Siouxsie and the Banshees were one of the most popular such groups, with "Siouxsie" as an emblem of punk style. Another punk band with a female singer, X-Ray Spex, was known for angry feminist lyrics denouncing objectification of women.

The greater participation of women was enhanced by the existence of a number of independent record labels. This commercial aspect of the music worked well with the democratic impulse of punk music—the notion that anybody could decide to learn the rudiments of an instrument and form a band. The proliferation of bands inspired by groups such as the Sex Pistols and The Clash was enormous. Among them were The Buzzcocks, The Vibrators, 999, Ian Dury and the Blockheads, The Jam, The Damned, and dozens more. It was the biggest explosion since the mid-1960s, but it was not destined to last. By the end of the 1980s, the collapse of independent companies in the face of multinational giants greatly restricted the range of new musical possibilities.

The punk rock phenomenon serves to illustrate the paradox with which this chapter began: whether "popular" culture is that which originates with actual people (e.g., alienated young Londoners forming bands in the late 1970s) or the calculated strategies of people in the so-called culture industry (e.g., the Sex Pistols' manager or the major record companies such as Warner Brothers with the Sex Pistols or CBS with The Clash). Perhaps it is more often the case that notable developments in the pop culture arena show a complicated admixture of the two possible explanations.

Suggestions for Further Reading

Brake, Mike. *The Sociology of Youth Culture and Youth Subculture: Sex and Drugs and Rock 'n' Roll.* London: Routledge & Kegan Paul, 1980.

Brantlinger, Patrick. *Bread and Circuses: Theories of Mass Culture as Social Decay.* Ithaca: Cornell University Press, 1983.

Hebdige, Dick. *Subculture: The Meaning of Style.* London: Methuen, 1979.

Hoggart, Richard. *The Uses of Literacy: Aspects of Working-Class Life with Special Reference to Publications and Entertainments.* London: Chatto and Windus, 1958.

Karnow, Stanley. *Paris in the Fifties.* New York: Times Books, 1997.

Nuttall, Jeff. *Bomb Culture.* London: Paladin, 1971.

Savage, Jon. *England's Dreaming: Anarchy, Sex Pistols, Punk Rock, and Beyond.* New York: St. Martin's Press, 1992.

Sklar, Robert. *Film: An International History of the Medium.* New York: Abrams, 1993.

Stovall, Tyler. *Paris Noir: African Americans in the City of Light.* Boston: Houghton Mifflin, 1996.

Chapter 10

European Culture, 1945 to 1970:
End of the "Modern"?

The quarter of a century that followed the end of World War II witnessed dramatic, sometimes baffling developments in European culture that began in reaction to the colossal destruction of the years between 1939 and 1945. The period drew to a close in the midst of new currents that signal, some have argued, the decline of Modernism and the emergence of what many cultural critics and theorists—often for lack of a better term—call "Postmodernism." Some have meant by this that modern history is tied to the consolidation of nation-states and the aggrandizement of their respective economies, the centralization of government apparatuses, the growth of internal transportation networks, and the all-important burgeoning development of cities. Most of these long-developing trends were on the wane or at least in crisis as the decade of the 1970s got under way.

Most of the artistic activity and intellectual debates that dominated the cultural scene from about 1945 to 1956 or so had begun during the war years. European artists in either temporary or permanent exile and intellectuals remaining in Europe, many of them active in Resistance movements, produced works and engaged in debates that posed serious questions of ethics and political allegiance. Such questions would reach a fever pitch of urgency with the revelations of the Holocaust's genocide on a massive scale and the detonation of atomic bombs on the civilian population of two Japanese cities.

Jean-Paul Sartre and Existentialism

By the time of the liberation of occupied France by Allied forces (August 1944), the intellectual movement known as Existentialism occupied the center stage of European philosophy and had an enormous impact on a variety of literary genres. Although it was "news" in the 1940s, Existentialist philosophy could be traced back into the mid-nineteenth century and the Danish philosopher Soren Kierkegaard (1813–1855). He was the first modern thinker to suggest that the central challenge of living was to find meaning in a world that seemed to negate it. Friedrich Nietzsche probed further along these lines, and the great Russian novelist Fyodor Dostoevskii (1821–1881) dramatized this struggle for meaning and moral certainty in his fiction. Edmund Husserl and Martin Heidegger, in the twentieth-century philosophical movement of Phenomenology, had deepened these inquiries, and religious thinkers such as Gabriel Marcel (1889–1973) and Martin Buber (1878–1965) had sought to wed ontological questions to, respectively, Roman Catholic and Jewish theology.

But it was the French philosopher/novelist/playwright (all-round man of letters) Jean-Paul Sartre (1905–1980) who became most identified with the term "Existentialism." His French colleagues Simone de Beauvoir (1908–1986), Maurice Merleau-Ponty (1908–1961), and Albert Camus (1913–1960) all made contributions, although with differing degrees of willed, conscious affiliation to the movement, but Sartre was the dominant figure. He also was to be the dominant figure (and some would say the last ever) of the French writer/intellectual as social prophet, the role reserved on French history for the likes of Voltaire, Rousseau, and Hugo. The popular perception of existentialism linked it to the Resistance and the Liberation, and Sartre did much to encourage these associations.

Sartre had established his literary reputation before the war, especially as a novelist. His 1938 novel *La Nausée* (*Nausea*) provided an extreme view of a man stymied by his confrontation with the horrors of his own existence. A trilogy of novels called *Les chemins de liberté* (*The Roads to Freedom*), completed in 1941 but published only after the war, dramatized the dilemma of protagonists torn by ambivalence regarding ethical and moral responsibility in an increasingly chaotic world. During the war itself, Sartre turned his hand to writing plays, plays that equally probed dilemmas of moral and political commitment. Briefly a soldier in the French army, Sartre was captured and held for a short time in a German prisoner-of-war camp. There he wrote and directed plays.

Returning to occupied Paris in 1941, he continued as a playwright. He could not approach themes of resistance to Nazi authority directly, but he did so more obliquely or allegorically, as when he drew on classical antiquity, reworking Sophocles for his 1943 play *Les mouches* (*The*

Flies). Use of Greek drama to express modern concerns and conflicts was not new in French theater. Jean Cocteau (1889–1963) adapted the myth of Orpheus and Eurydice in *Orphée* (1926, *Orpheus*) and offered his take on the Oedipus story in *La Machine infernale* (1934, *The Infernal Machine*) And Jean Giraudoux (1882–1944) explored similar territory but with greater emphasis on moral choice in *La Guerre de Troie n'aura pas eu lieu* (1935, *Tiger at the Gates*) and *Electra* (1937). *La Folle de Chaillot* (1945, *The Madwoman of Chaillot*), staged after the playwright's death resonated with audiences newly liberated from the Occupation, as had Sartre's *Les Mouches*.

Sartre's plays, however, underscored especially the existential situation of characters profoundly, terrifyingly alone in a hostile or indifferent world. His 1944 play *Huis clos* (*No Exit*) portrayed the horror of a character unable to escape the companions with whom he is trapped. The feeling of dread, of fear, of realizing that ultimately you are left to your own devices in order to make your way in a desolate, uncaring world received elaborate treatment in Sartre's monumental philosophical work *L'être et le néant* (1943, *Being and Nothingness*). Here, Sartre built on the foundations of phenomenology, on Husserl's insistence on our encounter with the irreducible phenomena we perceive in the "Life-World," and on Heidegger's interrogation of contradictory and overlooked aspects of "being," one sense of which is "existence."

Sartre went on to elaborate a distinction between the existence of inanimate objects or uncomplicated living beings on one hand and human beings on the other. The former category he designated as the *en soi*, or that which exists in and of itself; that which merely exists. The latter he gave the purposive label of the *pour soi*, that which exists for itself, with self-knowledge and awareness of its existence. An important part of this self-awareness is one's perception of being the object of other people's contemplation. One long, very important section of the book discusses the constitutive aspects of "the gaze" (*le regard*) for one's sense of self in an alienating, potentially threatening world. More than any of his predecessors in what can be described as the modern "Existentialist" tradition, Sartre placed radical emphasis on existence over essence, that is, that we have no essential qualities as human beings. What we are is what we become as a result of what we make of the fact of our existence. Failure to recognize that and to take personal responsibility for grappling with the brute reality of one's existence Sartre called "bad faith" (*la mauvaise foi*).

Being and Nothingness would continue to have a profound impact for decades, even after Sartre's equally ambitious work of 1964, *Critique of*

Dialectical Reason, which announced a newer preoccupation with history and adopted a consciously Marxist political stance. The appearance of *Being and Nothingness,* along with the publication of the first two volumes of his trilogy of novels and the success of his plays, served simultaneously to establish Sartre's reputation and the philosophical movement of Existentialism. His position was consolidated further when he assumed editorship in 1945 of *Les Temps modernes,* destined to be a very influential journal. Despite this, three other key intellectual contemporaries played significant roles in the Existentialist movement, although not all of them willingly accepted the label. Their ideas and works, just as is true of Sartre's, cannot be confined merely within that high-profile term. The three in question were Simone de Beauvoir (1908–1986), Maurice Merleau-Ponty (1908–1961), and Albert Camus (1913–1960).

Simone de Beauvoir was the author of numerous novels and memoirs, including volumes dealing with her years with Sartre. They were partners, famous for their open tolerance of each other's numerous liaisons, and remained devoted to each other despite occasional misunderstandings and estrangements. De Beauvoir's 1943 novel *She Came to Stay* and her book-length essay "The Ethics of Ambiguity" explored Existentialist themes, but in 1949 she published a groundbreaking book that signaled a most significant new direction in her writing. *Le Deuxième sexe* (*The Second Sex*) remains one of the towering works of the modern feminist tradition, and exerted enormous influence over the feminist movement, which became a major social force after 1970. The book offers a historical and philosophical examination of the persistence of women's oppression, and argued forcefully for the view that woman's role was not biologically determined but a learned cultural construct.

Merleau-Ponty, who joined Sartre on the editorial board of *Les Temps modernes,* was a philosopher influenced by Henri Bergson who also carried on the Phenomenological tradition. He was deeply interested in questions of language, aesthetics, and perception. His *Sens et non-sens* (1948, *Sense and Nonsense*) and *Signes* (1960, *Signs*) anticipate the later intellectual movements of Structuralism and Semiology. But in many ways the book with the most far-reaching implications for later cultural developments was his *Phénomenologie de la perception* (1945, *Phenomenology of Perception*), published posthumously in 1962. Using subtle, complicated argument and terminology, Merleau-Ponty offered a resolution to Sartre's harsh opposition between perceiver and perceived, describing instead the importance of a perceptual field within which one takes up various positions. Merleau-Ponty's attention to the nuances of spatial experience and perception has been influential for later French social theorists who have made social space a central focus of their inquiry. Merleau-Ponty's life was cut short by cancer, but perhaps he would have been as prolific as his colleague Sartre if he had been granted an equally long life.

The distinctive novels and essays Albert Camus published during the 1940s and early 1950s appeared to raise themes that complemented the Existentialist emphasis of Sartre, although Camus resented the term's application to his work. The 1942 novel *L'étranger* (*The Stranger*) features as first-person narrator a certain Meursault, an antihero in somewhat the same vein as Sartre's Roquentin in *La Nausée*. But where Sartre's protagonist reacted with dread and horror to his existence, Meursault exhibits an overwhelming indifference and lack of affect. In the novel's pivotal episode, he casually murders a man he does not know, having concluded that carrying out the act or not doing so are equally insignificant in the overall scheme of things. Camus presents human existence in a indifferent universe as, ultimately, an absurd proposition.

This harsh view of life took a different form in a collection of essays Camus published the same year called *Le Mythe de Sisyphe* (*The Myth of Sisyphus*). The title essay offers the myth of Sisyphus condemned forever to push the heavy boulder up the hill to the modern condition, where our actions seem futile. Yet in other essays in the same volume, Camus makes clear that, nevertheless, he affirms that reasons for action and political commitment still exist. His 1947 novel *La Peste* (*The Plague*), clearly inspired by the contagion of fascism, his powerful political testament *La Révolte* (1951, *The Rebel*), and his 1957 play *La Chute* (*The Fall*) are strong reminders that one should not confuse Camus with his famous fictional character Meursault.

Camus was a *pied-noir*, a product of a French family of colonists in Algeria. The colonial experience and the particular character of Algeria shaped his perceptions of life profoundly and provided the atmosphere for his novels and plays. When the Algerian war of independence began in 1954, Camus sided with the colonial power. This threw him into bitter opposition with prominent writers of the French Left, chief among them Sartre. Their quarrel was public and volatile, and produced an irrevocable break between them. Only after Camus's tragic death in an automobile accident did Sartre soften somewhat toward him.

Both writers had been associated with the French Resistance movement, and their literary fame was linked to the recently completed war in important ways. The war continued to cast a long shadow over European culture throughout the 1950s. The devastation of World War II had been even greater than that of the first, and Europeans endured many hardships and shortages in the immediate postwar years. Once again the cultural expression of the age expressed bitter disillusionment and loss of faith in the verities of a previous generation, yet there were also signs of renewed vitality in a variety of spheres, certainly in popular culture, as indicated in the previous chapter. The European film industry began to thaw from the frozen state the war and fascist cultural policy had imposed on it, but perhaps the single liveliest area of energetic activity was theater. Sartre, and to a lesser extent Camus, had been well-known for his plays in addition to other writings. At least as far back as Restoration England in the seventeenth century, often the theater is the milieu that registers the renewed buoyancy of a culture after a grim period.

Not that the plays that began to emerge in the late 1940s and early 1950s were lighthearted or escapist. Like most writers of the period, playwrights confronted the horrors of the Holocaust and the advent of nuclear weapons. Many of them concluded that earlier forms of theater were inadequate to confront the daunting realities of the nuclear age or the growing dominance of the culture of advertising and mass media of all kinds. Language itself seemed in crisis. A new kind of theater emerged that highlighted the absurdities of language debased by a culture of endless publicity and the stark dread produced by the real possibility of global catastrophe.

Samuel Beckett

The writer who broke most sharply with previous dramaturgical conventions and who created works whose starkness and apparent bleakness mystified their first audiences was Samuel Beckett. In 1952 his "tragicomedy in two acts," *En Attendant Godot (Waiting for Godot)*, opened before a Paris audience either baffled or outraged (and in some cases both). The play has since become one of the most often performed plays of the modern theater and the work for which Beckett, author of stories, novels, essays, plays, and one screenplay, is best known.

Not only did this Irish expatriate writer cast his lot with the French nation (see chapter 8), but he demonstrated in a particularly dramatic way his allegiance to his adopted country and its culture, for he began to write all of his work in French. In his earlier career as a writer, his prose was much under the spell of his mentor James Joyce, for whom he served for a time as a kind of secretary or assistant. The decisive turn toward French purged his writing of what the author came to see as its rhetorical excesses, giving it a more precise, streamlined—one might say Cartesian (Beckett being an admirer of Descartes)—quality. Over the years he translated his own works into English. By the late 1940s he had written several works of fiction in French, most notably his trilogy of novels (published 1951–1953) *Molloy, Malone meurt, L'innomable (Molloy, Malone Dies, The Unnamable)*, as well as the play that would make him famous.

In all of Beckett's plays, novels, and stories written after 1945, the physical circumstances and recognizable surroundings of the characters portrayed become progressively more reduced. Indeed the characters themselves eventually become little more than voices, even, in one later play, simply a breath. The trilogy completed at around the time Beckett wrote *Godot* demonstrates this process. In *Molloy* the title character becomes gradually crippled and then immobile. In *Malone meurt* Malone, who may or may not be the same person as Molloy, is confined to his bed. Finally, "The Unnameable" is some kind of human remnant wedged in a jar, although he (or it) soliloquizes all the more urgently for it.

In *Waiting for Godot* two tramps named Vladimir ("Didi") and Estragon ("Gogo") come upon a lone tree on an otherwise bare stage and discuss whether this was where they were supposed to wait "for Godot." While waiting (exactly the sense of the French title—*en attendant*), they engage in a sort of verbal tennis match punctuated by Gogo's frequent demands that they leave followed by Didi's protestation that they cannot because "We're waiting for Godot." Whoever Godot is (and the playwright himself claimed not to know), he never comes, although a small boy thought to be his emissary does, and once in each act a pair of characters named Pozzo and Lucky make their appearance. Pozzo leads "Lucky" by a rope round his neck. At least two important changes occur between the two acts. In the second act, the single tree on stage has lost its one leaf, and "Pozzo" has lost his eyesight. Finally the play ends with the tramps continuing their wait, despite Gogo's final "We're going," followed by Beckett's stage direction *They do not move.*

Understandably the play's first audience did not know what to make of this, and the famously interview-shy author offered few clues. Over the years actors have varied in their approach to the play, sometimes playing the roles in a kind of exuberant burlesque that calls into question what many have regarded as the play's bleak tone. There is much to support the view that Beckett is unrelievedly pessimistic. His second major play written in French, *Fin de partie* (1957, *Endgame*), shows four characters, two central and two marginal, who appear to be trapped within some dwelling as a result of a catastrophe outside (perhaps a nuclear holocaust) Once again, all they have are their words, although they inflict these on each other as if to suggest, like the characters in Sartre's *No Exit,* that this is a living hell.

Yet if Beckett's work was irredeemably pessimistic, it would be difficult for readers to sustain interest in it. The deceptively simple beauty of Beckett's language is what holds his admirers. Whether language is what passes the time or what we use to assault each other, in all of Beckett's work, whatever the genre, language is what remains when all else is exhausted. When humans have nothing else left as a resource, they cling to words or, in more extreme cases, to grunts, sobs, exhalations, or even ruder bodily noises. Sometimes the best you can say, as with Didi, is that discourse is what "passes the time." Yet at other times in Beckett's work, especially when the flame of hope most seems extinguished, a stubborn voice signals the determination to survive no matter what, as in the famous contradictory ending of *The Unnamable:* "I can't go on. I'll go on."

On one hand, Beckett's work seemed to suggest that literary language has run its course, that there is a sense that nothing remains to be said at a time when Western culture seems to be ending with Eliot's "whimper" instead of a "bang." On the other hand, Beckett paradoxically explored the ways in which language (writing) can operate despite the sense of its futility.

European Drama, ca. 1947 to 1967

Other playwrights of the early 1950s focused more on the absurdity of language in a modern culture in which people are increasingly distracted and overwhelmed by the messages coming at them from politicians, from leading institutions, and from ubiquitous advertising. No dramatist tackled this theme more energetically than Eugène Ionesco (1912–1994), a Romanian-born French playwright whose works most encouraged the subsequent critical vogue of the phrase "theater of the absurd."

Ionesco got the idea for his first play, which opened before a bewildered Parisian audience in 1950, from the stilted phrasing of an English-language instruction book for native French speakers. By definition, such a book would contain many phrases that, while technically correct, one would rarely hear spoken. In the play, *La Cantatrice chauve* (*The Bald Soprano*), a middle-class English couple relaxes after dinner (the contents of which the lady of the house recites laboriously) and are surprised by a sudden visit from another couple. The conversations in the play, as if lifted from a poorly written primer, are hilariously absurd, and references to a mysterious "Bobby Watson" abound. Needless to say, no soprano appears, bald or otherwise.

In Ionesco's next play, *La leçon* (1951, *The Lesson*), language goes from something absurd to something that can cause violence to erupt, as it does when an eager pupil arrives for her session with a private tutor. Despite the initial uncomprehending response to these two plays, they have enjoyed a long run on the Parisian stage. In fact, these two have been performed nightly for nearly fifty years in a small theater in the Latin Quarter. In later Ionesco plays, objects themselves, like the multiplying images in a Magritte painting, proliferate the way repeated statements do in the first plays. Thus in *Les Chaises* (1952, *The Chairs*), the stage becomes progressively filled with chairs that crowd out the actors themselves. In a later play, *Rhinoceros* (1959, *Rhinoceros*), one character after another turns into a rhinoceros, bellowing and charging about the stage in an apparent allegory of the rise of fascism. Ionesco also wrote essays and journals, which likewise give evidence of his mischievous spirit.

One of the most influential and disturbing French playwrights was Jean Genet (1910–1986), who was a talented writer and also a repeat offender as a thief. In the late 1940s Jean-Paul Sartre and a number of other prominent writers intervened to prevent Genet's serving a life sentence for his crimes, Sartre in particular arguing that France could not afford to be deprived of such a gifted writer. He expanded this argument into a full-scale philosophical treatise in *Saint-Genet: comédien et martyr* (1953, *Saint Genet: Actor and Martyr*). Genet was a writer in the tradition of Baudelaire, which is to say someone who wedded sordid themes to exquisite literary language. A more contemporary influence in this regard was Antonin Artaud (1896–1948), poet, actor, and madman (who struggled with mental illness nearly all his life), author of a provocative dramaturgical treatise called *Le Théâtre et son double* (1930, *The Theater and Its Double*). Artaud advocated a "theater of cruelty," by which he meant one that would treat extreme subjects in order to overcome audience complacency.

The themes of Genet's plays and other writings suggest he took this message to heart. A proudly defiant homosexual, he had been incarcerated repeatedly since his adolescent years, and filled his writings with episodes drawn from the depravity he had witnessed among fellow thieves and inmates. He was often compared to his American contemporary William S. Burroughs as a literary explorer of the underworld. *Notre-Dame des Fleurs* (1942, *Our Lady of the Flowers*), a novel, and *Le Journal d'un voleur* (1949, *A Thief's Journal*) were books that recounted the adventures of criminals and outcasts, showing their perspective on society to be an instructive one.

The plays were remarkable not just for their startling themes but for the ritual, almost liturgical quality they brought to the stage. The two actresses of *Les Bonnes* (1947, *The Maids*) move about the stage in a stylized pas de deux inspired by the notorious Papin sisters (see chapter 9) whose sensational murder case gave Genet his subject matter. Ritual positions are also adopted by the actors in *Haute surveillance* (1949, *Deathwatch*), a play about condemned criminals whose very title indicates something of the ritualistic, almost religious sense of theater (which, after all, is the oldest function of theater) for which the playwright was striving. Later plays like *Le Balcon* (1956, *The Balcony*) and *Les Nègres* (1958, *The Blacks*), make use of larger casts, which afford greater possibilities for highly stylized ritualistic movements and stage business. In this regard, Genet joined Cocteau, Giraudoux, Sartre, and Camus in their embrace of the ancient Hellenic sense of theater as mysterious spectacle.

Fairly or not, the work of the English playwright Harold Pinter (1930–) has commonly been grouped under the heading of "theater of the absurd." Characters in his plays stupidly mouth clichés and platitudes, but cause each other trouble in very real physical ways as well. Menace, whether conveyed by language or by gesture, seems to be the dark theme of Pinter's work. In *The Dumb Waiter* (1957), two down-at-the-heels companions show up for a job about which they are terribly vague. Awaiting further instructions, their only indication of impending intervention from their supposed employer is a dumbwaiter that communicates between their basement level and the story above. As they become more impatient and nonplussed by their situation the atmosphere of menace and dread becomes intolerable. In *The Birthday Party* and *The Homecoming*, families torment each other with their compulsively repetitious utterances. These plays offer no resolution and no hope of improvement, as the audience grows to share the agitation exhibited by the actors.

England in the 1950s was far from a happy country, as victory in 1945 gave way steadily to economic hardship and a sense of Britain's declining influence in the world. Pinter's theater was a part of that climate, although his innovative approach reminded critics more of such Continental figures in the modern tradition as Luigi Pirandello (1867–1936)—author of the psychologically fascinating play *Sei personaggi in cerca d'autore* (1921, *Six Characters in Search of an Author*)—or Beckett. The English playwright who seemed most to capture the spirit of resentment felt by the postwar generation was John Osborne (1929–1994), author of *Look Back in Anger* (1956) and *The Entertainer* (1957). Indeed, he was considered a member of a group of writers dubbed the "Angry Young Men," which included the successful novelist Kingsley Amis (1922–1995), author of the satirical novel *Lucky Jim* (1954). Especially in Osborne's case, his confrontation with English society moderated significantly with age, and in fact he became identified with a staunch Toryism.

The playwright who perhaps best captured the spirit of the 1960s was the Czech-born British author Tom Stoppard (1937–). His 1967 play *Rosencrantz and Guildenstern Are Dead* was a fresh, deliberately off-center look at the Hamlet story from the point of view of two minor characters in Shakespeare's tragedy. They are expendable representations of "everyman" and in Stoppard's treatment bring a kind of vaudeville quality to perhaps the world's most famous tragic play. Using marginal characters and odd juxtapositions to revisit historical episodes or literary classics of the Western tradition was typical of Stoppard's work. Stoppard did so to high comic effect in his 1972 play *Travesties,* which he based on the curious historical coincidence that Vladimir Ilyich Lenin, James Joyce, and such Dada artists as Tristan Tzara all happened to be residing in Zürich at precisely the same moment in 1916. His play rewrites history by having them encounter each other.

On the Continent during the 1950s and early 1960s, dramatic works in the German language often dealt with themes of political scandal and social responsibility. The Swiss playwright Friedrich Dürrenmatt (1921–1990) wrote the dark play *Der Besuch der alte Dame* (1956, *The Visit*), which is a disturbing exploration on how people will compromise every moral precept if they stand to gain monetarily. He also wrote a kind of historical play *Die Physiker* (1962, *The Physicists*), which used figures in the history of physics to raise questions about the power of science in modern culture, especially after the harnessing of nuclear energy. The German playwright Rolf Hochhuth (1931–) tackled the controversial topic of the refusal of Pope Pius XII to intervene to save Holocaust victims in *The Deputy* (1963) and treated the almost-taboo subject of German involvement in World War II in *Die Soldaten* (1967, *The Soldiers*).

By the later 1960s, the Austrian playwright/novelist Peter Handke (1942–) was the enfant terrible of German language drama, with his plays *Kaspar* (1968) and his contribution to the avant-garde impulse to shock the complacent bourgeoisie, *Publikumsbeschimpfung* (1966, *Offending the Audience*). In this turbulent decade, influenced by experimental theater from the United States as well as Eastern Europe, playwrights sought to push the limits of what could be represented on stage. A sensational example was *Die Verfolgung und Ermordung Jean Paul Marats, dargestellt durch die Schauspielgruppe des Hospizes zu Charenton unter Anleitung des Herrn de Sade* (1964, *The Persecution and Assassination of Jean-Paul Marat Performed by the Inmates of the Asylum of Charenton Under the Direction of the Marquis de Sade*) by the German author Peter Weiss (1916–1982). Based on the historical episode of Charlotte Corday's assassination of Marat and the fact that the infamous author Sade was held in the Parisian asylum of Charenton, the play was a kind of musical featuring Dionysiac revelry by the actors portraying mental patients. The play was a *succès de scandale* in Europe and the United States, and was adapted for the cinema by the British director Peter Brook (1925–).

Postwar Fiction and Poetry

Postwar German novelists also insisted on political and social themes guaranteed to unsettle conventional sensibilities, particularly in a country busy repressing its memories of the Hitler era. Intent on restoring dignity and moral conscience to German literature after the war, in 1947 a group of writers calling themselves Gruppe 47 (Group 47) formed, and it included a young Günter Grass (1927–). He would become the most important writer in post-1945 Germany for his novels, essays, and outspoken political participation. He won the 1999 Nobel Prize for Literature. Grass was from the free city of Danzig, which, renamed Gdansk, became part of Poland after 1945. Young men from this area were pressed unwillingly into service in the German army, as was Grass during the final months of the war. This area was the setting for his novels *Die Blechtrommel* (1959, *The Tin Drum*), *Katz und Maus* (1961, *Cat and Mouse*), and *Die Hundejahre* (1963, *Dog Years*). *The Tin Drum*, considered by many to be his greatest book, presents the Nazi years through the eyes of a boy who refuses to grow taller as his protest against what is happening. Heinrich Böll (1917–1985) was another German novelist who addressed the theme of the wartime years in such well-regarded novels as *Billard um halb zehn* (1959, *Billiards at Half Past Nine*), *Ansichten eines Clowns* (1963, *The Clowns*), and *Gruppenbild mit Dame* (1971, *Group Portrait with Lady*).

English novelists of the same era often wrestled with themes of politics, international conflicts, and social critique. Some of the most significant ones, such as the "Angry Young Men," discussed earlier, defied categorization in any particular school or movement. Graham Greene

(1904–1991) was a prolific and successful novelist, many of whose best works belong to the postwar period. He specialized in gripping tales that often featured doomed characters through whom the reader witnesses scenes of violent social upheaval, especially in Third World settings. Greene first employed such themes in his much-admired novel *The Power and the Glory* (1940), set in revolutionary Mexico. Among later books, *The Quiet American* (1956) and *The Comedians* (1966) were notable for exploring human predicaments of compromised morality in the explosive colonial milieus of, respectively, Vietnam in the last days of French rule and Haiti under the vicious François "Papa Doc" Duvalier.

The 1960s was the decade of greatest literary productivity for Anthony Burgess (1917–1993), a social satirist who claimed the comic tradition of James Joyce. In a burst of creativity, he published six novels between 1961 and 1964, including two very dystopic novels, *The Wanting Seed* (1962) and *A Clockwork Orange* (1962). The latter novel, which portrayed an unrelievedly bleak future English social landscape torn between violent youthful gangs and sinister totalitarian rulers using sophisticated techiniques of mind control, secured Burgess's fame when Stanley Kubrick adapted it for his extremely controversial film (see chapter 9). Burgess wrote dozens of books, many of them works of criticism. For all his literary productivity, he was even more prolific as a composer.

In terms of dominant figures or critical attention, the period from 1945 to 1970 was not a golden age of European poetry, or at least it is more difficult than usual to offer general descriptions of trends or schools. Some poets addressed war themes, but others turned to nature and their immediate surroundings. Some again took up the stylistic experiments of the prewar avant-garde, while others opted for a deliberate simplicity or matter-of-factness when it came to form. The English poets Stevie Smith (1902–1971) and Philip Larkin (1922–1985) were examples of the latter, Smith offering a personal touch informed by warm humor (reflected in offbeat titles like her 1957 collection of poems *Not Waving But Drowning*) and Larkin working to perfect simple, precise and decidedly anti-Romantic forms.

At the other extreme was the deliberately mythic pose of the Romantic bard struck by the Welsh poet Dylan Thomas (1914–1953), who celebrated the Welsh landscape (and seascape) and brooded on themes of death and our inescapable ties to nature. Something of an international poetic celebrity, his excessive drinking brought him to an early grave. Ted Hughes (1930–1999) was also a poet of nature, although far from a Romantic in inclination. In carefully crafted poems he emphasized the brutality of nature. Although he became England's poet laureate, for some his career was overshadowed by his controversial marriage to the American poet Sylvia Plath (1933–1963). The controversy had to do not only with her suicide during their separation but with his and his family's efforts to control access to her journals and diaries in later years.

If anything, examples of French poetry after 1945 show even more variety. One of the most widely recognized poets of the period was the French diplomat Alexis Léger, known by his pen name of St. John-Perse (1887–1975). He was fluent in English, having spent the period from 1940 to 1959 in Washington, D.C. He received the 1960 Nobel Prize for Literature for poems of a remarkable personal intensity, with an attention to imagery that called to mind such great Symbolist poets as Paul Valéry. Yves Bonnefoy (1923–) was one of the best-known poets of the new generation, and he also took his inspiration from the Symbolist tradition, especially from Rimbaud. René Char (1907–1988), the former Surrealist, devoted his poems to his rustic Provençal surroundings and to his experience as a member of the Resistance. But in some ways the greatest poetic presence in France during the 1950s and 1960s was a Romanian Jewish refugee, Paul Celan (1920–1970). Inspired by such great German lyrical poets as Friedrich Hölderlin and Rainer Maria Rilke, he wrote most of his work in German, but also wrote in French. He shared his predecessor Rilke's Francophilic tendencies. Celan's work dealt forcefully with the Holocaust, which gave his poetry a pessimistic cast. He committed suicide by drowning.

The Symbolist legacy extended beyond France, where it found expression in the work of Claudio Rodríguez (1934–1999), whose visionary approach to poetry led critics to compare him in stature to his great precursor, Federico Garcia Lorca. His greatest poems were simultaneously simple in imagery and mystical in tone, affirming life's basic themes and transcendent ones. If Rodríguez can be considered Spain's finest poet of the late twentieth century, the equivalent position in Italy is often assigned to Eugenio Montale (1896–1981). Unlike his younger contemporary, however, Montale shunned Romantic lyricism and Symbolist style for a highly refined, ultimately very private aestheticism. His distaste for Symbolism can be explained to a considerable extent by its association with Gabrielle d'Annunzio, the poet who became a vigorous supported of Italian fascism. Montale founded no "school" and remained wary of the modern avant-garde, where stylistic innovation sometimes lent itself to disastrous political uses.

The avant-garde had far from run its course, and the 1950s saw several examples of consciously new experimentation in many areas of the arts. In literature, this often involved radical experiments with language, especially in assailing the dichotomy between form and content. Just as abstract painters of the New York school sought to reduce painting to its simplest elements of surface, line, color, and texture, experimental writers of the 1950s set out to push writing farther than even deliberately baffling Modernist figures such as Joyce or Mallarmé had done. The best-known example of this came from the group of French writers associated with the so-called "new novel" (*nouveau roman*). The first contributions to this genre preceded the concept applied by critics and others. The Russian-born writer Nathalie Sarraute (1902–1999) produced the groundbreaking *Tropismes* (*Tropisms*) in 1939, and followed with *Portrait d'un inconnu* (*Portrait of a Man Unknown*) in 1949. These works were promoted by Jean-Paul Sartre.

By the early 1950s, Sarraute had been joined by Alain Robbe-Grillet (1922–), Michel Butor (1926–), and Claude Simon (1913–). In their works, familiar moorings of time and place are absent, and character development is held in check by the kind of radical narrative indeterminacy first introduced in French literature by Gustave Flaubert. Simon was influenced by William Faulkner, and employed his technique of interior monologue in his novels *Le Tricheur* (1945, *The Trickster*), *Le Vent* (1957, *The Wind*), and *La Route de Flandres* (1960, *The Road to Flanders*). He received the 1985 Nobel Prize for Literature. Michel Butor's novels, such as *L'Emploi du temps* (1956, *Passing Time*) and *La Modification* (1957, *Second Thoughts*), experiment radically with shifting time sequences, emphasizing action that leads to no fixed outcome.

In such Robbe-Grillet works as *Les Gommes* (1953, *The Erasers*), *Le Voyeur* (1955, *The Voyeur*), and *Jalousie* (1957, *Jealousy*), the reader enters a troubled atmosphere and adopts the shifting perspectives of several characters, but it becomes extremely difficult to determine what is afoot. Robbe-Grillet was conscious of the similarity between these narrative shifts and the editing techniques of cinema. He eventually wrote screenplays as well, most notable *La Dernière année à Marienbad* (*Last Year at Marienbad*), Alain Resnais's 1960 film. As for Robbe-Grillet's novels, ultimately one is most conscious of the spare, delicate beauty of the writing itself, like the aesthetic effect of a Japanese interior. In the hands of the New Novelists, the subject of fiction had become the materials and possibilities of writing itself.

Traditionally minded critics were at a loss when confronted with this kind of writing, one result of which was to call for a new kind of criticism—*la critique nouvelle*—that would focus nearly exclusively on the "texts" themselves, rather than on the kind of biographical information or investigation of social context upon which critics had long relied. A book published in 1953 by a critic named Roland Barthes (1915–1980) seemed to point the way. It was called *Le Degré zero de l'écriture* (*Writing Degree Zero*), and, as its title suggested, it called for the exclusive focus for criticism on the surface textual properties of writing itself. This version of new criticism would inform much of structuralism and semiology (see below), with which Barthes in particular was involved by the 1960s. But it was also generated in response to undercurrents in twentieth-century French literature that continued to operate in postwar France.

The undercurrents that had continued to flow especially through movements of the Modernist avant-garde represented versions of the erotic tradition in modern French literature that, borrowing from Symbolism along the way, ended up eroticizing, or making a fetish of, the written word itself. The "forbidden" author the Marquis de Sade had a number of prominent critical champions in the twentieth century, as did his late nineteenth-century literary descendant Lautréamont. Gaston Bachelard (1884–1962), best known as a philosopher of science, was the author of a critical study of Lautréamont, among other works of literary criticism. His *La Poétique de l'espace* (*The Poetics of Space*) was a direct influence on the critical essay *L'espace littéraire* (1955, *The Space of Literature*) by Maurice Blanchot (1907–), a prolific writer and critic with ties to the Surrealist movement. Blanchot also wrote an appreciative work on the "underground" tradition in French writing called *Lautréamont et Sade* (1963). His work, contemporaneous with new critical theories of "the text," also served to erase the boundary separating "writer" (i.e., novelist, poet) from critic/essayist.

Pierre Klossowski (1905–) was the writer who most embraced the legacy of Sade, writing pornographic novels of high literary quality such as *Roberte ce soir* (1954) and *La Révocation de l'édit de Nantes* (1959, *The Revocation of the Edict of Nantes*), and a critical appreciation of Sade called *Sade mon prochain* (1967, *Sade My Neighbor*). Klossowski also wrote philosophy, including a bold reinterpretation of Nietzsche called *Nietzsche et le cercle vicieux* (1969, *Nietzsche and the Vicious Circle*), part of a body of important French work that has done much to revise long-standing assessments of that controversial philosopher.

No less interested in Nietzsche, but even more so in Hegel, was Georges Bataille (1897–1962), an enormously complex and contradictory writer active in the Surrealist movement during the 1930s, then a pornographer by the late 1940s, finally turning more and more to political economy and ethnography. Of all the French writers just mentioned, he has had the most substantial influence during the late twentieth century. Bataille was fascinated with the idea of ritual violence as necessary to revivify social existence, and he was morbidly fascinated with the human sacrifice of the Aztecs. In the 1930s Bataille and a group of writers associated with Surrealism founded something called the Collège de Sociologie, dedicated to finding ways through ceremonies of controlled violence out of cultural stagnation and ennui. World War II appeared to do away with that idea.

In 1949 Bataille published his most famous pornographic work *L'histoire de l'oeil* (*The Story of the Eye*), a work of extreme violence mixed with eroticism. That same year he published the first volume of his ambitious work on political economy *La Part maudite* (*The Accursed Share*). In it Bataille offered an alternative model to the capitalist market economy, where value depends on scarcity, and the goal is to amass wealth through earned interest. Basing his alternative on studies by Marcel Mauss and later ethnographers of the "gift economies" of the tribes of the Pacific Northwest, Bataille took up the threads of his long-standing fascination with sacrifice and argued that a healthy society needs an economy based on ceremonies of squandering wealth. He offered his principle of "expenditure" (*dépense)* in place of the capitalist one of accumulation. Whether writing eccentric treatises such as this, pornographic stories, or critiques of Western philosophy, Bataille's writing, like that of Blanchot and Klossowski, was carefully crafted, further encouraging the growing critical preference for "textual" emphasis.

Equally attentive to carefully chiseled prose was a writer who entered French literature from an unexpected direction. This was Edmond Jabès (1912–1991), born in Egypt to a French Jewish family, who moved to France in 1957, as President Nasser's Arab nationalism began to threaten Egyptian Jews. Jabès shared Mallarmé's reverential attitude toward written language, often expressing it in an even more mystical way. His earliest publications were poems, but he turned more and more toward novels, although that word fails to do justice to books that seem as much like metaphysical excursions or theological meditations. The theme of most of his books, especially the series he began in 1963 as *Le Livre des questions* (*The Book of Questions*), is the Jews as the chosen people, as nomads subjected to great historical trials, none greater or more inexpressible than the Holocaust. The Jews, he pointed out, have been historically a "people of the book," that is, of the Torah. In exploring such questions through the guise of shadowy characters to whom the narrator of these texts addresses them, Jabès seemed to wed the Talmudic reverence for the word to the Mallarméan quest for a separate existence for literary language.

Music, the Visual Arts,
and the Avant-Garde

Powerful as this impulse was to follow Mallarmé's injunction to "cede the initiative to the words" in writing, it should be clear from the examples above that not all writers reduced their work so strictly to the material elements at hand. Similarly, in other arts, one finds examples both of creative work that pursued a kind of radical formalism and those of artists pursuing highly idiosyncratic subjective expressive impulses. For every artist who announced a desire to abdicate control of the creative process in order to follow laws of chance or be otherwise spontaneous, there was another who insisted on imposing his or her personal stamp on new forms of creativity. Music of the postwar era provides examples of this contrast.

In some ways, the radical innovations of the early part of the century, with the eccentric compositions of Erik Satie, the more experimental work of Debussy, Ravel, and Stravinsky, and the bold new twelve-tone system of Arnold Schönberg and Anton Webern, still had to be absorbed. Those following in this tradition had developed what was called "serial music" before World War II. Of the group of avant-garde French composers formed in the 1920s known as Les Six, one who remained active after World War II was Francis Poulenc (1899–1963), working particularly on operas. One of the most admired composers of the war years was Olivier Messiaen (1908–1992), who wrote his haunting *Quatour pour la fin du temps* (*Quartet for the End of Time*) while a prisoner of war in 1941. He continued to compose his highly personal, distinctive music, especially for solo piano and featuring scales he devised himself. His 1956 work *Oiseaux exotiques (Exotic Birds)* was similar in its ambitious scope to his groundbreaking *Vingt regards sur l'enfant Jésus* (1944, *Twenty Contemplations On the Infant Jesus*), also for unaccompanied piano.

One of the most radically experimental French composers, Edgard Varèse (1883–1965), had moved to the United States in 1940 but continued to influence European composers. Varèse liked to use percussion orchestras for his often austere, brooding pieces. He began after the war to explore electronic music, and collaborated with the Greek composer Iannis Xenakis (1922–2001) on *Poème électronique,* which he traveled to Belgium to have performed at the 1958 Brussels Exposition. Varèse continued to receive much more recognition in Europe than in his adopted country, although he was a major influence on the very successful American composer/pop musician Frank Zappa (1940–1993).

Electronic music, using early versions of what would become the first synthesizers, increasingly found a home among the new generation of composers. Xenakis, one of the pioneers in the field, made use of the twelve-tone system, and also used mathematical probability in such compositions for orchestra as *Métastasis* (1955, *Metastasis*). In France Pierre Boulez (1925–) experimented with serial and electronic music, but also embraced so-called aleatory music, music based on the laws of chance. Fascination with chance elements of music somewhat mirrored developments in the United States, where the internationally influential John Cage, himself directly inspired by the artist Marcel Duchamp, subjected much of his music, both in composition and performance, to chance. One of the most adventurous European composers was Luciano Berio (1925–) of Italy. Working both with serial and electronic music, he composed *Visage* (1961, *Visage*) for electronically altered voice. He also composed electronic pieces to be used as settings for poems by e. e. cummings and texts by James Joyce.

Some visual artists embraced the same kind of neo-Dada spirit found in composers willing to use chance in their compositions. So-called Pop Art in the United States seemed a kind of reassertion of Dada, and had its imitators in Europe. The English painters Richard Hamilton (1922–) and David Hockney (1937–) were examples, although Hockney would go on to develop a highly personal figurative style. Hamilton's best-known work was the eye-popping collage *Just What Is It That Makes Today's Homes So Different, So Appealing?* (1956). In France the painter Yves Klein (1928–1962) emulated the Dada penchant for shock and outrage, as when he exhibited an entire show of nothing but painted white canvases, so that the "show" consisted of the shadows gallery-goers cast on the paintings. On another occasion he staged an exhibition of "Nothing at all," an ultimate anti-art statement. The Italian conceptual artist Piero Manzoni (1933–1963), taking the German Dadaist motto "Kunst ist Scheisse" at its word, produced a series of signed, numbered tins of what he claimed was his own excrement—*Merda d'artista*. Of course, at the same time he was making a wry comment on the arbitrariness of the art market.

The greatest exemplar of the abstract tradition in Modern art at this time was the English sculptor Henry Moore (1898–1986). The immediate postwar period saw his international fame soar, thanks initially to a first-ever retrospective at the Museum of Modern Art in New York. For this 1946 occasion, the sculptor, who had weathered wartime hardships in England that included severe shortage of materials for his art, made his first voyage to the United States. The economic success that came his way after the New York show and the 1948 Venice Biennale, where he received the sculpture prize, enabled him to fund the larger projects he had dreamed of. He now moved from smaller works in stone to large-scale works in bronze, resolutely abstract, as always. Alberto Giacometti (1901–1966) of Switzerland, having participated earlier in both the Cubist and Surrealist movements, began in the 1950s to produce the tall, extremely elongated sculptures for which he is most recognized today. The Catalan artist Joan Miró (1893–1983), whose previous affiliations were the same as Giacometti's, moved from Surrealistic images increasingly into abstract shapes. He also began to produce tapestries, many of them quite large, rather than paintings. In addition, he was in demand as a painter of murals, and in 1958 completed the murals for the UNESCO buildings in Paris.

Some of the most original and disarming images in postwar art came from Jean Dubuffet (1901–1985) of France. His paintings and often enormous sculptures featured deliberately childlike renderings, incorporating sand, stones, and other rough surfaces. For all the importance and critical prestige (especially in New York, where Abstract Expressionism reigned supreme) of abstract art, a number of important painters opted for a figural direction. In England, Lucian Freud (1922–), Sigmund's grandson, embraced a starkly realistic approach to portraits and nudes. And while never as deliberately realistic, David Hockney moved increasingly toward portrayal of the human figure.

Certainly one of the most powerful and disturbing painters of the age, also from England, was Francis Bacon (1909–1992). A flamboyant homosexual and extreme alcoholic, he was as shockingly notorious in his personal life as he was on the canvas. His style of portraiture acknowledged very traditional models, as in his *Study After Velázquez: Portrait of Pope Innocent X* (1953). But Bacon disrupted the calm that usually prevails in portraits by presenting faces in states of distortion, mutilation, or decay. In one of his paintings he displayed a bloody side of beef suspended alongside his subject, and, indeed, his figures often appear as if in eviscerated states like so many animal carcasses. A number of Bacon's figure studies are displayed as triptychs, multiplying the perspectives from which one might regard them, as if to suggest a fragmented, multiple sense of the human subject by definition.

The Colombian-born painter Fernando Botero (1932–), who moved to Spain and then settled permanently in Paris, shared with Bacon an interest in the human figure and a penchant for reworking themes from traditional paintings, such as the ones he admired in The Prado in Madrid. His approach was far more humorous. His signature style has been to crowd his canvases with bloated, obese figures who look as if they are about to explode with pressure from within. In *Mona Lisa at Age 12* (1959), the young girl fills the canvas to bursting like Magritte's apple in *La Chambre d'écoute*. In addition to the figures borrowed from the Golden Age of Spanish or Dutch art, Botero populated his canvases with stereotypes (priests, nuns, generals, dictators) drawn from South American society.

One of the central ironies in any discussion of seemingly radical or disturbing artists is that their shock value inevitably seems to ebb away and they become incorporated within standard histories of art (or literature, music, etc.). But certainly one of the most radical impulses of the modern avant-garde tradition has been to attack the special status of "artist" and to seek to break down the barrier between art and everyday life. This has been the lasting legacy of Dadaism, even though individual artists associated with Dada found their way into the museums and official art histories. During the period from 1945 to 1965 or so, at least three radical cultural movements took up anew this demand that "Art" be reclaimed and demystified by everyday life, wedding their critique of the social institution of art to a general critique of the alienating abstractions of advanced commercial urban civilization. These movements were Lettrism, Situationism, and Fluxus.

Lettrism was the name given a new concept of literature, even of language, by a Frenchman named Isidore Isou (1925–). He began to advocate the new "ism" in the late 1940s, and was assisted during subsequent years by Maurice Lemaitre (1926–). Lettrism built on the ambitious linguistic experiments of literary Modernism but with the aim of erasing the distinction between literature as an institution and the rest of society. To bring about this rapprochement, Lettrists advocated a completely new language, returning to the radical sound experiments of such Dada artists as Hugo Ball and Kurt Schwitters. Lettrist manifestos referred approvingly to the Dadaist aim of returning literary language to the poetry of shouts heard in the street, of a new poetics of "found" sounds.

By the mid-1950s several people involved with Lettrism went on to establish a new movement they called "Situationism." A key figure in this regard, a member of both groups, was Guy Debord (1931–1994), a writer, filmmaker, and activist. Situationists borrowed something of the stance and style of left-wing European political parties, as their founding in 1957 of something called the "Situationist International" would suggest. Debord and other French members of the movement (which would gain adherents from other European countries, especially England) were influenced by the maverick Marxist theories of French sociologist Henri Lefebvre (1901–1991), who argued for a communism that made access to urban space a central aim for the amelioration of the working class. He had articulated this view with the modern history of Paris in mind, especially since the Commune of 1871.

Situationists called for strategic interventions into the urban landscape, which they viewed as held in thrall to the totalizing demands of the market economy, with its emphasis on purposive activity and the free flow of goods. Debord and his colleagues proposed strategies of *détournement,* of deliberate disruption of the daily urban routines of modern capitalism. One way to bring this about, they argued (and practiced), was to set out on random wanderings crisscrossing the city, refusing to adhere to timetables and schedules. This practice, which they called the *dérive,* harked back to Baudelaire's concept of the *flâneur,* or "idler" who decides spontaneously where to venture and what to do next in occupying urban space. The point was to devise ways to attack the tendency of life under advanced capitalism to become passive and vicarious, to attack the "society of the spectacle," to borrow the title of Debord's most sustained critique of the dominant urban culture he saw around him.

Situationism influenced related social movements throughout Europe down through the 1960s, including the emergence in Amsterdam of a group called the Provos, who staged various interventions of that city's routines, most famously in their "white bicycle" campaign (painting hundreds of bicycles white and leaving them throughout Amsterdam for anyone who needed to use them). A number of historians credit Situationists with directly influencing the events of May 1968 in Paris, in which case they represent a kind of bridge between the Paris Commune and the Sorbonne student uprising. A link to 1970s punk rock in England has also been established, through the manager of the band the Sex Pistols. (See chapter 9.) And whether a causal link can be established or not, Situationism was complemented by an international movement in the arts knows as Fluxus.

Founded in 1960 in New York City by a Lithuanian immigrant named George Maciunas, Fluxus spread both to Europe and Japan and was associated at times with the so-called Happenings, free-ranging art performance/dance/multimedia parties that were staged at first by the American pop artist Allen Kaprow. One of the most notorious European examples was a performance organized by Yves Klein and held at the Galérie Internationale d'Art Contemporain in Paris on March 9, 1960. Titled *Anthropométries de l'Époque bleue* ("Human Measurements of the Blue Epoch"), it consisted of two nude female models who smeared their bodies with blue paint and then dragged each other across an unmounted canvas spread on the floor. Meanwhile, an orchestra of twenty musicians accompanied by playing a single note for ten minutes separated by silent intervals of equal duration. A photograph of the event shows elegantly dressed members of the audience seated stiffly and looking decidedly grim.

Fluxus, not unlike Lettrism, advocated that artists refuse to hold themselves apart from their audiences and argued for a deliberately simple, Minimalist kind of art. The Korean American artist Nam June Paik and the Japanese conceptual artist Yoko Ono were two of the most visible members of the movement. Ranging from the creation of childlike objects and simple poems to decibel-shattering Minimalist vocal performances, Ono was by far the most uncompromising of the Fluxus artists. After moving to England, she met and eventually married John Lennon of The Beatles (who was interested in Fluxus art), and together they exercised a strong influence on the alternative youth culture of the late 1960s and early 1970s.

Structuralism

A major new body of theoretical work in linguistics, literary criticism, anthropology, philosophy, and related fields in the human sciences (as they are called in contemporary Europe) came in the 1960s to function as another kind of avant-garde, one that, in its style of theoretical presentation, challenged the divide between "criticism" and other kinds of writing. This was Structuralism, including its related discipline of Semiology, or the "science of signs." At its peak of development (ca. 1966), Structuralism at its most ambitious appeared to offer a way of understanding all of human culture in relation to the structures of language and perhaps even the mind. By this point the movement began to unravel from within through internal critique and debate. The origins of Structuralism, while possible to trace out through a number of fields and important modern thinkers, can be found most specifically in the theories of an obscure (in his lifetime) Swiss linguist named Ferdinand de Saussure (1858–1913).

As adumbrated in his posthumously published work *Cours de linguistique générale* (1916, *Course in General Linguistics*), Saussure broke with the long-standing tradition in linguistics of studying isolated words, documenting their entry into a given language, and so forth. He argued that no one element of language, spoken or written, has any meaning or significance apart from its membership in the overall system of that language, his term for which was *langue*. Any individual component of language, what he termed *parole*, meant only whatever it meant through its position vis-à-vis the totality of that *langue*. Saussure also taught that language produces meaning through what he called "signs," each composed of two elements: a "signifier" (*signifiant*) or material element of language (e.g., a syllable or mark on the page) and an intangible "signified" (*signifié*), what a combination of context and cultural convention suggests is referenced. Saussure implied that signs could be nonlinguistic, and suggested the eventual establishment of a broadly defined science of signs, or "Semiology." Two additional ideas of Saussure's that have had continued influence are that all language functions according to the "binary opposition" of paired opposites, such as *langue/parole* or signifier/signified, and that the meaning of any one element of language is arbitrary, there being no necessary reason in human biology or cognition why a sound like *arbre* ("tree") should refer to the particular kind of object we agree it does.

Structuralism was primarily a French intellectual phenomenon, and Structuralists built on Saussure's foundation in several ways. The anthropologist Claude Lévi-Strauss (1908–) proposed a structural anthropology that, among other things, would carry out a study of the structural nature of myths, something he himself applied to the Bororo people he studied during his fieldwork in the Amazon Valley. Lévi-Strauss viewed all of culture through the lens of Saussurean linguistics, and likened kinship structures, cooking, and sexual practices to language. Applying the idea of binary opposition, he argued for the need to understand culture through such oppositions as "raw" and "cooked," terms analogous to nature and culture. Saussure had explained that linguistic constructions can be mapped along the intersecting axes of "synchrony" and "diachrony," the former referring to the structure of language at a fixed point in time and the latter to linguistic performance taking place in the flow of time.

Lévi-Strauss described mental patterns of the "primitives" he studied as a kind of *pensée sauvage* (literally "savage thought") that, he argued, is radically synchronic. Historical consciousness, he insisted, is alien to this and can be understood as the imposition of Western societies intent on excluding indigenous peoples from history. The book (*La pensée sauvage*, 1962, *The Savage Mind*) in which he developed this argument was indirectly an attack on Jean-Paul Sartre's *Critique of Dialectical Reason*. Sartre's hybrid of Marxism and Existentialism had privileged history, particularly his version of Marxist historical materialism. Although

Lévi-Strauss was no less indebted intellectually to Marx, as a Structural-ist he was bound to reject Sartre for the latter's emphasis on individual human agency and responsibility. The most radical thrust of Structural-ism, instead, was to portray individual human subjects as dissolved within complex determinant systems of meaning and sign-production, language in a sense "speaking" or "writing" people, and not the other way round.

The French literary critic Roland Barthes (1915–1980) was equally interested in myth, although by "myth" he meant the historically con-tingent processes that culture misinterprets as essences. In this sense he was consistently Marxist. As a Structuralist, he approached texts as self-contained systems of meaning, his job being to reveal the structures that accounted for the peculiar textual properties to be admired. In the early 1960s, Barthes became embroiled in a heated polemic with a critic named Raymond Picard (1917–) over a book the former published on the classic French tragedian Racine. In *Sur Racine* (1963, *On Racine*), Barthes set aside the traditional kinds of biographical/philological crit-icism applied to such a canonical author in favor of a system of struc-tures and codes by which the texts themselves produce meaning in the form of signs. He singled out Picard, a Racine scholar, for particular scorn. Picard, for his part, responded even more scornfully with a full-scale assault on Structuralist interpretation called *Nouvelle critique ou nou-velle imposture?* (1966, *New Criticism or New Fraud?*).

Before moving gradually away from Structuralism, Barthes went on to apply his methodology most relentlessly in *S/Z* (1970), an elaborate "decoding" of a minor novella by Balzac. But before publishing this book he carried out a number of studies that in a real sense redeemed Saussure's wish that a general "science of signs" or Semiology be estab-lished. Barthes turned his critical eye to such aspects of mass culture as advertising, cuisine, sport, and fashion. His *Mythologies* (1957) was an en-tertaining collection of short pieces on these subjects. Then in *Système de la mode* (1967, *The Fashion System*), he presented his most exhaustive ever structural analysis of the "signs" to be detected in the writing pub-lished in women's fashion magazines. The very scholarly rigor with which Barthes approached this subject may not have earned him many readers, but his critique was rich with suggestions for cultural criticism along class and gender lines.

Jacques Lacan (1901–1981), the so-called French Freud, applied Struc-turalism to the unconscious, which he viewed as being "structured like a language." Lacan has been credited with introducing Freud, very belatedly, to France. Freud's theories had been known, of course, and championed notably by Breton and the Surrealists. But French culture, for complicated reasons, resisted Freud and psychoanalysis for decades. Once psychoanalysis gained acceptance there, it was embraced fervently, especially in the late 1960s and early 1970s. Lacan's ability to mediate Freud in a distinctively French way, especially one that presented psychoanalysis as a kind of linguistic practice, had everything to do with this.

Lacan's Freudianism was highly idiosyncratic, and for his theories as well as for his unorthodox analytic practice, he was drummed out of the International Psychoanalytic Association in 1953. His tampering with the standard length of the analytic session (either greatly reducing or lengthening the "fifty-minute hour") and his aggressive manner with his analysands (for example, mimicking their peculiar verbal styles) provided scandal enough for the analytic establishment, but the single most controversial idea of Lacan's was his concept of the so-called mirror stage as the formative one in the development of the psyche. Although he by no means abandoned the Freudian concept of the Oedipus complex, Lacan argued for heavy emphasis on an early stage of human development, before motor skills have been mastered. He described a scenario in which, probably with the assistance of a parent or guardian, the toddler views itself full length in a mirror. This primal scene of gazing at one's reflection does two important things: It creates a sense of physical wholeness (in the earliest months the infant interacts with its environment one body part at a time, so to speak), and it drives home the realization that the person is someone who exists as an object to be viewed by others. The first such mirror experience, Lacan argued, creates a primal "splitting" of the personality that is deepened with the acquisition of language, including pronouns that designate subject/object distinctions.

Lacan's most radical insight (in many ways), that human beings are divided (sometimes his teachings made it seem "divided and conquered") and prevented from claiming truly autonomous status, was certainly in keeping with the Structuralist tendency to diminish the importance of human agency in the face of vast systems of meaning and sign production. Lacan also argued vigorously that his insight was consistent with Freud. Calling for a "return to Freud," Lacan claimed that Freud's texts had not received a properly attentive reading. As a result, clinical, institutional uses had been made of psychoanalytic theories that not been understood properly. In particular, Lacan scorned the so-called Ego Psychologists, primarily German American émigré analysts who had forged a kind of analytic practice with the restoration of the unified ego as its goal. This goal, Lacan observed, had more to do with the extreme individualism of American culture than with the discoveries of Freud.

Reading Freud with emphasis on specific terms in the German, Lacan was struck by the images of splitting (*Spaltung*) and fragmentation he encountered. He reasoned that Freud gained an insight into the nature of the unconscious that even he found too terrifying and, to use one of his own most famous terms, "repressed." Enlarging on this idea, Lacan offered his own scheme to explain how culture and the permanently divided personality operate together, with language as the nexus. The mirror stage introduces the first register along which human existence unfolds, and Lacan called it the "imaginary." This is where we hallucinate, so to speak, the actual conditions of our existence, imagining a kind of unitary identity that is false. With the acquisition of language, we enter what Lacan termed the "symbolic" order. And Lacan, believing himself true to Freud in this regard, argued that language is the key to the unconscious. He especially delighted in the puns and verbal slips that would seem to signal the irruption of the stubborn, unruly, obscene unconscious into the controlled routines we seek to impose on the personality. Lacan posited a third register he called "the real," but, however much we may need to believe in it, we approach it from within the symbolic order we inhabit. As a Structuralist, Lacan dismissed the idea that we can stand apart from language in order to be free of its rhetorical devices and transformations.

Unlike Freud, who was a prolific writer, most of Lacan's teachings were presented in regular seminars, where what he uttered was transcribed for eventual publication. In 1966 the publication of his collected *Écrits* (which, though untranslated in the English version, means simply "Writings") created a stir in Parisian intellectual circles, but the title was somewhat misleading, as most of these texts began as talks. In the seminars, Lacan's method was to speak as the unconscious speaks, which is to say elliptically, sometimes chaotically, indulging in complicated word play. This did not make for intelligibility, to say the least. Many frustrated auditors reacted by calling him an intellectual charlatan, but Lacan, steeped from his early years in Symbolist and Surrealist literature (for a time he was a member of the Surrealist movement), embraced the Mallarméan principle of addressing only the "happy few." Paradoxically, by the early 1970s Lacan's regular audiences seemed more like the "many." It was not uncommon for a "seminar" to boast an attendance of perhaps one thousand people, mostly young denizens of the Left Bank, crowding the aisles and bending solemnly over the copious notes they took as the flamboyant *maître* (famous as something of a dandy) carried on in his deliberately baffling way.

Most well-known French intellectuals of the day attended at least occasionally. One of those most directly influenced by Lacan was Louis Althusser (1918–1991), a leading French Marxist philosopher of the century and one who insisted on a Stucturalist reading of Marx. He based his concept of ideology on Lacan's "imaginary." As Lacan had done in insisting on revisiting what Freud had written, Althusser called for a return to the text of someone (Marx) in whose name so much has been proclaimed and practiced. With a philosopher named Etienne Balibar (1942–), he wrote a book called *Lire le Capital* (1966, *Reading Capital*), a follow-up to his manifesto claiming Marx for Structuralism, *Pour Marx* (1964, *For Marx*). What Althusser claimed to find in reading Marx was a "scientific" thinker whose crowning achievement was *Das Kapital*. Marxist thought in France since 1945 had been dominated by Sartrean Existentialism and, relatedly, by a surge of interest in the writings of the "young Marx" of around 1843 to 1845. The rediscovered texts of those years appeared to reveal a "humanist" Marx, one in close touch with Romanticism and Idealist philosophy.

Althusser sharply disagreed with this emphasis, arguing that these youthful writings were something Marx had to get out of his system before he could take up his real work of systematically—structurally—critiquing the capitalist order and establishing his own "science of society." Borrowing a concept first introduced to French history of science by Gaston Bachelard, Althusser identified an "epistemological break" (*coupure épistémologique*) separating the early writings of Marx from the texts leading up to and including *Capital*. As opposed to the officially approved view of Marxist (i.e., the work of Marx and Engels) theory as "historical materialism," Althusser, being a Structuralist, assigned relatively slight importance to historical stages of development. He viewed "ideology," defined in neo-Lacanian terms, as the imaginary way we represent the conditions of our social existence to ourselves, as a constant in all periods, a kind of glue holding together what he called the "social formation."

Althusser formulated his own distinctive version of the typical Structuralist attack on the Humanist shibboleth of the "autonomous subject." Again borrowing from Lacan, Althusser argued that language, wielding pronouns as weapons, plays an ideological role that designates us as what we misunderstand to be autonomous subjects. In one of his most influential essays of the late 1960s, "Ideology and Ideological State Apparatuses," Althusser introduced the term "interpellation" to explain this phenomenon. Ideology in class society under capitalism (which appears to be an ahistorical constant to Althusser) "hails" us (interpellates us) as subjects, beckons to us and gets our attention in a way similar to the mirror for Lacan's hypothetical transfixed infant.

As a Communist intellectual, Althusser was curiously aloof from politics and activism, even though many of the students he influenced would take part in radical movements, including the events of May 1968. While his theories were by no means orthodox, he never questioned the notoriously doctrinaire Parti Communiste in France. Even though the French Communist Party did not embrace his views, Althusser was one of the few French Marxist intellectuals to remain in the party even after the Soviet invasion of Hungary in 1956. By the 1960s many French intellectuals were consciously *gauchiste*—"leftist"—but few wished to remain party members.

In retrospect, it becomes easier to see how Structuralism was at odds certainly with Marxism if not with all reformist movements or social critiques that depend on the idea of human agency in order to bring about transformation. For a combination of reasons, Structuralism was felt to be on the Left even as it occupied the French intellectual establishment. One influential review that captured the heady mix of Barthesian semiology, Althusserian Marxism, Lacanian psychoanalysis, and the emerging "Poststructuralist" critiques of Michel Foucault and Jacques Derrida (see chapter 11) was *Tel Quel,* founded by the writer Philippe Sollers (1936–). In addition to his pieces, *Tel Quel* frequently included the contributions of two brilliant Bulgarian émigrés, Julia Kristeva (1941–), wife of Sollers, and Tzvetan Todorov (1939–). Todorov specialized in Structuralist analysis of rhetoric and poetics. Kristeva shared this interest, and also worked in psychoanalysis. (She became an analyst.) The ensemble of writers active in *Tel Quel* constituted a kind of crucible for what was soon to become an internal crisis for Structuralism, especially after the cultural explosion of May 1968.

Cultural and Intellectual Dimensions of May 1968

The intellectual associations surrounding the upheaval of May 1968 are difficult to sort out. Few of the supposedly progressive new intellectuals could be said to have taken an active role in the uprising, which was genuinely student-led. The French Communist Party was actively hostile toward the largely anarchist (with a sprinkling of Maoist) students. Among intellectuals, it was the old warhorse Sartre who most clearly showed common cause with the students. He shared their opposition to the Vietnam War and understood completely their criticism of the rigidity of the French educational system from which he himself had held aloof.

On one level, the Sorbonne uprising (which began in solidarity with radical students expelled from the suburban University of Nanterre) was but one of the most sustained and dramatic examples of protest during a highly explosive political and cultural climate worldwide, especially as opposition to the Vietnam War increased. There had been "Prague Spring" as Czech dissidents tried unsuccessfully to liberalize their regime and a student occupation of university buildings at Columbia in New York. Later that summer there would be the brutal murder by police of students in Mexico City. As was true elsewhere, the concerns of the French students ranged from international politics to demands for fewer social restrictions in their own lives, and the events of May were, so to speak, at the intersection of multiple emancipatory demands and frustrations.

Those conscious of the influence of Situationism emphasized the "festival" atmosphere that prevailed in the streets of Paris, and indeed there was a kind of youthful exuberance and joyousness, mixed with sardonic humor, to be found especially in the posters and graffiti by which the events especially are remembered. Examples include *Sois jeune est tais toi* ("Be young and keep your mouth shut"—showing a silhouette of De Gaulle in a gendarme's uniform, his hand clapped over a young man's mouth), *La Beauté est dans la rue* ("Beauty is in the street"—a stenciled image of an attractive young woman hurling a brick, presumably at police), *Il est défense de défenser* ("It is forbidden to forbid"—perhaps the slogan that best encapsulates the philosophy of May), and, to remind us of the lightheartedness of many in the midst of all this tension as well as to answer those who have wanted to see the Communists' hand in the uprising: *Je suis marxiste, tendance Groucho* (which translates roughly as "I am a Marxist of the Groucho persuasion").

True both to historical arguments about the Paris Commune and to the views of Situationists, the movement was consciously decentralized. If there was anything most participants agreed on, it was their emphatic distrust of leaders. Loosely organized *comités d'action*—action committees—sprang up throughout France during the weeks that followed the May uprising, and many would evolve in following years into activist groups that would seek to address a wide array of social problems. As was the case in the United States relative to its civil rights and antiwar movements, both feminist and gay liberation movements evolved out of the struggles of 1968. In the short run, what the May movement did was to disrupt the normal order of things in France. In this regard as well as in what many have called the "festival" atmosphere, particularly in Paris, *les événements,* as the French often refer to the episode, seemed a fulfillment of the Situationist program of *détournement.*

However dramatic such events may have been, the grand revolution some expected did not materialize, and, as the decade of the 1960s ended with continued war in Vietnam, Arab-Israeli tensions in the Middle East, the breakup of The Beatles, the drug deaths of many leading rock stars, and the first signs of a global economic crisis that would be evident by 1973, many of the features of cultural life associated with Modernism were beginning to disappear. Looking back on this era, many more recent observers have been led to characterize the period that followed as "Postmodern."

Suggestions for Further Reading

Cohen-Solal, Annie. *Sartre: A Life.* New York: Pantheon Books, 1987.

Cronin, Anthony. *Samuel Beckett: The Last Modernist.* New York: HarperCollins, 1997.

Esslin, Martin. *The Theatre of the Absurd.* Revised Edition. Garden City, NY: Anchor Books, 1969.

Fowlie, Wallace. *Dionysus in Paris: A Guide to Contemporary French Theater.* London: Victor Gollancz, 1961.

Hollier, Denis, ed. *A New History of French Literature.* Cambridge, MA: Harvard University Press, 1989.

Jay, Martin. *Downcast Eyes: The Denigration of Vision in Twentieth-Century French Thought.* Berkeley: University of California Press, 1993.

Marcus, Greil. *Lipstick Traces: The Secret History of the Twentieth Century.* Cambridge, MA: Harvard University Press, 1989.

Marwick, Arthur. *The Sixties: Cultural Revolution in Britain, France, Italy, and the United States, c. 1958–1974.* New York: Oxford University Press, 1998.

Poster, Mark. *Existential Marxism in Postwar France: From Sartre to Althusser.* Princeton: Princeton University Press, 1975.

Stoekl, Allen M. *Agonies of the Intellectual; Commitment, Subjectivity, and the Performative in the Twentieth-Century French Tradition.* Lincoln: University of Nebraska Press, 1992.

Sturrock, John, ed. *Structuralism and Since: Lévi-Strauss to Derrida.* New York: Oxford University Press, 1979.

Turkle, Sherry. *Psychoanalytic Politics: Freud's French Revolution.* Second Edition, Revised. New York: Guilford Press, 1992.

Chapter 11

The Aftermath of 1968:
Poststructuralism and Postmodernism

One unfortunate drawback to using the term "Postmodern" to designate recent cultural trends is that the first syllable implies something coming after, as if a break has occurred between the periods. However, and this is a point that creates confusion and not a little frustration with the term "Postmodern," much of what gets labeled this way can be understood more as exaggerated tendencies of what was already under way in Modern culture. To use one important example from the last chapter, Samuel Beckett can certainly be understood as a member of the Modernist tradition in literature, heir to Flaubert, Proust, and Joyce. But he has been claimed also for "Postmodern" literature, one definition of which for some critics is the deliberate way the artist calls attention to the act of creation, something Beckett certainly does in most of his texts.

In some ways the term "Postmodern" is little more than shorthand for ongoing processes of cultural transformation not yet definitively understood. By definition historians usually are reluctant to comment on the very recent past, but a book like this one that seeks to examine as much as possible of late twentieth-century European cultural history cannot help but tread on this still-forming ground. The reader will want to keep two things in mind about this: (1) nothing encountered here can be understood as anything like orthodoxy or "the last word" on the subject, and (2) no historical writing on whatever subject can claim to have provided "the last word."

Throughout this chapter, we will examine ideas that may or may not exhibit characteristics some are encouraged to call Postmodern. In most cases they can be called a little of both, that is, "Modern" and "Postmodern." Some cultural critics, such as Jürgen Habermas (see chapter

12) argue therefore for the inclusive term "Modernity," rejecting the need for a problematic term like Postmodernism. But if by Postmodern one means the decline of modern nationalism, heavy concentration of resources almost exclusively in cities, and centralization of national systems of transportation or communication, then there is some justification for the term's use. In any case, ending the previous chapter with the events of May 1968 was far from an arbitrary dividing point. For many cultural/intellectual historians of contemporary Europe, May 1968 has become the hinge on the door that opens onto Postmodernism.

Intellectual Legacies of May 1968

Among other things at work, May 1968 represented the overthrow of Structuralism's intellectual dominance in France. By 1970 the term "Poststructuralism" was increasingly in use. Like the term "Postmodernism" relative to Modernism, the other "post" term can also be understood less as a dramatic break or rupture with its predecessor than as a coming to fruition of tendencies already emerging from it. Both Structuralism and Poststructuralism were preoccupied with language and systems of sign production, and they shared a sense of profound skepticism about the ability of individual human subjects to stand apart from language and systems of meaning within which human beings are positioned socially. The two thinkers most identified with Poststructuralist thought, both of whom rose to great prominence after 1968, were Michel Foucault and Jacques Derrida. They also both represent larger patterns of the reorganization of French thought in these years, which have everything to do with the abandonment of Marxism and the concomitant vogue for Nietzsche, although a Nietzsche that would be scarcely recognizable to previous generations.

The first period of Nietzsche's reception in Europe, beginning soon after his death in 1900 and mediated decisively by his sister (see chapter 6), created the proto-fascist philosopher, the apostle of brute strength and theorist of a master race. Later interpreters, especially those influential by the mid-1960s in France, argued that these were gross distortions of Nietzsche's thought. Ironically, the pivotal role in bringing about a revision of Nietzschean thought was that played by Martin Heidegger—ironic because of his own support for the Nazi cause. The Heideggerian reading of Nietzsche that flowered especially in an age of new linguistic and critical theories (see chapter 11) saw him as a master of indeterminacy, as one who broke with the tradition of Western philosophy by giving priority to written language in its full figural richness and complexity.

This view was embraced by Bataille and Klossowski, and by a French philosopher named Gilles Deleuze (1925–1995). Foucault and Derrida were likewise influenced along these lines, as was Sarah Kofman (1934–1994), an influential French feminist philosopher. Particularly in the wake of the failed (at least in an obvious political sense) revolution of 1968, a generally leftist (*gauchiste*) version of Nietzsche suited a generation disillusioned with Marxism or any system of thought offering sweeping, total explanations and interpretations. In France, the immediate source of disillusion was the unrepentantly Stalinist Parti Communiste.

For some French thinkers, what now needed to be explained was why the revolution failed. Their situation was similar to that of the Frankfurt School theorists of the 1920s, who sought explanations for the resistance in other European countries to Bolshevism. Those thinkers had forged a kind of synthesis of Marxism and Freudian psychoanalysis, most evident in the works of Herbert Marcuse. Half a century later, Marx and Freud remained the reference points, but now in a negative sense. Distrustful equally of Marxism and psychoanalysis, two French philosophers published a highly original and rather baffling work in 1972 that was shaped decisively by the experience of May 1968 in France. The authors were Deleuze and Félix Guattari (1930–1992). Deleuze was the more prolific writer, but both were known for their progressive political activism. Guattari in particular was identified with the so-called antipsychiatry movement (he was a psychiatrist), critical of psychiatric professionals and advocating rights for patients.

Their book, called *Capitalisme et schizophrénie: l'Anti-Oedipe* (1972, *The Anti-Oedipus: Capitalism and Schizophrenia*), was well timed to excite reaction among new post-1968 social forces such as women's and gay rights movements and to detonate in intellectual circles that had been engaged in a stampede toward psychoanalysis of the Lacanian variety. Deleuze and Guattari's work is notoriously recondite and deliberately defiant of one's usual expectations of what to find within the covers of a book, so it is understandably difficult to summarize their arguments. However, the significance of the title would seem to be that the oedipal triangle (what they call the "mommy-daddy-me" scenario) is to blame for creating the kinds of wounded, self-limiting creatures who are incapable of staging a successful cultural revolution. There is a "cop within," they explained, who must first be killed in order to remove obstacles to the kind of personal emancipation upon which a truly free society can be founded.

By attacking the oedipal emphasis of psychoanalysis they were dismissing Lacan, for whom the oedipal drama of early childhood represented the internalization of paternal authority in the guise of language, plunging the subject into an inescapable symbolic order. Although hostile to Lacan and psychoanalysis, Deleuze and Guattari shared the antihumanism of leading Structuralists like Lacan, and went them one better. Their prevailing metaphor is that of the schizophrenic whose condition is an understandable response to the fragmentation and processes of social control the exist in society. Paradoxically, only a schizophrenic stance can permit the emergence of the "full body without organs" that can survive the indignities of modern social domination.

They may have been anti-Lacan, but they certainly shared his penchant for baffling statements that, more than anything else, seem calculated stylistic interventions. In 1980 the two authors published an even longer, more complex follow-up volume called *Mille plateaux: Capitalisme et schizophrénie* (*A Thousand Plateaus: Capitalism and Schizophrenia*), which they recommended being read not necessarily in numerical sequence, but in whatever order the reader chose—even comparing the reading process to that of dropping the tone arm of a record player down onto some random track of the album. (This was pre–compact disc.) This time around, Deleuze and Guattari offered new metaphors to stand for escaping domination and subjection, such as the *rhizome,* a complex botanical root structure that shoots out underground in all directions.

Michel Foucault and Jacques Derrida

The author of the preface to the first Deleuze/Guattari volume was Michel Foucault. Foucault often took time to praise Deleuze, and shared his political commitment to resisting excessive power and social control. In the early 1970s Foucault increasingly became a theorist of power and its complex operations in modern society, always seeking assiduously to avoid reliance either on Marxist explanations involving ideology and class consciousness or on psychoanalytic explanations of unconscious desire, introjection, or sublimation. In 1970 he had been named professor at the Collège de France, a position that gave him considerable visibility as he propounded his views resulting primarily from the historical research seminars he conducted as his principal duty as holder of a chair in History of Systems of Thought (the title he had suggested when appointed to the Collège de France).

Foucault started out as a philosopher, initially concerning himself with questions of madness and mental illness. In 1961 he published a major study of the origins of the modern asylum called *Histoire de la folie à l'age classique* (*Madness and Civilization*). Foucault's emphasis in this book was on the establishment of procedures designed to isolate or exclude forms of consciousness once tolerated in Western culture. Both in the book and in interviews and occasional pieces written in the early 1960s, Foucault made clear his admiration for a number of modern figures judged insane, from the Marquis de Sade and Francisco Goya (in the eighteenth century) to Gérard de Nerval (nineteenth century) to Antonin Artaud (twentieth century). He also acknowledged his intellectual debt to Georges Bataille, and played a significant role in the revival of interest in that unique writer, now claimed for Postmodernism by several trendy publishing houses. Foucault wrote a laudatory preface for the four-volume *Oeuvres complètes* (*Complete Works)* of Bataille, whose publication by the distinguished house of Gallimard he did much to bring about.

Turning his attention to other kinds of modern institutions, Foucault moved on to a study of the emergence of the modern medical clinic in *La Naissance da la clinique: Une archéologie du regard médical* (1963, *Birth of the Clinic: An Archaeology of Medical Perception*). Here Foucault advanced a characteristically iconoclastic argument he would employ in his examination of other modern professions and scholarly disciplines, that, in this case, the function of the clinic was to "produce" disease, i.e., as an object of study, description, classification, and treatment. In this sense, the field of modern medicine constituted what Foucault would soon begin describing as a "discourse."

The modern human sciences as discursive systems for the production of knowledge provided the focus of Foucault's next book, his most ambitious work to date. This was *Les Mots et les choses: Une archéologie des sciences humaines* (1966, *The Order of Things: An Archaeology of the Human Sciences*), a comparative discussion of the consolidation by the nineteenth century of such fields as political economy, comparative linguistics, and morphology as modern practices for the definition and classification of knowledge. One of Foucault's objectives was to reveal the arbitrary rules by which the human sciences organized themselves, something he implied strongly by beginning his book with a discussion of a humorous parable by the Argentine writer Jorge Luis Borges of an ancient Chinese encyclopedia based on an absurd classificatory scheme. In subsequent pages Foucault would make clear that the "joke" was on "we" modern Europeans who imagine our systems of knowledge to be based on unshakably logical principles.

Oddly enough, this most difficult and demanding of all of Foucault's books was a great commercial success. For one thing, the timing (1966) was right. This was the heyday of Structuralism, the same year that saw the much heralded publication of Lacan's *Écrits.* (See chapter 10.) Despite the author's strenuous objections to the label, in 1966 Foucault was viewed as a Structuralist. And indeed he shared the Structuralist preoccupation with language (despite eschewing its terminology), and certainly its antihumanism, made clear in a ringing diatribe against the concept of "Man" that closed out *Les Mots et les choses.* The sense of Foucault as a new "Structuralist" heavyweight joining the movement's already well-established figures was captured in a famous political cartoon by Maurice Henry called *Le Déjeuner des structuralistes.* It appeared June 1967 in *La Quinzaine littéraire,* and depicted Foucault holding forth to Lévi-Strauss, Lacan, and Barthes. At once a tribute to Manet's *Le Déjeuner sur l'herbe* and to Lévi-Strauss's research, the artist portrayed the four men wearing only grass skirts, although Lacan, ever the dandy, sports a bow tie.

Both to clear up misunderstandings about his work and to signal a new direction for his historical research, Foucault published a theoretical work in 1969 called *L'archéologie du savoir* (*The Archaeology of Knowledge*). He contrasted his methods with those of a more traditional history of ideas, comparing his work of sifting through layers of accumulated documents and sources to that of an archaeologist digging at a site. Again rejecting the Structuralist label, he went to considerable lengths to explain his approach to language embedded in written sources and the kinds of evidence they can be said to provide. The latter part of his treatise took the form of a manifesto claiming the right to strike out in new intellectual directions. "Do not ask me who I am, and do not ask me to remain the same," he wrote, adding "Leave it to the police to see that our papers are in order."

The following year Foucault provided a detailed schema for the direction at which he was hinting in his previous book. He announced his intention to carry out historical investigations of the operation of what he called "discourse," defined as the sum total of statements, pronouncements, and writings produced by a culture that can be shown to operate by certain principles of affirmation, comparison, distinction, and exclusion. He chose as the occasion for this prolegomena his inaugural lecture as professor at the Collège de France. The title of the lecture, published as a short book, was *L'ordre du discours* (*The Order of Discourse*). On this very ceremonial public occasion, Foucault was deferential toward his own mentors and intellectual predecessors and was quite self-effacing. Speaking softly and precisely, he expressed the desire, quoting Beckett, to be able to disappear behind his own story or his own discourse.

Instead of the lecture series chosen by many holders of chairs at this august institution, Foucault opted to conduct research seminars and chose as his subject the history of crime, penology, and incarceration in France. This complemented his political activism on behalf of prisoners' rights as well as gay rights. All during the 1970s and early 1980s Foucault became increasingly visible as a gay spokesman. What was always central in the research he supervised was attention to the operations of discourse in modern penology and related professions, such as law and psychiatry. In 1973 Foucault and his seminar colleagues published a kind of dossier called *Moi, Pierre Rivière, ayant égorge ma mère, ma soeur, et mon frère. . . . Un cas de parricide au XIXe siècle (I, Pierre Rivière, Having Slaughtered My Mother, My Sister, and My Brother. . . .A Case of Parricide in the Nineteenth Century).* This book contained accounts of the arrest and trial of a self-confessed murderer of the 1830s, along with the man's own narrative in which he expressed a fervent desire for martyrdom. Instead of being guillotined, however, he was the first example of a parricide judged criminally insane and given life imprisonment instead. Decisive in this sentence were the statements of psychiatrists, and for Foucault and his team this was striking evidence of the emerging power of modern discourses of mental health and an avowedly rehabilitative penology.

Foucault's fascination with the penal system culminated in a major work published in 1975 called *Surveillir et punir: Naissance de la prison (Discipline and Punish: Birth of the Prison).* As with his previous studies of the asylum and the medical clinic, he contrasted an earlier period when the prison in the modern sense was unknown with one just a few decades later, and set out to explain the attitudes and practices that had to change to bring this about. The crucial difference in this book is that here Foucault seemed ready to propound a general theory of power's operation in the modern world, arguing that the prison offered an advantageous way to discover this since power is unmasked within that institution. According to Foucault, the modern prison aims at total surveillance of the inmate and the production of "docile bodies." The author performed several chilling moves in this haunting study, as when he compared prisons to schools and factories, suggesting their functions are identical in that each aims to produce compliant citizens who have internalized the relations of power. Most famously, *Surveiller et punir* opens with a horrific account of a spectacular 1757 public torture and execution and then shifts to a description of the daily routine in a modern prison, implying that the latter is a greater horror, for it seeks to achieve permanent mastery over those incarcerated.

The shift he described held great importance for Foucault's subsequent research topics, for what he found most meaningful in the evolution of the penal system was the control being exerted increasingly over the physical bodies of inmates. In an interview given at the time of his book's publication, Foucault said he wished to show how the relations of power, defined by now as *pouvoir-savoir,* or "power/knowledge," seeped into actual bodies, especially as their care and regulation increasingly became the business of modern societies (e.g., combating alcoholism or sexually transmitted diseases). Foucault's concept of power was deliberately differentiated from such influential models as those provided by liberal democratic theory (rights, representation) or Marxism (class, ideology). He offered no moral condemnation of power, observing that it was both repressive or controlling and productive or enabling. If power was completely denying or forbidding, consensus would be easy to form against it.

But all people, he explained, are positioned in a social field where power circulates through discourse, for example, through the educational system, where people acquire knowledge and skills that give them advantages but also absorb or internalize a profound sense of conformity and limits they assume and impose on themselves. Foucault shared with Deleuze and Guattari an awareness of how human beings are complicit in their own regulation and policing. The sum total of all the social procedures whereby people are so many nodal points in grids or networks through which power flows in its always contradictory ways creates or produces them as subjects. More and more Foucault came to locate the unquestioned sense of the self as subject at the center of power's operation in modern society. In his book on the prison he broached the topic of the body as a target of regulation by the "carceral society" that was the prison writ large. After 1975 he made the history of sexuality or, more specifically, how human sexual identities or proclivities came to be viewed as the key to defining and understanding personality, his object of research.

In 1976, Foucault published a kind of prologue to the research that was to occupy him until his last days. Called *La Volonté de savoir: Histoire de la sexualité 1* (*The History of Sexuality, Volume 1: An Introduction*), it was planned as the first of a series of several related volumes (though the subsequent volumes he came to write differed significantly from his original conception). Here Foucault more fully elaborated his theory of power as more than merely prohibitive and called for an end to the emphasis on "repression" of sexuality. Too much had been made, he felt, of the repressiveness of the Victorian period (and, conversely, he dismissed what he viewed as exaggerated claims made for the sexual liberation of the later twentieth century). For his purposes, whether sex is being affirmed or denied, the important thing is that in the modern period, both through phases of prudishness and hedonistic "liberation," sex and sexuality become topics for discourse. Foucault announced his intention to show through specific kinds of historical research how the primacy of sexuality came to be the principal means whereby the "subject" was made the central emphasis of Western civilization and the primary locus for the discursive flow of *pouvoir-savoir*. As the title suggested, the "will to knowledge," to know the essence of a person through sure knowledge of that person's sexuality, was the impetus for this modern preoccupation.

Once again he and his associates used the seminar format to examine sources produced by another unusual episode from the annals of nineteenth-century French medico-juridical activity. This was a case from the 1820s involving a person called Herculine Barbin who was born a hermaphrodite, judged to be a girl and raised primarily in a convent. At the age of twenty, Barbin was examined by a doctor who pronounced him male. A judge ordered him to dress and live in every way as if male from that point on. The eventual result was despair and suicide. The dossier *Herculine Barbin* (1978) published under Foucault's supervision includes contemporary descriptions of the events, doctors' reports, and the judicial ruling. But what most preoccupied the historians, Foucault in particular, was the striking way the case showed that social and cultural categories had to triumph over the ambiguous facts at hand. Of utmost importance was the need to declare the person's "true sex," seen as the principal index to identity. This assumption becomes the foundation that underlies modern psychology, psychoanalysis, and especially the late-nineteenth-century studies by Havelock Ellis and others known as "sexology."

By the early 1980s, Foucault shifted direction, radically redesigning his project. Up until then, all of his books had been concerned with the period covering ca. 1700 to 1900, depending on the specific subject. His method, described in his essay "Nietzsche, Genealogy and History," had been of working back from present situations to preceding points that might explain not origins with a capital "O," but steps by which modern "problematics" had evolved. He embraced the Nietzschean concept of *Herkunft,* a kind of zigzagging vertical descent as opposed to the overdetermined linear trajectory of Hegelian of Marxist temporality. Now, for his historical investigation into the emergence of sexuality as the overriding category defining modern subjective existence, he decided he needed to investigate classical antiquity and describe an extremely prolonged trajectory that produced the exaggerated preoccupation with the sexualized self.

There, in the moral and ethical philosophers of Hellenistic Greece and Roman pagan and early Christian schools, Foucault believed he had located the beginnings of the obsessive concern with the self as an object of cultivation, care, and discipline. Originally, he observed, all forms of bodily and personal behavior were part of this preoccupation, but gradually sexual conduct and the regulation of one's erotic desires became paramount. In the second and third volumes of his series on the history of sexuality—*L'usage de plaisir* (1984, *The Use of Pleasure*) and *Le Souci de soi* (1984, *The Care of the Self*)—Foucault described the building of the theoretical edifice that supported this central feature of Western culture, moreover the one that most enshrined the subject as the center of social existence and therefore most facilitated the operation of regimes of power working within discursive systems. The drama of these claims was heightened by the author's own race against time. He died of complications from AIDS just days after the publication of these two volumes.

Always oriented toward specific objects of study and distrustful of grand theoretical claims, Foucault was in many ways the Poststructuralist thinker par excellence, especially for those concerned with history, society, and the sociocultural deployment of discursive systems. For those more concerned with very detailed philosophical or literary questions about the complex properties of texts, Jacques Derrida was the Poststructuralist of note. First attracting attention while a little-known member of the faculty of the École Normale Supérieure in Paris with his simultaneous publication of three ground breaking books in 1967, Derrida was the first to demonstrate the internal contradictions of the Structuralist enterprise. He did this in an essay called "Structure, Sign, and Play in the Discourse of the Human Sciences," included in his book *L'ecriture at la différence* (1967, *Writing and Difference*).

Derrida's essay was a direct attack on the principle of binary opposition so fundamental to Structuralism. He demonstrated that the work of Lévi-Strauss depended excessively on the opposition of culture to nature and that a careful, nuanced reading would show how the strain created by the opposing terms, with preference always going to culture over nature, produced confusion and instability in the writing itself. Derrida's way of calling attention to this unwarranted opposition at the expense of the less privileged term was an example of the textual operation of "deconstruction," the concept that came to be most associated with Derrida. It quickly took on the connotation of a kind of demolition or nihilistic attack on all meaning in texts. In fact, what Derrida was largely suggesting in 1967 was that a comprehensive study or science of writing was necessary and long overdue.

In the three books he published in 1967—*La Voix et la phénomène* (*Speech and Phenomena*), *De la grammatologie* (*Of Grammatology*), and *L'écriture et la différence* (*Writing and Difference*)—and in several more published down through the early 1970s, Derrida elaborated a distinctive argument about writing, Western philosophy, and by extension, the entire civilization. He claimed that the close readings he carried out in these books demonstrated a fear and distrust of writing based on the desire to control and stabilize meaning. The working assumption has been that speech is superior to writing for communicating philosophical argument, Socrates standing as the model for this preference. Derrida called this bias "logocentrism" and described it as based on the desire to foster an illusion of "presence" in texts, as if the author is there speaking to the reader.

Focusing particularly on texts by writers who exhibit versions of this fear of writing's inability to preserve unitary, coherent meanings (Plato, Hegel, Husserl, Rousseau, among many others), Derrida dramatized the forms of confusion such contradictory attitudes about writing can produce in readers. His own versions of close readings show the many ways that quirks of syntax, rhetorical complexities, and undue emphasis on one term or category at the expense of another create effects other than those intended by their logocentric authors. The reader, who after all comes to the act of reading with the accumulated associations and experiences of other texts (Roland Barthes and others in the Structuralist tradition had developed the notion of "intertextuality," that is, that texts open up into other texts in endless combinations), is subject to distractions, points of confusion, and baffling choices among multiple possible meanings. Derrida's imagery for this includes *aporia,* a term meaning loss of path or inability to decide on a correct one, and also the "abyss" of nonmeaning that opens up before the reader.

Derrida's distinctive style mimics these nonlinear fits and starts of actual readings, showing the impossibility of an author's ability to fix meanings in texts. Occasionally he went so far as to show the possibility of reading a text completely against the grain of what might appear to be the author's intent. For example, in a 1978 essay called *Éperons/Les styles de Nietzsche* (*Spurs: Nietzsche's Styles*), he considered the subject of Nietzsche's misogyny apparent in *Die fröhliche Wissenschaft* (*The Gay Science*), but brought together several different contradictory passages that can add up to the conclusion that the style(s) of Nietzsche's text end up affirming woman.

Beginning with his first books, Derrida developed a very specific terminology to describe the features of a written text that bring the dream of logocentrism to grief. One such term was "trace," which refers to way any one text refers to others, even if only indirectly, because of the ability of certain combinations of written syllables to invoke others and because of the associations, unforeseen by an author, that some point in the writing triggers in the reader's mind. All written language, Derrida argues, bears the "traces" of other writings. Every text, in a way, is a kind of palimpsest on which one can detect the partial erasures of other texts. Another key Derridean term was *différence,* but often deliberately misspelled as *différance.* It is a fundamental principle of linguistics (and most certainly was for Saussure) that meaning in language depends on similarity and difference, that is, one sound or word has meaning because we have a sense of its opposite.

But Derrida wanted a term that would express not only how meanings in a text depend on differentiation but how they also come about through displacement, shiftings or veering off of meaning in this or that direction. The French verb *différer* can mean both "differ" and "defer," so Derrida invented his term *différance* to suggest deferral, the second meaning. Derrida, a very capable reader of Freud, showed how this kind of linguistic displacement is similar to displacement in Freud's sense, as in the odd and unpredictable sequences followed by the unconscious mind in the dreaming state. Derrida was also a very knowledgeable reader of Lacan, who had borrowed the Russian linguist Roman Jakobson's notion of metaphor and metonymy representing two intersecting axes of language and applied them to Freud's concepts of Condensation (metaphor) and Displacement (metonymy).

Having developed both a terminology that described the ways texts produce meaning but also make it often "undecidable," and having performed so-called deconstructive readings of texts where these phenomena can be observed, Derrida intensified his critique of logocentrism, implying as well a feminist direction to be pursued. He coined the term "phallogocentrism" to suggest, in a quasi-psychoanalytic sense, that desire for control of meaning was based on an idealized notion of full phallic presence in speech, something deeply involved with patriarchal prerogatives, including those found in major world religions. Responding to a critique of his work by an American philosopher and "Speech Act" theorist named John Searle (1932–), Derrida pushed his argument further (in *Limited, inc.,* 1977) to say that not only can speech not subdue writing or subject it to control but that speech itself is a kind of writing. That is, it can be shown to be composed, filled with traces of other statements, and subject to the same kinds of rhetorical volatility that can be found in texts.

Like Foucault, Derrida frequently accepted positions as visiting professor in leading American universities. By the late 1970s, in fact, he was probably more recognized and commented on in the United States than in France. For several years he divided his time between the École Normale Supérieure in Paris and Yale University. (Subsequently he joined the faculty of the École des Hautes Études en Sciences Sociales and the University of California-Irvine.) He and colleagues there in English and comparative literature became known as the "Yale School" of more or less "Deconstructionist" critics. Their notoriety produced no end of polemics and fed into the late-twentieth-century American "cultural wars" about humanities education and the literary canon.

In later writings Derrida experimented adventurously with the book format (something already implied by his theory) and expanded into other topics, including the visual arts. In 1974 he published *Glas,* an extra-large-format book in which two dense columns of writing appeared separated by a white expanse between them. One contained Derrida's essay on a text of Hegel, while the other dealt with Jean Genet. It was as if Derrida wanted to suggest that the two texts were in a position to unravel each other across the chasm that separated them. For some years Derrida had been interrogating the nature of the book as an object that creates certain expectations and makes certain determinations. In 1978 he turned this skepticism toward framing devices in visual representation in *La Vérité en peinture* (*Truth in Painting*). Another physically striking book was *La Carte postale de Socrate à Freud et au-delà* (*The Post Card: From Socrates to Freud and Beyond*), which consisted of a series of meditations on an ancient engraving depicting Plato lecturing to a seated Socrates as scribe, a group of love notes sent as postcards, and three long essays on Freud and Lacan.

During the last two decades of the twentieth century Derrida branched out into additional areas. Two long-standing criticisms of his work had been that he ignored politics and that his elaborately textual emphasis ignored history. Sharing with Foucault a penchant for confounding his public's expectations, he involved himself in such political causes as the anti-apartheid movement in South Africa and the rights of immigrant populations in Europe. And his growing concern with history and memory came to be expressed in writings dealing with the Holocaust and with the revelations about the degree to which his intellectual precursor Heidegger had championed the Nazi cause, as well as the painful disclosure of the youthful Nazi collaboration of his friend and Yale colleague Paul de Man. Born in Algeria to a French Sephardic family, Derrida had long been conscious of the importance of his Jewish identity, and had written important essays on Edmond Jabès and Emmanuel Lévinas (1906–1995), a Lithuanian-born French Jewish philosopher.

French Intellectuals and Politics, 1974 to 1987

Other French intellectuals brought renewed attention to the Holocaust during the 1980s and 1990s, including Alain Finkielkraut (1949–), one of the most visible of a younger generation of philosophers, and the historian Saul Friedlander (1933–). And it was a French filmmaker, Claude Lanzmann (1925–), one of Sartre's colleagues on the editorial board of *Les Temps Modernes,* who gave the subject the most exhaustive treatment in his just-under-ten-hour long documentary film *Shoah* (1985), whose title is the Hebrew word meaning "Holocaust." Derrida's preoccupation with Jewish history and the Holocaust was consistent with the urgent work of facing up to France's Vichy past, the focus of a series of celebrated trials and episodes beginning with the capture in 1986 of Klaus Barbie, "the butcher of Lyon," in Bolivia. Barbie was the subject of another long documentary film by Marcel Ophüls (1927–) called *Hotel Terminus* (1988), a film that dealt especially with the delaying tactics French officials used to prevent Barbie, who died while in custody, from ever coming to trial. The fear was that he would implicate prominent French politicians who had sought to present themselves to the public as resolutely antifascist and even as heroes of the Resistance. When it came to light after his death in 1994 that French president François Mitterand had originally been pro-Vichy, these suspicions seemed confirmed.

Perhaps predictably, the new attention to France's shameful past rekindled new expressions of anti-Semitism, often to be found among adherents to the neo-Nazi Front Populaire (Popular Front) of Jean-Marie Le Pen, a French veteran of the Indochina War who made opposition to African immigrants the center of his political effort. By the late 1980s, France was in the throes of a profound rightward political shift that was not unrelated to the declining fortunes of Marxism as a guiding principle of the French Left. It had everything to do with the stodgy, neo-Stalinist character of the French Communist Party under the leadership of Georges Marchais, and in any case had been under way

since at least 1974, when the publication in Paris of Aleksandr Solzhenitsyn's *Gulag Archipelago* dropped like a bomb on the French Left, especially the youthful veterans of May 1968, many of whom had flirted
with Maoism and been favorable toward Mao's Cultural Revolution.

Solzhenitsyn's three-volume historical account of the *gulag,* or Soviet
prison-camp system where millions had perished especially under
Stalin, appeared as its author was already in the news for being expelled
from his homeland. Almost overnight, several young French philosophers who had been part of radical elements of the 1968 generation
rushed into print with books that turned on their previous political al-
legiances, now denouncing all Marxist thought as just so much elaborate rationale for totalitarian abuses. The two best known of these
nouveaux philosophes of "New Philosophers," as they were dubbed by the
media, were Bernard-Henri Lévy (1948–) and André Glucksmann
(1938–). The latter had been especially visible in radical Maoist circles
around the time of May 1968.

Late in 1974, Lévy published to great fanfare his *La Barbarie au visage
humain* (*Barbarism with a Human Face*), and Glucksmann followed in
1975 with *La Cuisinière et le mangeur d'hommes* (*The Cook and the Eater
of Men*). The two books denounced the end-justifies-the-means logic of
existing socialist regimes and lamented the way political philosophies
purporting to ameliorate human suffering actually create it anew. Both
writers expressed the distrust of "totalizing" systems of thought found
in the ideas of Foucault and other neo-Nietzscheans. Glucksmann carried the argument to even greater extremes with his book *Les Maîtres-
penseurs* (1977, *The Master Thinkers*), where he denounced not only
Marxism and Leninism but all of German idealist philosophy, Hegel in
particular, as if the step from Kant's categorical imperative or Hegel's
Geist to Auschwitz or the gulag was only a short one.

For those accustomed to thinking of France as a country whose
prominent intellectuals were positioned clearly on the Left, where ordinary citizens voted for Communist candidates and Marxism had not
been a dirty word as it had been in other Western countries, this was a
jolt. On one level, it could be dismissed as trendiness, especially given
the way the media lionized the handsome Bernard-Henri Lévy, customarily photographed in a brooding pose, wearing his dark hair long
and keeping the top several buttons of his shirt unbuttoned. But it was
also an important sign of the serious decline of French Marxism, always associated in most people's minds with the sclerotic Communist
Party. And Louis Althusser, the most prominent Marxist theorist (although not officially; that designation was reserved for a writer named

Roger Garaudy), was in eclipse for a number of reasons, including tragic personal circumstances.

By the mid-1970s Althusser could claim only a few "disciples" in France. Nicos Poulantzas (1936–1979), his brilliant Greek-born protégé, committed suicide after publishing several books on the themes of the state and social class. Beyond him, Althusser's coauthor Etienne Balibar remained loyal, and there was the philosopher Dominique Lecourt (1944–) and Pierre Macherey (1938–), an important Marxist literary critic. After the manner of Cultural Revolution–era Chinese intellectuals, the maître himself had published an auto-critique, and he had suffered throughout the decade from bouts of extreme depression and mental illness. This culminated in the 1981 murder of his wife, for which he escaped criminal prosecution on grounds of insanity (a decision that outraged French feminists among many others). He was held in an asylum for the criminally insane and eventually released, a broken man. Before his death in 1990, however, he completed a very revealing autobiography.

Suggestions for Further Reading

Bennington, Geoff. *Derrida*. Chicago: University of Chicago Press, 1995.

Bogue, Ronald. *Deleuze and Guattari*. London: Routledge, 1989.

Dreyfus, Hubert, and Paul Rabinow. *Michel Foucault: Beyond Structuralism and Hermeneutics*. Second Edition. Chicago: University of ChicagoPress, 1983.

Eribon, Didier. *Michel Foucault* Trans. Betsy Wing. Cambridge, MA: Harvard University Press, 1991.

Halperin, David. *Saint Foucault: Towards a Gay Hagiography*. New York: Oxford University Press, 1995.

Massumi, Brian. *A User's Guide to Capitalism and Schizophrenia: Deviations from Deleuze and Guattari*. Cambridge, MA: MIT Press, 1992.

Poster, Mark. *Foucault, Marxism, and History: From Mode of Production to Mode of Information*. Cambridge: Polity Press, 1984.

Ulmer, Gregory. *Applied Grammatology: Post(e)-Pedagogy from Jacques Derrida to Joseph Beuys*. Baltimore: Johns Hopkins University Press, 1985.

Chapter 12

Literature and Postmodern Cultural Politics,

ca. 1975 to 2000

Much of the writing produced in the years since the introduction of Poststructuralist theory has in certain ways illustrated some of its themes: continuing experimentation with a decentered authorial presence and point of view, minute attention to the body and its demands, a complicated relationship to history and memory, and increasingly insistent narratives from members of social categories long obscured and marginalized within modern European culture. Yet it remains difficult to generalize about recent European writing in genres from fiction to historical writing to cultural criticism. But lack of ability to offer definitive thematic claims for an increasingly diverse European literary scene in no means negates its vitality.

English Historians and Cultural Studies

Chapter 11 ended at a point where French Althusserian Marxism had run out of steam. Yet French ideas have a way of gaining a second life when exported. If Althusser's star had dimmed in France, it shone brightly across the English Channel. There, during the 1970s, Althusserian Marxism became part of a complicated mix of theoretical ingredients that informed an intellectual and educational movement known as Cultural Studies. It also became a topic of intense interest and sometimes bitter debate among Socialist and Marxist English historians, including E. P. Thompson (1924–1992), Rodney Hilton (1916–), Eric Hobsbawm (1917–), Sheila Rowbotham (1943–), and Christopher Hill (1912–). Cultural Studies as a term derived from the Centre for Cultural Studies at the University of Birmingham, directed by a historian named Stuart Hall (1932–). Hall, a Jamaican immigrant, was a pioneer in the academic study of popular culture, including the products of the mass media and their cultural uses and impact. He later founded Britain's television-based Open University.

In addition to such French imports as Althusser's philosophy and Lacanian psychoanalysis, Hall and his colleagues drew on previous work done in England in the fields of social history and literary criticism. The most important figure whose work they adopted was Raymond Williams (1921–1988), a Welsh literary critic whose many books promoted the broadening of the term "culture" to encompass what he liked to call "the whole way of life," a more or less cultural anthropology position. In his view classics of English literature should be considered along with the popular press, pulp fiction, and, more recently, cinema and television. In later years Williams more openly embraced Marxism, of an especially eclectic variety. His two most important influences from modern Marxism were Gramsci and Althusser.

By the 1980s, Hall was very interested in using Cultural Studies to address themes of class conflict and police abuse of power, both much in evidence during Prime Minister Margaret Thatcher's regime beginning in 1979, visible on the terrain of popular culture. Several studies focused on Brixton, the London neighborhood home to many Jamaican immigrants where police had clashed with residents, and on the xenophobic anti-immigrant politics that appealed to many whites. Dick Hebdige (1951–)—who demonstrated considerable intellectual debts to Barthes and Althusser—and Angela McRobbie (1951–), younger colleagues at the Birmingham Centre, published interesting work on punk rock, Rastafarian culture in England, and gender differences (McRobbie's emphasis) within groups of young music fans.

Historians, while interested in Marxist theory, were quick to seize upon the surprisingly (for a Marxist) ahistorical character of Althusser's ideas, especially in his monolithic use of the term "ideology." E. P. Thompson, a courageous social activist who gained worldwide prominence during the 1980s as the leader of the European Campaign for Nuclear Disarmament (or END), argued emphatically that England had sufficient native radicalism, traceable through medieval peasant revolts (the focus of Hilton's research as well as Hobsbawm's), the radical messianic politics of the English Civil War (as explored by Christopher Hill), the visionary radicalism of Blake and Shelley, and the distinctive socialism of later nineteenth-century figures such as William Morris (topics Thompson explored). Thompson had first asserted his views on this score in his groundbreaking history *The Making of the English Working Class* (1963), a book that influenced an entire generation of labor historians. His 1977 polemical essay "The Poverty of Theory" was an excoriating attack both on Althusser and on the vogue his ideas enjoyed in England.

Along with Barthesian semiology, with its obvious applicability to the study of popular culture (see chapter 9), Lacanian thought was another crucial component of the Cultural Studies influence. In England it merged with feminism and with film criticism, best illustrated by the appearance of a new journal of film theory and criticism called *Screen*. Feminists, especially in England and the United States by this time, were intent on exposing and critiquing what could be called the politics of representation, most obvious in visual imagery, that worked to the detriment of women. Despite Lacan's own apparent hostility to women, feminists both in France and England found in his concept of the "imaginary" a theoretical means of developing their critique of representation.

English and French Feminists
in the 1970s and 1980s

Juliet Mitchell (1940–) and Jacqueline Rose (1949–) were two British feminist theorists who turned Lacanian thought into such a feminist direction. American feminists, by contrast, tended to be much more hostile to psychoanalysis. Probably the single most influential article in *Screen* that applied such a perspective to cinema was "Visual Pleasure and Narrative Cinema," by Laura Mulvey (1941–), an art historian, critic, and filmmaker. It was published in 1975. English feminists put theory into practice, as evidenced by an ongoing campaign during the late 1970s and early 1980s of "talking back" to sexist messages by spray-painting graffiti on billboards and similar advertisements. By no means were all British feminists inclined toward continental theory. Germaine Greer (1939–), an Australian immigrant, remained the best-known feminist author for her book *The Female Eunuch* (1971), which denounced the way patriarchal culture "desexualizes" women by imposing passivity and dependency on them. Elizabeth Wilson (1936–) was a critic whose special domain was popular culture, which she explored in such books as *Hallucinations* (1988) without being dependent on well-known theorists.

French feminism, like its counterparts in England and the United States, emerged from the radical politics of the late 1960s, especially from 1968. The first French feminist groups organized themselves into collectives modeled along the lines of the *comités d'action* of the May uprising. Although they called for reforms and rights as feminists in other countries did, they followed a strongly theoretical direction whose ultimate goal seemed to be the shaping of a mode of thinking and expression that would be inherently both feminine and feminist. Unlike Anglo-American feminist thought, which intellectually gravitated toward searching for "mothers" in the form of important female precursors who could inspire women in the present, French feminist theory defined itself through confronting masculinist thought, including such modern masters as Marx and Freud (although the great importance of the "maternal" influence of Simone de Beauvoir was always acknowledged).

The project of defining feminist politics through confronting the great male theorists continued to receive much more attention than the search for matriarchal lineage. One of the most influential of French feminist groups was Psych et Po, or Psychanalyse et Politique, whose very name showed the overwhelming influence of psychoanalysis—*à la Lacan*—in the years after 1968. Much like Mitchell and Rose in England, feminists in this circle sought to purge psychoanalysis of its misogynist tendencies and maximize the implicit feminism that could be seen in the Lacanian critique of the "phallus" as the imaginary "signifier" par excellence, the marker of male privilege constructed through oedipal castration anxieties and similar hallucinatory exaggerations of biological sex difference. Catherine Clément (1939–) has been an important example of a French feminist who took Lacan seriously and tried to put his ideas to feminist use.

The most profound French feminist philosopher made her name first for her attack on Lacan. This was the Belgian-born Luce Irigaray (1932–), a Parisian psychoanalyst herself, who opened fire on Lacan with a dense, enormously wide-ranging philosophical treatise called *Spéculum de l'autre femme* (1974, *Speculum of the Other Woman*). This work engaged Western patriarchal thought from Plato to Lacan in order to demonstrate that "woman" is always the topic that cannot be faced or addressed, always the "other," to borrow an important Lacanian term. In a move she would repeat in other writings, and one that remained part of her strategy to employ the female body as metaphor, Irigaray arranged her chapters so that the title essay formed the middle of the book. The open book, with its central chapter parted before the reader, thus would imitate the spread legs of a gynecological patient—hence the title Irigaray gave her book—for a speculum is a gynecological instrument for probing the cervix and viewing the interior of the uterus. The most striking (and paradoxical) combination of effects familiar to readers of Irigaray's other books can be seen here: vivid female bodily imagery yet discussion of—argument with—male texts.

Irigaray consolidated and sharpened her argument in a 1977 book called *Ce Sexe qui n'en est pas un* (*This Sex Which Is Not One*). Once again the subject was the inadmissibility for patriarchal thought of the way the world might be viewed from a female perspective. The title, which can be read two ways, suggested the continuing assault on the phallocentric tradition as represented most recently by Jacques Lacan. The French title can read "This sex which is not one," or "This sex of which there is not (only) one." Against the vaunted isolate status of the all-powerful phallus, Irigaray opposed the labia, two halves of the female genitalia in a state of mutual contact. She made this metaphor most explicit in an essay that forms a crucial part of this book called *"Quand nos lèvres se parlent"* ("When Our Lips Speak to Each Other"). Elaborating the metaphor further, she suggested that masculinist thought seeks always to establish singular categories and hierarchical structures that depend on separations and distinctions, whereas feminine/feminist (the two are conflated in her work) thought, modeled on the female anatomy, is always plural and about flowing over boundaries. In a later work called *Amante marine de Friedrich Nietzsche* (1978, *The Marine Lover of Friedrich Nietzsche*), she imagined herself as the female counterpart to Nietzsche, challenging his misogyny (along lines Derrida had suggested). She extended her metaphorical explorations still further, suggesting that masculine meant solid, isolated, fortresslike categories, while "the feminine" was all about liquid, flowing over boundaries, menstrual blood, and breast milk.

Such metaphors figured prominently as well in the work of Hélène Cixous (1937–), a versatile writer (critic, novelist, playwright, essayist) and, like Derrida, of French Algerian Jewish origin. After publishing a major critical work on James Joyce, Cixous began by the early 1970s to write plays with feminist themes, one of which dealt with Freud's famous patient "Dora," the one whose lesbianism he refused to acknowledge. Her most widely publicized contribution to feminist theory was an essay *cum* manifesto called *"Le Rire de la Méduse"* ("The Laugh of the Medusa"). It introduced her most characteristic themes, that women must use their bodily, reproductive experience as women to produce a unique *écriture féminine* ("feminine writing") long overdue for recognition, stylistically and otherwise. She called for a writing with "white ink," that is, breast milk.

Julia Kristeva's writings of the 1970s and 1980s also made use of female reproductive experience to advocate woman-centered, if not feminist (Kristeva expressed qualms about the term) writing. She also dealt with painting, one of her great interests. Several of her essays in art criticism dealt with such classic representations of maternity as the Madonna motif. This kind of emphasis, like the metaphorical use that Irigaray and Cixous both made of the female body, brought charges of "essentialism," or reducing women to their anatomical destiny, both from within and without French feminist circles. A collaborative work of 1975 by Cixous and Catherine Clément, *La Jeune née* (*The Newly Born Woman*), dramatized this debate, Clément especially objecting to imagery that limited women in their social or intellectual roles. For her part, Cixous took up Jacques Derrida's theme of the "phallogocentric" prejudice that ran throughout Western traditions of philosophy and literature.

An additional limitation of the French feminist "poetics," one might say, of the female reproductive system, was that a theory founded thereon could not account for lesbianism. As in the United States and elsewhere, the Gay Rights movement in France was launched in the late 1960s. One of the most important early theorists of the movement, Guy Hocquenghem (1946–1988), was a 1968 veteran. His death from AIDS in 1988, like that of Foucault, another significant figure in the movement, dramatized the urgency of the struggle against homophobic prejudice. French literary history supplied important resources for gay culture in the lives of such important writers as Proust, Gide, Cocteau, Colette, and Genet. Perhaps appropriately, one of the most imaginative and original writers of the 1970s and 1980s was Monique Wittig (1935–), a novelist and lesbian activist. Her novel *Les Guérillières* (1969—the title, not translated in English editions, means roughly "The Female Guerrillas") was based on the idea of a band of amazon warriors, and her subsequent book *Le Corps lesbien* (1973, *The Lesbian Body*) was a stylistic tour de force, pushing language to its limits in order to represent a gender that might be said to go beyond the standard dualism of that category.

Wittig's writing was very much a sign of the times for the last decades of the century, especially in the sense that previously silenced or underheeded groups and constituencies were gaining a hearing in literature, art, media, and academe. For many, whatever their viewpoint, these gains represented a progressive movement in Western culture. But it must also be mentioned that these developments took place simultaneously with the decline of Marxism as both a political and cultural force. For some, the replacement of revolutionary class struggle with so-called identity politics (e.g., feminist, gay, racial minority) was an enfeebling kind of fragmentation of the political Left, the consumer economy being always prepared skillfully to market products to each identity group as just another market cohort.

Marxism, History, and Postmodern Theory

Remaining European Marxist theorists (and their number was dwindling) used various strategies to cope with these developments. In addition to the Cultural Studies approach just discussed, some Continental thinkers sought to synthesize Marxism with related political movements. The early work of Jean Baudrillard (1929–), a French sociologist, was an attempt to use semiology in conjunction with Marxism to produce a "critique of the political economy of the sign," to borrow the title of a book he published in 1972. In Italy, Antonio Negri (1933–), a political scientist at the University of Bologna, wrote a series of books, including *Marx oltre Marx* (1979, *Marx Beyond Marx,*) which drew on a variety of social and cultural theories that were increasingly coming to be called "Postmodern." Negri was also associated with anarchist groups, including the *Brigate Rossi* (Red Brigade), and served a prison sentence on a charge of abetting their terrorism.

One of the most significant political movements of the late 1970s and early 1980s was the ecologically minded "Green" movement. The Greens formulated a critique of capitalism emphasizing environmental degradation and the immorality of putting profits before the health of the population and surrounding environment. Die Grünen were able to elect a number of deputies to the West German Reichstag and, after German unification in 1990, to the new German Reichstag. Rudolf Bahro (1935–) was the most prominent German Marxist theorist with a Green emphasis. In France, André Gorz (1929–), another of Sartre's protégés, formulated similar theories. He also argued, as had Herbert Marcuse some years earlier in the United States, that the concept of the revolutionary working class, or proletariat, had to be set aside in favor of a new coalition of various oppressed groups, including women, gays, and indigenous peoples immediately threatened by environmental crises.

Important debates about the continued theoretical value of Marxist historical materialism took place among European historians. The English polemics provoked by the reception of Althusser were discussed above. France proved to be the European country most inclined to discard Marxist perspectives. The historiography of the French Revolution, especially as France neared the observance of its bicentennial (as a republic) in 1989, showed the greatest retreat from the Marxist paradigm. François Furet (1927–1997) led the attack on earlier historians who had emphasized class conflict in the revolution, arguing instead for an emphasis on "political culture," seeing the revolution as the series of events that ushered in concepts and practices of modern politics.

Despite this, the so-called Annales School, named for the journal *Annales: Économies, Sociétés, Civilisations* founded in 1929 by Lucien Febvre (1878–1956) and Marc Bloch (1886–1944), continued to exert enormous influence. It was clear that the *annaliste* emphasis on enduring social structures viewed over long periods of history depended in part on Marxist perspectives. Like Marx and Engels, historians of this school wished to encompass as much of human historical life as possible in their studies, pioneering especially in demographic studies and even history of climate and the soil itself. Fernand Braudel (1902–1985) was the historian in this tradition who most attempted to understand the emergence of modern capitalist civilization in a comprehensive way, focusing especially on the Mediterranean area.

Georges Duby (1919–1996), a medievalist, concentrated his research on rural life in all its aspects. Emmanuel Le Roy Ladurie (1929–), who assumed a chair at the Collège de France and served for a time as director of the Bibliothèque Nationale, used bizarre episodes in southern France during the Early Modern period to uncover complex layers of social codes and structures of everyday life, a tactic also pursued for a later period by Alain Corbin (1936–), who first worked on the social history of prostitution, then took up the project of a "sensory" history of modern culture, researching the growing modern intolerance for certain smells people had tolerated for centuries or writing about the many kinds of bells that pealed and tolled in the sonic atmosphere of the traditional countryside. And Duby, together with the modern social and feminist historian Michelle Perrot (1928–), edited a five-volume *Histoire de la vie privée* (1985–1987, *History of Private Life*), which attempted a comprehensive survey of daily life in all its intimate aspects from the Middle Ages to the late twentieth century.

It was the abiding accomplishment of the "Annales" school to establish social, economic, and cultural topics as central to the discipline of history, previously the nearly exclusive preserve of political, diplomatic, or military subjects. One of the most gifted of the new social/cultural historians was Carlo Ginzburg (1939–), a professor at the University of Bologna who came eventually to accept a specially created chair at UCLA. Ginzburg's speciality was the peasant culture of northern Italy during the time of the Catholic Counter-Reformation. He was interested in instances of peasants or other subaltern groups defying or speaking defiantly to elite groups and authorities. His earliest studies dealt with the persecution of witchcraft, which he showed to be a misunderstanding of very ancient pagan folk rituals. Ginzburg applied Gramsci's concept of "counterhegemony" to examples of isolated groups that showed through their words (as preserved in mediated fashion through court and Inquisitorial records) or actions that they did not accept the worldview of their social superiors. He was also one of many contemporary cultural investigators influenced by the work of the Soviet sociolinguist Mikhail Bakhtin (1895–1975), whose studies of premodern Europe revealed a "carnivalesque" subordinate culture of irreverence and contempt for social hierarchies.

Armed with these theoretical perspectives as well as borrowing some from Foucault's concept of discourse, Ginzburg produced his most remarkable book in *Il formaggio e i vermi* (1976, *The Cheese and Worms: The Cosmos of a 16th-Century Miller*). Using the thorough records kept by the Inquisition, Ginzburg narrated the story of an eccentric northern Italian miller called Menocchio, the subject of repeated investigations for heresy and the eventual victim of a public burning. What Ginzburg revealed as most interesting about this character was his prodigious reading, unusual for anyone of peasant background, especially in the infant years of printed books. Menocchio had read with interest the forbidden writings of Luther and even a translation of the Qur'an. He did not hesitate to bend the ear of anyone who brought in grain to be milled about the views he derived from these and other readings. Among the opinions he proclaimed loudly was contempt for people in powerful positions, most notable the Church leadership. By showing that historians could find examples of rebelliousness where none might be expected, Ginzburg demonstrated that the topic of social class in the study of the past was far from exhausted.

The topic was increasingly absent from the prevailing philosophical currents and social or cultural theories of the day. The influence of Foucault as a social theorist had left little room for emphasis on class and, by extension, for the application of Marxist theory in general. By the early 1980s, especially in France, much attention was being commanded by theorists who were eager to explore the dazzling new terrain of what they had begun to call "Postmodernism." It was a term that surfaced first in critical discussions of architecture and recent literature, often in the United States. The ongoing work of Deleuze and Guattari, with their emphasis on decentralization and the strategic need to seek multiple social spaces to escape domination, seemed well suited to the new "regionalism" that many associated with Postmodernism.

Postmodern thought was difficult to locate clearly on a political spectrum. Deleuze and Guattari considered themselves leftists, and their work at times seemed complemented by that of philosopher Jean-François Lyotard (1925–1998), the first in Europe to use the term "Postmodern" with any degree of frequency. Anti-Marxist yet vaguely leftist like many French thinkers of his generation, Lyotard emphasized the multiple, often contradictory possibilities afforded by Postmodern culture. An aficionado of avant-garde art, he called for a return to its playful spirit, which could now be pushed further. He advocated strategic use of "gaming," recalling for many the ideas of the Situationists. He summed up his arguments in *La Condition postmoderne* (1979, *The Postmodern Condition*), a book that describes a world where people travel as never before; consume food, fashion, music, and culture from all over; and live with new senses of both time and space. As disorienting as this might be, Lyotard remained optimistic about the emancipatory potential provided by such a "condition."

Other Postmodern thinkers emphasized technology, as Deleuze and Guattari did to a great extent in their 1980 work *Mille plateaux* (*A Thousand Plateaus: Capitalism and Schizophrenia*). There they were indebted to a French philosopher named Paul Virilio (1932–), who was preoccupied with the social role of technology, including especially military technology. Virilio argued that advanced technology leads quite literally of a speeding up of life, with profound social consequences and potential for totalitarian political uses. His most significant book on this subject was *La Vitesse et la politique* (1977, *Speed and Politics*).

By far the most influential of French thinkers who were consciously Postmodernist was Jean Baudrillard. After an initial attempt to apply Marxism to semiology in order to analyze the social role of advertising and other media phenomena, Baudrillard gradually moved away from Marxism and into ideas as well as a style of writing that showed the pervasive influence of Nietzschean thought. In 1973 he mounted a strong critique of Marx's political economy in *Le Miroir de la production* (*The Mirror of Production*), and went on to write a series of books arguing that social class and any sense of "the masses" was becoming increasingly irrelevant due to the growing hypnotic power of the media-instilled society of "spectacle." Here he went beyond even Debord's earlier critique, arguing that "the real" was disappearing in the face of the simulated reality of a world of screens displaying ever more intimate aspects of what used to be called "life."

His tone became increasingly shrill and apocalyptic about this through *A l'ombre des majorités silencieuses* (1978, *In the Shadow of the Silent Majorities*), *De la séduction* (1979, *Of Seduction*), and a series of books during the 1980s and 1990s based on his travels in the United States, which he argued was most advanced on the path toward "hyper-reality," that is, a world in which Disney realities have replaced what used to pass for social reality. Baudrillard even went so far as to argue in

1991—in *La Guerre du Golfe n'a pas eu lieu* (*The Gulf War Did Not Take Place*), borrowing from Giraudoux's famous title—that the Persian Gulf War was an ultimate example of his point about the "hyperreal," as if it were a war existing only on video display terminals. Whether there were actual casualties seemed beside the point, he appeared to argue.

From Germany, from the leading Marxist philosopher who was heir to the Frankfurt School tradition (Adorno had been his mentor), came a withering critique of French Postmodern thought, especially of the ideas of Foucault and Lyotard. The source was Jürgen Habermas (1929–), a prolific and difficult critical theorist whose books brought about a kind of intellectual synthesis based on Kant, Marx, Freud, and linguistic theory and whose political theory was unabashedly utopian and democratic. Habermas, in an argument echoed by other Marxist theorists, charged that the Postmodernists were "neo-conservatives," like the former political progressives who now championed the politics of Thatcher or Reagan, that ultimately they were apologists for a stage of late capitalism that benefited tremendously from fancy theories that explained away the need for class or for clearly stated political theories and programmes.

Habermas was particularly alarmed by the gleeful neo-Nietzschean contempt for rational thought that seemed to run throughout contemporary French theory. Certainly for him the Nietzschean-Heidegerrean tradition was tainted by association with the Third Reich. More important for his argument, however, was the assertion that reason and Enlightenment still spoke to today's needs, that one only had to look at the fascist era to see what came of abandoning those principles. The stance Habermas took was based on his particular social vision, summed up by the concept of "Ideal Speech." In a just society, he asserted, communication is free and unconstrained among people who hold no power over each other. It was in this direction that modern Western political society had been moving beginning with the Enlightenment.

The Enlightenment culture of newspapers, books, and coffee shops has created the "public sphere" that progressive societies should do everything to nurture. Habermas explored this particular aspect of his theory at length in *Strukturwandel der Öffentlichkeit* (1962/1976, *Structural Transformation of the Public Sphere*). There he argued that Postmodern theories (including Poststructuralist linguistic critiques) that either celebrate or seek to rationalize the communicative instabilities and disruptions of this public sphere are thus hostile to the emancipatory potential still to be gained from the Enlightenment impulses that flourish in the public sphere. And now, he charged, just when new, previously excluded groups are able to be heard within the public sphere, theories that cast doubt on the clarity of discourse or the possibility of democratic intervention into a kind of public space still intelligible to the rational mind are profoundly undemocratic and threatening.

The Novel, History, and Memory

European writers of the last quarter or so of the twentieth century wrestled with many of the same themes found in philosophy and cultural criticism: gender roles, the loneliness and disorientation of late twentieth-century life, and the challenges to human beings posed by new technologies. At the same time, older concerns continued to haunt their pages. The Holocaust, for one, was a topic that demanded to be addressed. An unlikely Italian writer named Primo Levi (1919–1987) did so most powerfully in books that carried even more impact for the calm, matter-of-fact tone he adopted. Levi was a chemist who joined the Italian partisans against the occupying Nazi forces in 1943. Captured, he admitted to being a Jew (having heard that captured partisans were summarily executed) and was sent to Auschwitz. He chronicled his experiences in several memoirs, the first of them published in 1958. Its title was *Se questo è un uomo* (*If This Be a Man*), and it was later published in English as *Survival in Auschwitz: The Nazi Assault on Humanity.* The success of that book especially brought him international acclaim by the 1980s, when he published the last of his memoirs as *I sommersi e i salvati* (1986, *The Drowned and the Saved*). In 1987 Levi was killed when he fell from over a banister on the top floor of his apartment building in Turin. The death was ruled a suicide, and many speculated that his memories of Auschwitz provoked this end. But doubts have persisted about the ruling and some suspect murder. Others have pointed out that he suffered dizzy spells from a medication he was taking at the time.

The so-called Neo-Realist movement just after World War II had included a number of women writers whose books muted the topic of fascism and the war years. One of these, Elsa Morante (1912–1985), finally turned to these topics in her 1974 novel *La Storia* (*History: A Novel*). She resented those critics who began every review by discussing her gender, saying she wanted to be regarded as simply a writer, not a "woman writer." But there were other Italian writers of the 1970s whose main purpose in writing was to bear witness to women's lives. The label "documentary fiction" was applied to this genre. Dacia Maraini's (1936–) *Memorie di una ladra* (1972, *Memories of a Female Thief*), the story of a very picaresque thief based on research in women's prisons was an example.

The most famously politically minded Italian writer of the last part of the century was Dario Fo (1926–), winner of the 1997 Nobel Prize for Literature. Primarily a playwright (and actor and mime), Fo was a radical anarchist who delighted in clowning, spoofs, and "agitprop" theater. He founded an acting company in 1968 called Nuova Scena, which had ties to the Communist Party. Earlier in the decade he began to contribute comedy sketches to a popular variety show on Italian television called *Canzonissima* (which might be translated as "Really Big Song"). During the period Fo was associated with it, *Canzonissima* often ran afoul of the censors. He often collaborated with his wife, with whom he wrote some of his plays. Among his best-known plays are *Morte accidentale di un anarchico* (1974, *Accidental Death of an Anarchist*) and *Il papa e la strega* (1989, *The Pope and the Witch*). Frequently his themes drew threats of censorship. The awarding of the prize drew loud cries of protest on the political Right.

Other Italian writers produced books of fantasy, in the case of Italo Calvino (1923–1985), or complicated brain-teasing historical novels, in the case of the best-selling author (as well as prominent semiologist) Umberto Eco (1932–). Calvino's fiction, which some compared to the "magic realist" novels of contemporary Latin America, displayed a fascination with the art of storytelling and with fragmented, puzzling narratives, as in *Se una notte d'inverno un viaggiatore* (1979, *If, On a Winter's Night, A Traveler*). In such lengthy, complex novels as *Il Nomme della rosa* (1981, *The Name of the Rose*) and *Pendolo di Foucault* (1988 *Foucault's Pendulum*), Eco achieved readable, mind-twisting narratives by combining linguistic theory, medieval history and philosophy, and a good detective writer's sense of intrigue and suspense.

One of the most important writers in France during these years was Marguerite Duras (1914–1996), a versatile talent as a novelist, playwright, screenwriter, and film director. She was born in Indochina (now Vietnam), and the Southeast Asian setting figures prominently in her work. Much of her writing is autobiographical, having to do with her origins in a privileged French colonial family. She was a member of the Communist Party for a number of years and engaged in dialogue with many prominent French intellectuals, including Sartre. Her most acclaimed screenwriting was for the Resnais film *Hiroshima mon amour,* and her own film *L'amant* (1992, *The Lover*) was based on her Goncourt Prize–winning 1984 novel. It was the somewhat autobiographical story of a love affair between a teenage French girl and a Chinese man. *Le Ravissement de Lol V. Stein* (1964, *The Ravishing of Lol Stein*) was another of her most significant novels. Duras's work was marked by its combination of themes of sexual awakening and political engagement.

The French novelist J. M. G. Le Clézio (1940–) is another contemporary author who has ranged widely, and in fact far from Europe, in his fiction. Ancient Aztec culture holds a particular fascination for him, and he has written scholarly studies on this topic. His novels, such as *Desert* (1980), explore dreamlike states and express a longing for a way of life free of European cultural baggage. Fantastic literature or "magic realism" does not always turn up where it might be expected. Even though South American writers have been known for this style (which is not necessarily a retreat from political topics, more often a way around censorship), Spanish and Portuguese writers, even though faced with considerable burdens of history especially before the end of the Franco and Salazar dictatorships in the mid-1970s, have more often looked to European Modernism for their inspiration.

The Spanish Nobel Prize–winning (1989) author Camilo José Cela (1916–) created a style that bore comparison in some aspects to that of Kafka. Cela is a rare example of an admired Spanish writer who fought on Franco's side in the Civil War. He was best known for his earliest works *La Familia de Pascual Duarte* (1942, *The Family of Pascual Duarte*) and *La Colmena* (1951, *The Hive*), texts of dark, troubling intensity. Later important novels include *Mazurca para dos muertos* (1983, *Mazurka for Two Dead Men*), based on his civil war experiences, and *Cristo versus Arizona* (1988, *Christ versus Arizona*). He was also known for his colorful travelogues. The novels of José Saramago (1922–), the first Portuguese writer ever to win the Nobel Prize (1998), feature constant interplay with historical realities and imagination, with great attention to the seemingly autonomous realm of language. One of his most important books in this regard is *Memorial do convento* (1982, *Balthasar and Blimunda*), set in Lisbon at the time of the late-eighteenth-century Inquisition. Portuguese history is also creatively reimagined in *O ano da morte de Ricardo Reis* (1984, *The Year of the Death of Ricardo Reis*).

Meanwhile, the dramatic changes in Central and Eastern Europe after 1989 have preoccupied writers there and elsewhere. Christa Wolf (1929–) is one example of an East German author who, after unification, continues to address important political and cultural topics, especially dealing with the role of women. Her *Kassandra* (1983, *Cassandra*) critiques nuclear weaponry in relation to patriarchal culture, while *Was bleibt: Erzählung* (1990, *What Remains*) confronts the subject of East German state-sponsored police brutality.

Several women have been among the most prominent recent English authors. One of the most acclaimed was Iris Murdoch (1919–1999), known for a highly intellectual style featuring characters tormented by the clash between intellect and life's messiness. Her best-known novel remained *A Severed Head* (1961), but she produced important novels in later years, including *The Sea, the Sea* (1978) and *The Good Apprentice* (1986). An equally cerebral approach to fiction can be found in the novels and novellas of Antonia S. Byatt (1936–), especially *Possession* (1990) and *Angels and Insects: Two Novellas* (1994). The former resembles Eco's fiction with its attention to literary theory, although Byatt adds the crucial category of gender. Byatt's vast knowledge of literature was apparent in the critical essays and reviews she contributed frequently to publications in Britain and abroad.

Another novelist who shared Byatt's penchant for scholarship but who tilted more often than Byatt toward works of criticism was Anita Brookner (1928–). Brookner's area of scholarly expertise was art history, and she became a well published authority on eighteenth-century French painting. Her novels are psychologically subtle stories presented through the narrative viewpoint of intelligent, detached mature women, often dryly observing the foibles and eccentricities of those around them. Remaining aloof from male companionship, they occupy a position similar to that of the narrator in Jane Austen's novels. Brookner's most successful achievement in fiction was *Hotel du Lac* (1984), which received the distinguished Booker Prize. This book's protagonist is an English writer vacationing at a Swiss resort hotel whose gentility is beginning to fade a bit. Reluctantly, but gradually, she begins to be drawn into the lives of her somewhat mysterious, occasionally unpleasant fellow guests. Other novels of Brookner's include *Providence* (1982), *Brief Lives* (1990), *Visitors* (1997), and *Undue Influence* (1999).

Eva Figes (1932–), born Eva Unger, is a highly lyrical, subtle English stylist of fiction and critical essays whose family emigrated from Germany when she was an infant. Her books often emphasize the experiences that mark the stages of women's lives, especially true of her 1981 novel *Waking* as well as *The Seven Ages* (1986). Her powerfully concentrated tale *Light* (1983) is a fictional account of a day in the life (late in his life) of Claude Monet at his home at Giverny. The description of the elderly painter gathering his supplies to go out in his boat to catch the water lilies at first light weaves around the story of an important family dinner being planned, one at which an engagement of marriage will be announced.

Angela Carter (1940–1993) was a prolific novelist whose feminism combined improbably with the "forbidden" tradition of European writing that passes from Sade through Lautréamont (after a detour through Poe) to Bataille. This legacy can be seen in her books *The Infernal Desire Machines of Doctor Hoffman* (1972), *The Bloody Chamber*

(1978), and *Nights at the Circus* (1984). She was also the author of *The Sadean Woman,* a work of criticism that is as well a feminist defense of pornography.

The body and its desires as a lesbian experiences them are at the center of the novels of Jeanette Winterson (1959–), far and away the most stylistically imaginative of contemporary English authors. Her autobiographical first novel *Oranges Are Not the Only Fruit* (1985) was followed by *The Passion* (1987) and *Sexing the Cherry* (1991), books that made wildly imaginative use of history, including the mid-seventeenth-century period of the English civil war (in *Sexing the Cherry*). *Written on the Body* (1994) is her most sustained exercise in an exploration of style that can convey the lesbian experience in ways that defy usual description and categorization. It bears comparison to Wittig's *Lesbian Body.* Winterson continued to explore the theme of lesbian relationships in *Gut Symmetries* (1997). In *The World and Other Places* (1998), she began to explore themes of myth and spirituality, while her next novel, *The Power-Book* (2000), addressed the cyberworld of internet communication.

London life is the subject of books by Martin Amis (1949–), son of novelist Kingsley Amis. Examples include *London Fields* (1989) and *Success* (1991). That same year he departed from his usual theme with *Time's Arrow: The Nature of the Offense,* a dizzying stylistic challenge in which the Holocaust is remembered and then reexperienced through a process of reverse time travel. The book was controversial, as some felt it trivialized the events, while others argued that the reversal of time, with victims restored to life, intensified the shock of what happened. Julian Barnes (1946–) is another contemporary English novelist (and also a television commentator), obviously influenced by Continental traditions of Modernism, as in his second novel *Flaubert's Parrot* (1985). The tongue-in-cheek title of *A History of the World in 10 1/2 Chapters* (1989) is an indicator of its satirical style. Later books, such as *Before She Met Me* (1992) and *England, England* (1999), provide witty contemplation of the pretensions and despairs of Londoners watching the century wind down. William Boyd (1952–), who, like Barnes, is a best-selling author in translation throughout Europe, brings to contemporary English fiction the perspective of someone born to an English family living abroad, Ghana in his case. His novel *Brazzaville Beach* (1990) is set memorably in the Congo, while *Armadillo* (1998) is a witty examination of nouveau-riche London dwellers. Boyd is also the author of several screenplays.

As philosophers, with rare exceptions, retreated increasingly into topics remote from most people's concerns, the best novelists of the age often played the role formerly handled by philosophers, that is, raising and debating crucial questions of morality, ethics, and purpose in a world of daunting complexity.

At this point it would make sense to turn to visual artists and film-makers, for after all visual experience has figured at the center of Post-modern cultural concerns. But before taking up this theme in a final chapter dealing with additional aspects of new European culture, we will turn now to an entire chapter on photography and its enormous role in the shaping of modern culture.

Suggestions for Further Reading

Arac, Jonathan, ed. *Postmodernism and Politics.* Minneapolis: University of Minnesota Press, 1986.

Berman, Russell A. *Cultural Studies of Modern Germany: History, Representation, and Nationhood.* Madison: University of Wisconsin Press, 1993.

Burns, Rob, ed. *German Cultural Studies: An Introduction.* New York: Oxford University Press, 1995.

Dennis Dworkin, *Cultural Marxism in Postwar Britain: History, The New Left, and the Origins of Cultural Studies.* Durham, N.C.: Duke University Press, 1997.

Forgacs, David, and Robert Lumley, eds. *Italian Cultural Studies: An Introduction.* New York: Oxford University Press, 1996.

Foster, Hal, ed. *The Anti-Aesthetic: Essays on Postmodern Culture.* Port Townsend, WA: Bay Press, 1983.

Grossberg, Lawrence et al. eds. *Cultural Studies.* New York: Routledge, 1992.

Hutcheon, Linda. *A Poetics of Postmodernism: History, Theory, Fiction.* New York: Routledge, 1988.

Jay, Martin. *Marxism and Totality: The Adventures of a Concept from Lukács to Habermas.* Berkeley: University of California Press, 1984.

McCarthy, Thomas. *The Critical Theory of Jürgen Habermas.* Cambridge, MA: MIT Press, 1981.

Moi, Toril. *Sexual/Textual Politics: French Feminist Theory.* London: Methuen, 1985.

Chapter 13

Photography and the Culture of Modernity

We are so thoroughly accustomed to photographs that we probably have an even harder time imagining a world without them than we do one devoid of automobiles or telephones. If we think about their significance at all, perhaps it is merely to reflect that the technology of photography afforded human beings the ability to capture little slivers of reality a bit at a time and thus leave behind a record of existence more rapidly and more reliably (we assume) than that within the capability of even the most skilled painter. What we consider less often, or less automatically, is how photography has shaped the reality of our world, the way we see it, what we have come to expect of it. Aspects of photography's use in recent times have become so familiar that we have become cynical and dismissive of them. We joke about politicians scheduling "photo opportunities," or we have a laugh at the tourists in the Louvre snapping photos of the *Mona Lisa* behind the painting's thick Plexiglas barrier. We know those snapshots will look even worse than the cheapest postcard reproduction.

This chapter explores not only important photographers of the Modern age in Europe but also attempts to examine the role photographed images have played in modern European culture. The uses of photography have been multiple, and the more types and genres of photography have proliferated, the more varied have been the kinds of things we can say about their intervention in cultural life. For photography has not only held a mirror up to fleeting glimpses of reality, its dramatic presence—its witness—has shaped cultural reality to a profound extent. The result is that photographed images have played roles that are documentary, evidential, available for advertising come-ons, titillating, propagandistic, and more.

Early Photography

Long before the first cameras were invented, as early as the fifteenth century, painters experimented with the camera obscura, an apparatus that projected objects or scenes being viewed onto a flat surface where they could be traced or in other ways used to teach perspective. In the early 1820s a Frenchman named Joseph Nicéphore Niépce (1768–1833) succeeded in using the camera obscura principle to capture images on treated metal plates. He needed eight hours of exposure to do this with his first "photographs" of a set table and a view through a window. Influenced by Niépce, an inventor named Louis-Jacques Mandé Daguerre (1787–1851) came up with a process (first advertised in 1839) based on principles of optics and chemistry that, through long exposure, created a mirror-reversed image etched into silver-coated copper. These monochromatic pictures, using the inventor's name, were known as daguerréotypes. Only one image at a time could be created, but the fact that the image could be capture in less than thirty seconds made it a convenient procedure for portraits.

Then, in 1844, an Englishman named William Henry Fox Talbot (1800–1877) invented the photo negative process that made multiple reproductions from a single print possible and thus became the basis for modern photography. He titled his first group of photographs using the new method *The Pencil of Nature*. One of the most famous images showed several shelves containing china. Due to the great popularity of the daguerréotypes, however, at first Talbot's method did not take hold. For one thing the image was less precise than that of a daguerréotype (although the negative process meant photographs could be reproduced as book illustrations, for example). Thus it would not be until the 1850s that photographers began using the process in earnest. The earliest forms of photography filled the need for popular diversion, as was the case with stereoscopic images, dual images that composed one single image in three dimensions when viewed through a special stereoscopic device. The technology was invented by Charles Wheatstone (1802–1875) in 1838. Often lighthearted scenes of everyday life or travel themes proved especially popular with stereoscope users.

The single most immediate use for the first photographs was portraiture. It was important especially for families to have some document of how loved ones appeared, even if stiffly posed for the camera. In an era of low life expectancy, a photograph of a family member too soon departed might provide a small measure of consolation, and almost immediately portraits of deceased infants and children laid out in their coffins became common. Some of the earliest photographers of note were accomplished portrait photographers, such as Alexander Gardner (1821–1896) in the United States, whose works include the haunting portrait of Abraham Lincoln—late in his life—and also a series of portraits of the Lincoln assassination conspirators. In France, Gaspard-Félix Tornachon (1820–1910), known as Nadar, established himself as a sought-after photographer especially of notable people of the day, from writers like George Sand and Victor Hugo, to the composer Giaccomo Rossini, to the aged French chemist Eugène Chevreul, photographed alone and seated with Nadar on the occasion in 1887 of Chevreul's 101st birthday. (He lived to be 103.) In all there were twenty-one photographs of Chevreul, each with captions containing questions Nadar asked with the scientist's responses. It was the world's first photo interview. Nadar also created a sensation in 1870 when he went aloft in an observation balloon from besieged Paris (during the Franco-Prussian War) to take the first-ever aerial photographs.

But photographic portraits were not only for society's notables. Many citizens who could afford to engaged photographers to create small photographic *cartes de visite,* which were printed out in sheets containing multiple exposures, much like later versions of contact prints. And photographers themselves were motivated, like painters before them, to capture the likenesses of people around them whom they found attractive or interesting. Two photographers of Victorian England provide well-known examples. One of the greatest photographers of the nineteenth century was Julia Margaret Cameron (1815–1879), a patrician Englishwoman who took up photography as a pleasant hobby, but became quite consumed by it. She photographed notable contemporaries such as Charles Darwin and the astronomer Sir John Herschel (1792–1871), who, as it happens, originated the term "photography," that is, "writing with light." He was a friend of Talbot's.

But Cameron was best known for her fanciful, highly idealized photographs of young girls, posed sometimes as angels, complete with wings. The photographer used deliberately blurred focus to enhance the ethereal quality of these pictures. The English mathematician and parson Charles Dodgson (1832–1898), better known under his pseudonym Lewis Carroll, similarly made use of young girls in his photographs, including Alice Liddell, the "Alice" of his books *Alice's Adventures in Wonderland* (1865) and *Through the Looking-Glass* (1871). (See figure 13.1.) In the cases of both Cameron and Dodgson, the complexities of Victorian morality are on display. Even more important, the power of these distinctive images no doubt helped to shape and define what we call the "Victorian" sensibility. On one hand, the pictures appear to celebrate the almost desperate belief in childhood innocence (angel wings being a none-too-subtle means to this end). On the other hand, the use of the young models' nudity or seminudity eroticizes the content in ways that jolt a contemporary viewer but that Victorians might not have considered troubling or particularly remarkable.

Stiffly posed portraits and highly sentimentalized images may strike today's viewer as quaint, but examples of humor as well as such extremely transgressive uses of photography as explicit pornography emerged quite early in its history. One of the most famous early instances of at least mildly provocative sexual expression in photography featured the Comtesse de Castiglione. Born Virginie Oldoini (1837–1899), she was a great Italian beauty of the mid-nineteenth century with a reputation for amorous adventure and a penchant for having herself photographed. She married a French count and moved to France in 1861, where she embarked on her most famous affair with Emperor Napoleon III, right in the Tuileries Palace, and with the knowledge of a most unhappy Empress Eugénie. Her cousin, Count Cavour, had encouraged this *amour,* believing it to be of diplomatic advantage.

The countess often posed in states of partial undress and was particularly keen on having her bare feet photographed, a throwback in some ways to the daring Madame Récamier, the subject of a controversial painting by Jacques-Louis David. With a Paris photographer named Pierre-Louis Pierson, the countess collaborated in setting up more than 400 "self" portraits. Together they tried things that shattered the conventions of portraiture, photographic or otherwise. The countess would often be positioned at odd angles toward the camera, and in one striking photograph taken around 1860 she peers through an empty oval frame in semiprofile. Her hair is arranged loosely, and her shawl droops down to reveal a bare shoulder, while most of her bare arm is exposed to the viewer as she holds the frame to her face. The overall effect is playful, sexual, self-mocking, and irreverent.

It was as if the countess anticipated by well more than a century contemporary debates about pornography and whether a woman can challenge its conventions from within, so to speak—while participating in it. Indeed, pornography was one of the very earliest uses of photography, even in the heyday of stereoscopy. Photographers in major cities such as London found it easy enough to pay prostitutes and a variety of other marginal social characters to perform for their cameras.

Figure 13.1   Charles L Dodgson "Edith, Lorina, and Alice Liddell." 1859 Courtesy of the Gernsheim Collection, University of Texas at Austin.

Photography's Uses:
From Criminology to Photojournalism

The other use for photography that emerged just as early was criminological. The Parisian police expert Alphonse Bertillon (1832–1898) was a profound believer in the value of the camera for compiling a record of the facial features and other characteristics of criminals. Drawing on the popular nineteenth-century pseudosciences of phrenology (which studied the surface features of skulls), craniometry, and anthropometry, where skulls were measured and their general proportions compared and contrasted, Bertillon supervised the accumulation of an exhaustive record of ears, eyes, noses, and mouths of criminals, most of which would later be rendered obsolete by the introduction of fingerprinting. Assumptions of the importance of skull measurements also determined the kinds of photographs Charles Marie Debierre took in 1895, showing multiple views (frontal, in profile, etc.) of the severed heads of guillotine victims.

Bertillon believed that his kind of empirical evidence could not but lead to general patterns and typologies that would enable criminal investigators to find suspects much more quickly, even to prevent crime in the first place.

Bertillon's confidence in the ability of photography to produce such a valuable archive of evidence bespoke a naive faith in the power of technology, as well as an underestimation of the human agency involved in selecting a pose, the moment to make the exposure, and so forth. In England the eugenicist Sir Francis Galton (1822–1911) undertook a similarly exhaustive task of using the camera to record human physiognomies, but in his case the purpose was to further a racialist kind of taxonomy. (See chapter 4.) Galton's method was the composite photograph, constructed through multiple superimpositions to achieve a generic stereotype of each subcategory of humanity he deemed worthy of separate classification. In a move that prefigured the racist theories of the Nazis, he documented "Jewish types," emphasizing head shape, noses, ears, brows, and the like. Galton even mapped regions of the British Isles according to physiognomy, producing composites for the West Country, Midlands, North, Scotland, Wales, and Ireland. Not surprisingly, Londoners stood at the top of his hierarchy and the Irish at the bottom.

The second half of the nineteenth century also saw the first uses of photography to document military campaigns and to play the role that would later be associated with photojournalism. The military use of photography began in Europe as early as the Crimean War (1853–1856), with the photographs of a British journalist named Roger Fenton (1819–1869). He photographed soldiers taking their ease after a day of battle, as well as the landscape of the famous "valley of the shadow of death" at Balaclava. And a decade later the American photographer Matthew Brady (1823–1896) became world renowned for his work on the Civil War, from formal portraits of notable generals (the above-mentioned Alexander Gardner began his career as Brady's assistant for portrait photography) to somber battlefield scenes with stiffened, bloated corpses crowding the foreground (as in his famous photographs of the dead at Gettysburg). The power of images like these for the public had to so not only with morbid curiosity but with the sense they conveyed of authenticity, "this is what it was like." Therefore, it was with some degree of disillusionment that historians later learned that Brady had positioned corpses to suit his artistic purposes in the composition of his photographs.

Some of the most dramatic European photographs of military fortifications and the ensuing carnage of warfare came from the bloody events of the Paris Commune in 1871. Communards recorded such symbolic events as the toppling of the Napoleonic Vendôme column and, as Versailles troops marched on Paris, posed heroically standing at

Figure 13.2   Anonymous, Dead Communards in their coffins. (Supplied by the Gernsheim Collection.)

artillery batteries ready to defend the city. Then, with the defeat of the Commune after a bloody week of fighting, the victorious Republican forces of Versailles produced their own propagandistic documentation, most famously with a picture taken by an anonymous photographer of slain communards in their coffins. (See figure 13.2.) Meant to advertise the fate that awaits those who would rise up against the legitimate government, the effect of the haunting photograph may serve instead to win more sympathy for the communards.

It was one thing to be able to photograph corpses, but photojournalists longed for the ability to record movement; action. This was soon to come, for in the very year of the Commune an Englishman named Richard Maddox (1816–1902) began to coat photographic plates with an emulsion of gelatin, which resulted in a much faster exposure time—a fraction of a second—to record an image. This, along with the invention of the Kodak box camera in 1888 by George Eastman (1854–1932) of Rochester, New York, made photographing far less cumbersome. The way was paved for action photography, and far more people could begin to practice photography as a leisure activity. Eastman's other great innovation was flexible film. And although the English physicist James Clerk

Maxwell (1831–1879) demonstrated as early as 1877 the possibility of projecting color images, it would be some decades before color film was available. (First on the market was Kodak Kodachrome in 1935.) Many late nineteenth-century photographers hand-painted black-and-white photographs to transform them into color.

Photography as Art

By the late nineteenth century, the relationship between photography and painting was beginning to become complicated. Some still condemned the upstart activity of photography as something banal, and they dismissed the skill or aesthetic judgment that might be involved. Some painters (including Impressionists, one of whose exhibitions was held in Nadar's gallery in 1874) began to use photography the way they might use preliminary sketches, simply to produce studies that would result eventually in the real work on canvas. But what if photography could aspire to being another of the fine arts, neither beholden to painting nor in need of being judged according to similar aesthetic criteria? In the nineteenth century there were only a few isolated examples of photographers using the camera and the print-making process in ways that experimented with abstraction or began to move beyond the merely representational mode. One was the American photographer Gertrude Käsebier (1852–1934), whose pictures of women and children in domestic settings were deliberately distorted and blurry in the extreme, the result being that one of her photographs was as instantly recognizable as a Käsebier, the way lines, colors, or telltale brush strokes provide the "signature" for a modern painting.

By the early twentieth century, startling new approaches to photography began with experimenters who rejected the strictly representational role of their métier and sought to establish photography as an art in its own right. Most of the avant-garde circles of the early decades of the century included photographers. The Italian Futurists embraced photography as they did all new technology, and Gertrude Käsebier and Alfred Stieglitz (1864–1946) founded a group called Photo-Secession in 1902 whose goal was to promote photography as an art form. They were joined in this effort by Edward Steichen (1879–1973), a photographer born in Luxembourg who move to the United States in 1882. His twilit mist-shrouded photograph of New York's Flatiron Building in 1905 could serve both as an example of Futurist worship of technology (i.e., the skyscraper) and the aesthetic claims he and Stieglitz advanced for photography. Stieglitz associated closely with painters all his life, marrying Georgia O'Keeffe in 1924, and at the time of World War I was active in New York Dada circles with such artists as Marcel Duchamp and Man Ray.

In New York and later in the 1920s in Paris, Man Ray experimented with a kind of "pure" photography that at times completely abandoned representationalism. He accidentally left some keys and some other small objects on a piece of photographic paper that then became exposed to light. The result was an arrangement of ghostly images outlining the objects placed on the paper's surface. Ray immediately set about making a series of these works which he called "Rayograms." He and other Dadaists saw this as happily in keeping with the "laws of chance" they hoped would govern the creation of their "anti-" art objects. The Hungarian photographer Laszlo Moholy-Nagy (1895–1946), a leader of the "Constructivist" movement in art and architecture and a professor at the Bauhaus in Germany from 1923 to 1928, likewise produced photographs that bypassed the use of negatives. He called his works "photograms." Man Ray's experiments were not limited to the Rayograms. In his Surrealist phase of the later 1920s and 1930s, he often took photographs that he would alter in some bizarre way, as in his *Le Violon d'Ingres.* For this picture, he posed the famous model "Kiki" of Montparnasse with bare back, wearing a turban and in every way reminiscent of the dominant figure in the exotic *Bain turc* of the nineteenth-century painter Ingres. In the preparation of the final photograph, Ray cut the outlines of the elegantly curved sounding holes of a violin, hence the title.

German Dadaists applied collage techniques to photographs, thus producing photomontages. Hannah Höch (1889–1978) was one of the most prolific, and she would continue to produce photomontages long after most Dada artists had abandoned them. Raoul Hausmann (1886–1978) was another Berlin Dadaist—by way of Cologne—who used this technique, although he often incorporated fragments of photos into assemblages of other more typical kinds of collage material. Photomontage lent itself to pointed commentary of contemporary German politics, and no artist was more inflammatory in this regard than John Heartfield, né Helmut Herzfelde. German militarism and the emergent Nazi movement were the favored targets of his coruscating satire.

Heartfield worked in relative isolation and was part of no artistic movement, but one of the most important proponents of photography as an autonomous art was Eugène Atget (1857–1927), who primarily photographed scenes and aspects of life in Paris, including neighborhood characters such as prostitutes. One of his "signature" styles was in his photographs of shop windows reflecting the streets outside. The most famous example of this motif is his 1925 photograph *Avenue des Gobelins.* The window simultaneously displays merchandise, specifically children's hats and clothing, and reflects the exterior, including buildings across the street. It may also provide commentary on consumer society, where advertised commodities begin to crowd out the rest of the urban surroundings.

Atget was unknown to most of his contemporaries until his "discovery" by Berenice Abbott (1898–1991), an American photographer in Paris who had worked as Man Ray's darkroom assistant. In her long career working primarily in Paris, she befriended many writers and artists and became best known for her sensitive photographic portraits of them. Her 1928 portrait of James Joyce became one of her most famous works. Other photographers preferred to record more anonymous human subjects. In Cologne the German photographer August Sander (1876–1964) set out to document the social classes and various occupations of his country. Sander's subjects were posed rather formally and with great dignity, all the more powerful for the humble circumstances of many of them. Some of his most striking subjects were a well-to-do gentleman posed with his rail-thin Weimaraner dog, a laborer bearing a hod of bricks fitted about his neck and shoulders, and a sturdy baker in his white smock holding a large bowl and mixing spoon. Nazi cultural policy condemned Sander's work, perhaps for its implicit class consciousness but certainly for the failure of his subjects to conform to their notions of racial purity.

Twentieth-century art photography was a transatlantic phenomenon, with several important photographers spending phases of their careers on both sides of the ocean, a practice well under way even before Hitler caused the large exodus of European artists able to escape to the United States. For the early twentieth century, Paris surely must have been one of the most thoroughly photographed cities, although at first only some milieus were featured. Jacques-Henri Lartigue (1894–1986) became well known for his camera's attention to the haut monde world of the privileged class, as in his famous picture of a sumptuously dressed lady walking her dog in *Avenue du Bois de Boulogne* (1911). He was almost a photographic equivalent of Proust, documenting a social world that would recede from view after 1914.

During the interwar period, Paris continued to be the base of many of the most ingenious and original photographers. One of the most influential was the Hungarian-born André Kertész (1894–1985), who settled in Paris in 1925. He made deliberate use of distortion and bizarre camera angles, which he practiced with a variety of genres. One can witness these strange effects in *Danseuse satirique* (1926, "Satiric Dancer"), in which a woman dressed as the quintessential 1920s' "flapper" viewed from above lies in a contorted position on a sofa in the corner of a room. At the end of the sofa near her feet a small stand holds a dramatic sculpture of a male torso, and a small framed female nude hangs on the wall above her head. Kertész applied his vertiginous distorted perspective to exterior shots, as in his *Carrefour, Blois* (1930, "Blois Crossroads"), where the photographer, from several stories above, has captured a scene of cyclists and a horse-drawn cart turning a corner.

Kertész began to explore new directions after acquiring his first Leica camera in 1928. Introduced in Germany in 1924, the Leica, which used 35 millimeter film, was a great technological advance allowing spur-of-the-moment candid photography, since it could fit easily in a pocket. Kertész now began to concentrate on scenes of everyday life, schoolchildren, old men browsing in bookstores, people going about daily routines, "capturing" them in fortuitous split-second poses. This would become the approach of a whole generation of Paris photographers, and certainly those elsewhere. In 1936 Kertész emigrated to the United States, becoming a U.S. citizen in 1944.

Paris photographers of the 1930s continued to explore and document examples of social life and social classes, celebrated people, and, spurred on by the convenience and reliability of the Leica, serendipitous moments of people in motion, their sudden gestures creating surprise and beauty. Like Berenice Abbott, Gisèle Freund (1908–2000) became known for her photographs of writers and indeed for her profound friendships with them. Both she and Abbott claimed James Joyce as a subject, and Freund also photographed Colette, André Malraux (one of her most famous portraits is a 1935 shot of a windswept, tousled Malraux, stub of a cigarette clasped between his lips), and Walter Benjamin, her friend and fellow exile. Freund left her native Frankfurt in 1933 for Paris, but was more fortunate than Benjamin and was able to escape to the United States in 1940. She returned to France in 1946.

Gyula Halász (1899–1984), a Hungarian photographer who took the name Brassaï and made Paris his home, likewise befriended writers, especially those drawn like himself to the seedy side of Paris, including bohemian haunts and areas like the infamous Place Pigalle. Henry Miller, literary chronicler of that Paris, befriended Brassaï, who also enjoyed the friendship of such artists as Picasso and Dali. Brassaï posed picturesque characters of his acquaintance seated in the cafés they haunted and photographed anonymous Parisians in candid moments, such as young lovers embracing under a streetlight. Indeed, as the title of his

1933 collection of photographs *Paris la nuit* reminds us, he was very much the photographer of Paris after dark. Brassaï's subjects form a gallery of Parisians indulging themselves in pleasures, furtive or otherwise, in the last desperate years preceding the cataclysmic outbreak of World War II.

Henri Cartier-Bresson (1908–) likewise made Paris life his subject, though he would become known during an extremely long career for photographs taken in many regions of the world. Perhaps more than any other photographer he was the master of the Leica camera (which he began using in 1932), and would linger for long stretches of time waiting for what he liked to call "the decisive moment." Perhaps no photograph captures this better than his *Derrière la gare Saint-Lazare* (*Behind the Saint-Lazare Railway Station*), taken that same year. In it Cartier-Bresson has caught a man in business attire, replete with bowler hat, leaping across a broad puddle that reflects both the jumper and the sky above. The composition of the photograph is rich with ominous shadows, adding to the sense of drama that seems to tell us that the gentleman stood there fretting for the longest time before summoning up the determination to attempt his great leap, and that leaves us in permanent suspense wondering whether he made it to dry ground or splashed down despite his effort. And the photographer waited patiently to record exactly this moment. Like Kertész, Cartier-Bresson enjoyed scenes of Parisians going about their daily routines, as seen in his photograph of a young boy coming down the Rue Mouffetard (a famous Left Bank street for food markets) bearing two large bottles of red wine, perhaps his family's supply for the day. He smiles broadly with the importance of his errand and the sense of his triumphant return home.

No photograph conveys the perhaps troubling sense of the photographer as predator ready to pounce on the moment in someone's life he deems most photo-worthy more than Cartier-Bresson's *Dimanche sur les bords de la Marne* (1938, *Sunday on the Banks of the Marne*). Given the date, this is very much a "calm before the storm" scene. Two middle-aged probably lower-middle-class couples are enjoying a Sunday picnic on the Marne riverbank. In the background we see a small skiff, which they face, tied up by the shore. The photographer has stolen up behind the quartet taking their *déjeuner sur l'herbe* (their picnic lunch). It appears to be a hot afternoon, for one of the women has removed her blouse and sits in her slip and skirt. The two men wear short-sleeved shirts. The dirty plates and other remains of their picnic sit in the grassy bank around them. Cartier-Bresson has snapped the photograph just as the man in the near foreground has begun to pour himself another glass of red wine. It is a beautiful photograph, but it remains invasive, and could be used to raise ethical questions about photography. Do other people exist for the photographer merely to provide dramatic moments that flash up before his trained eye, so that (s)he can seize them for another use?

This is not to single out Cartier-Bresson for the voyeurism that is probably inescapable both in photography and in a culture shaped by its power and influence. Any number of fine photographers on both sides of the Atlantic made memorable photographs of anonymous subjects captured in fleeting moments in the streets. Garry Winogrand (1928–1984) and Arthur Fellig (1899–1968), a.k.a. "Weegee," were American photographers whose work displays sudden emotion (Winogrand) or scenes of disaster or the immediate aftermath of extreme violence (Weegee). Lisette Model (1901–1983) was an Austrian photographer who emigrated to the United States and often photographed people in moments of leisure that seemed to suggest something important about their character. Like a latter-day Lartigue, she devoted a series of photographs to the idle rich along the boardwalk at Nice, France. Then, in New York City, she turned her lens toward the common folk taking their ease at Coney Island. As in the case of Cartier-Bresson's subjects, most of hers were not aware of being photographed. Model was also fond of photographing New York City night life, a task made easier by the introduction of the stroboscopic flash in 1939.

Twentieth-Century Photojournalism

War photography is another genre in which the relationship between the photographer and the subject is paramount, and troubling in different ways. In the era of Roger Fenton or Matthew Brady, when action photography was not yet possible, the photographer was removed from the immediate moment of violence and carnage. But the horrific wars of the twentieth century had more than their share of photographic eyewitnesses, many of whom met their deaths in the service of photojournalism. One of the most famous examples was Robert Capa (1913–1954), whose 1936 photograph *Death of a Republican Soldier* must surely be one of the most famous war photographs ever. In it, a fatal bullet has just entered the skull of an advancing soldier who falls backward, still clutching his rifle. For many years some disputed the authenticity of the photograph, until surviving comrades vouched for it and named the victim.

Capa was born Andrei Friedmann in Budapest but went to Paris in 1931 and apprenticed himself to a photographer. He made a reputation for brash self-promotion and for a playboy's inclinations, and numbered among his friends such artists as Picasso and Matisse. He fell in love with a Polish photographer named Gerda Taro (1911–1937), and they became engaged shortly before both embarked for Spain to cover the Spanish Civil War for the Paris illustrated magazine *Vue*. They both displayed great physical courage as they documented the Republican forces combating Franco's troops. Tragically, Taro was crushed and killed by a tank during a hasty retreat after the battle of Brunette. Devastated by grief, Capa went off to China on an assignment but returned for the last years of the war in Spain.

World War II was the new chapter in Capa's career as a photojournalist, and he was in the thick of things at the Allied Landing in Normandy June 6, 1944. Like the famed photojournalists Margaret Bourke-White and Eugene W. Smith, Capa sold a number of his photographs during these years to the illustrated American magazine *Life*, founded in 1936 by Henry Luce. One of Capa's most dramatic sequences of photos published there records the events as he huddled in a Paris apartment defended by an American soldier during the last hours of the liberation of Paris in August 1944. The soldier was stationed at a window firing at Germans outside. In the final photo, one sees the body of the soldier slumped to the floor as the pool of blood from his fatal wound flows over the floorboards, reflecting the light from the open window. The photograph, at once horrible and beautiful, again directs our attention to the ethical dimension of this kind of eyewitness. Could the photographer have prevented the death? Did Capa place the slain man at greater risk in order to set up a dramatic photograph?

After the war, Capa resumed using Paris as his base (he had spent some time in New York earlier during the war), and, in 1947, with his friends and fellow photojournalists Henri Cartier-Bresson and David Seymour (1911–1956), founded the Magnum Photo Agency, the world's first autonomous international photographic cooperative. To the present day, Magnum has been the home for a distinguished number of photojournalists. The end of World War II certainly did not mean the end of wars that could be documented by photography. Capa covered the French Indochina war in Vietnam and was present with the French army as it retreated from its decisive defeat at the battle of Dien Bien Phu in 1954. Advancing across a field on foot after the convoy he was riding with got bogged down on the road, he stepped on a land mine and was killed instantly. Capa's Magnum colleague Seymour was to be another war casualty, killed in the Suez in 1956 during the Arab-Israeli War.

After World War II photographers once again turned to everyday themes, often emphasizing the relief and pleasure of people newly able to enjoy life's simple routines and events. In the United States, *Life* published a seemingly endless stream of photographs depicting (typically) white middle-class suburbanites pursuing a carefree materialistic existence. But most countries in the world were not as materially well favored as the United States. In the immediate aftermath of the war, photographs of the near-dead brutalized survivors of Nazi concentration camps issued from Europe (the Nazis themselves had compiled a proud photographic record of the Final Solution), as did heart-rending photos of frightened, disoriented refugees.

It would take years for most Europeans to be able to enjoy material well-being and stability again. Perhaps for this reason, people enjoyed photographs that captured lighthearted moments, showing that *joie de vivre* could be realized once again. Easily the most beloved practitioner of this sentimental genre of photography, and one whose technical skill has been widely admired, was the French photographer Robert Doisneau (1912–1994). The Paris streets were his setting, but unlike his predecessor Brassaï, his subjects were the wholesome, proper bourgeois set, glimpsed strolling together in the streets, young lovers stealing a kiss, friends enjoying the sociability of café life. Although he had been hired shortly after the war as a fashion photographer for *Vogue*, by the early 1950s Doisneau typically plied the streets of Paris, armed with his Leica, to take the pictures that made his name, pictures he was able to get published regularly in *Life*, among other illustrated magazines.

One of Doisneau's most famous photographs features the shop window of an antique store. The camera's view is of a proper looking middle-aged couple window-shopping. The wife points to some object that interests her in the middle of the window display, trying to direct her husband's attention to it. His gaze, however, strays to the side of the display window, where he admires the derrière of a voluptuous nude in the small ornate frame that hangs on the wall. The photograph's appeal was in the conceit that the shot had been snapped just at the moment the husband, unbeknownst to his wife, begins greedily to devour this view. But as so often turns out to be the case with "candid" photographs, it seems that Doisneau staged the shot, instructing his models exactly how to pose. For French people to this day, Doisneau photographs are as evocative of the 1950s as the music of Edith Piaf or Jean-Paul Sartre and Simone de Beauvoir together at the Café de Flore or Les Deux Magots.

The last decades of the century saw increased global travel, new migrations of previously isolated populations, and a growing sense that older ways of life were vanishing forever. Photojournalists often turned to this theme. One of the first examples after World War II was Paul

Strand (1890–1976), an American photographer who studied with Lewis Hine in New York early in the century, exhibited at Stieglitz's Gallery 291, and later spent time in Mexico photographing the Mexican Revolution. The Mexican government appointed him chief of photography and cinematography in 1933. In the last phase of his life he was active primarily in Europe, and died near Paris. His early 1950s' photojournalistic study of traditional peasant life in Sicily and southern Italy presents its subjects with simple, straightforward dignity, displaying the ultra-clear direct approach Strand brought to his photography. This is demonstrated clearly in his *The Family, View II, Luzarra, Italy, 1953.* (See figure 13.3.)

One of the greatest figures in this photographic tradition by the 1960s was the Czech photographer Josef Koudelka (1939–). He joined the Magnum Agency, making Paris his base. Koudelka was fascinated by the ethnic complexity of Eastern Europe, and especially by the Gypsies, the ancient nomads universally despised, persecuted, and hounded from one European country to another. His book *Gypsies* (1968) collected his many photographs of Gypsies in various European locales. Koudelka's powerful images often contrast a foreground detail, such as a man's anguished face, with the broad vista of a stark, windswept hillside stretching away into the background. Depicting Gypsies in everyday situations, he strikes a balance between exotic stereotyping and a facile humanism that declares "after all, they are like us."

By late in the century the most celebrated photographer of the Magnum group was the Brazilian photojournalist Sebastaio Selgado (1944–). While making his headquarters in Paris, Salgado has traveled throughout the world, emphasizing such themes as work and migration of peoples everywhere. He has worked often on a vast scale, using wide-angle lens and enlarging prints to enormous size. The most stunning example is his spectacular series of photographs of Brazilian gold miners, scurrying up and down crude rickety ladders, risking their lives to haul the heavy precious ore up great heights from deep in the earth. Salgado has also made ecological disasters one of his important themes, which he documented in the wake of the Exxon *Valdez* oil spill in Alaska in 1990 and in the burning oil fields of Kuwait in the 1991 Persian Gulf War.

Cultural Impact of Photography: Critical Questions

Clearly a photojournalist like Salgado intends to appeal to the conscience of a viewer of his photographs, to instill sympathy for oppressed

Figure 13.3 Paul Strand: *The Family, Luzzara, Italy, 1953.* © 1955, Aperture Foundation Inc., Paul Strand Archive.

workers and to stir the political will to take action. Unfortunately, a growing body of critical literature about photography and about the overdetermined "visual culture" of late Modernity argues that photographs have done the opposite. Photographs, and even more so television and advertising, so saturate everyone with images that a kind of psychological numbness sets in. Or so goes this kind of critique, in a direction quite opposite of that which argues that photojournalistic (print or televised) coverage of key events in recent history awakened sensibilities to social ills and calamities that need to end. Examples have included images of southern police brutality against civil rights activists, coverage of the Vietnam War, or horrific images of starving Ethiopians.

While there seems to be no consensus on what the impact of proliferating visual images on Western culture is, there seems to be general agreement that it is enormous. For much of the later twentieth century, philosophers, critics, and other observers have offered various kinds of critical interpretations of photography. Walter Benjamin (1892–1940) wrote an influential essay called "The Work of Art in the

Age of Mechanical Reproduction." Benjamin, the friend of Gisèle Freund, appreciated photography and even collected photographs. In his essay he was concerned with the photographic reproduction of works of art, the significance, for example, of the mass circulation via reproduction of a classic painting that in previous eras could have been viewed only by those with the means to travel to Rome, Florence, or Paris. The greatly expanded availability of art through reproduced images produced contradictory results. On one hand, the "aura" of the work, its special legendary or exemplary status, was threatened by reproduction. Think of how banal the *Mona Lisa* has become through overexposure. And yet, on the other hand, Benjamin saw something appealingly democratic in this, that more people could be included in the experience of art. He even hinted at the extreme argument that any person selecting reproductions to decorate his or her own surroundings was expressing a kind of personal artistic sensibility.

The English critic, novelist, and filmmaker John Berger (1926–) used Benjamin's essay as the basis for his illustrated book *Ways of Seeing* (1972), also a BBC television documentary. Berger emphasized the blurring of lines between art and advertising in a culture of commodification where everything, precious art works included, is available for the packaging of products—a world in which Botticelli's Venus, her long tresses streaming out behind her, is a perfect emblem for a shampoo bottle. As a writer concerned with the vanishing way of life of the southern French peasants where he lives in voluntary exile, Berger has wrestled with the dilemma of using photographs to represent their existence, wondering whether this creates distancing and stereotyping rather than empathy.

The American critic and novelist Susan Sontag (1933–) published an influential book called *On Photography* in 1977. She too cited Benjamin's argument; in fact, she was one of the very first American writers to comment on his work. Largely, however, her little book was a somber meditation on memory, death, and longing as embodied in the experience of taking, collecting, and, most important, perceiving the world through photographs. Sontag was more concerned with the everyday role of snapshots than with "art" photography. She argued that taking pictures is a means of attempting to hold onto the moments of our lives, not just in a vain attempt to defeat death but in a desperate effort to affirm our existence here, there, in these moments and particular places. Eventually memory itself begins to be constructed according to these little vignettes, and our memory of our lives becomes dependent on their photographed moments.

Roland Barthes's highly personal, often lyrical, essay on photography *La Chambre claire: Note sur la photographie* (1980, *Camera Lucida: Reflections on Photography*), published the year of his own death, was also initially a meditation on the relationship between photography and death. In his case, he began thinking about such questions after his mother's death, as he was going through some photographs of her, looking for the one that best "captured" who she was. Barthes then went on to describe his reaction to a number of photographs from throughout the history of photography, emphasizing frequently the theme of death, that the person in the photograph is alive at that instant but is going to die; has already died in most of the examples Barthes cited. Despite the fact that the books Barthes wrote in his last decade moved away for the most part from the sometimes forbidding framework of his influential works of semiology and adopted a more flexible, playful spirit, in *La Chambre claire* he offered a kind of structuralist means of interpreting photographs. Using Latin terms, he distinguished between the *studium,* or general subject matter of a given photograph, and the *punctum,* the detail within the photograph that pricks or "lacerates" the viewer. It might be a gesture, a peculiar article of clothing, even the awkward expression of someone not central to the photograph.

One of the most important things to note about photographs is the way they "freeze" instants of ongoing time, as if one had snipped one small frame out of a reel of film, relying on it to provide a narrative. The cumulative effect of all these frozen moments may interfere with a sense of time as flow, even the realization of the arbitrariness of the camera's isolation of one particular instance. In the case of a famous news photograph, the power of the image can make it seem as if history had been leading to just that point, which sums up all that can be said about the temporal complexities surrounding the concatenation of objects that make up the photographed image. In other words, it could create the same sort of distortion for collective historical memory that snapshots do, as Sontag argued, for personal memory.

Photography, Representation, and Postmodernism

Stuart Hall (see chapter 12) has echoed Sontag's argument somewhat in the case of news photographs. He believes they do violence to a full sense of lived time, interfering with our sense of what came before the photographed moment and making it more difficult to imagine possible futures except in terms of the visible present reality of the news photographs that come at us on a daily basis. In short, they foster the kind of "this-ness" that flourishes in advertising, where all efforts are expended on the present moment, as we heed this or that promise of immediate gratification. The overall effect, Hall has argued, is to stifle imagination, especially the ability to envision alternative social realities. His is a version of the growing body of Postmodernist commentary on representation and even the politics of representation.

Feminist critiques of masculinist objectification of women's bodies have found their way into contemporary photography. One strategy adopted by feminist photographers, like that of filmmakers, has been to disrupt the standard practices of sexual representation from within. The internationally influential and controversial American photographer Cindy Sherman (1954–) has attempted to do so by posing herself in a variety of clichéd vamping, cheesecake poses (in part a throwback to the Comtesse de Castiglione), creating a satirical commentary that is quite chilling and disturbing. Some men, influenced by these moves and mindful of the feminist complaint that Western artists have relied on female nudes but have been reticent about male nudes, have turned their cameras on their own nude bodies. The American photographer John Coplans (1920–) produced photographs of enormous size mercilessly mapping the terrain of his aging body in relentless detail. The Greek-born American artist Lucas Samaras (1936–) produced enormous color Polaroids (making use of another of photography's technological milestones) as nude self-portraits, and cut them into strips and sections, piecing them back together—but not quite—to call even more attention to the body's objectification.

Gay artists have used photography to explore similar issues, the paramount one often being to insist that others see and acknowledge gay existence. One of the most prolific and influential gay photographers was Robert Mapplethorpe (1946–1989), known for his stunning enlarged color photographs of flowers in bloom as well as for the explicit gay male imagery that brought notoriety and controversy in his last years and well after his death from AIDS. Whether gay artists or straight, feminist or not, the prominence of the body as a theme in recent visual arts, including photography, continues to spark controversy. One feminist photographer, artist, and writer, Martha Rosler (1943–), has opted for a strategy of refusing to photograph human subjects, even when human problems are implied, as they certainly are in her very socially conscious work in her home in Brooklyn, New York.

Some photographers on either side of the Atlantic have adopted what might be considered a compromise between graphic representation and its refusal by combining text with photographs. The French photographer Sophie Calle (1953–) is an important example. Her *Histoires vraies*

(1994, *True Stories*) use semifictional narratives, both photographic and textual, to describe female experience. Meanwhile, she calls attention to the voyeuristic impulse in photography by carrying it to great extremes, equating photography with a kind of espionage. For one project she even took a job as a hotel chambermaid in order to photograph the personal items of the guests whose rooms she cleaned.

At the end of the twentieth century, new digital technologies were poised to alter the nature of photography even more radically, and the use of the Internet has already become central to photography's dissemination. As noted at the outset of this chapter, it has become impossible to imagine contemporary culture without photography, for all its contradictions. Important museums housing photographic collections flourish, all major museums of modern art have photography sections, and a photograph by a celebrated master can fetch nearly as much in an elite auction house as a Modern painting. Yet cameras ranging from high-tech models with breathtaking price tags to disposable pocket cameras are found wherever people are found, people for whom the camera has become an essential appendage.

Whatever may be said for recent technological innovations, the haunting power of photographs has remained tied to some basic, powerful human emotions and preoccupations. Consider the three photographs used as illustrations in these pages: They deal with voyeurism, morbid fascination, and the desire to hold on to stages and ways of life already in the process of vanishing. Perhaps photography has altered something important about our humanity, but it also engages something very deeply rooted within it.

Suggestions for Further Reading

Barthes, Roland. *Camera Lucida: Reflections on Photography.* Trans. Richard Howard. New York: Hill & Wang, 1981.

Berger, John. *About Looking.* New York: Pantheon Books, 1980.

Berger, John, and Jean Mohr. *Another Way of Telling.* New York: Pantheon Books, 1982.

Phillips, Sandra S., et al. *Police Pictures: The Photograph as Evidence.* San Francisco: San Francisco Museum of Art/Chronicle Books, 1997.

Rosenblum, Naomi. *A World History of Photography.* 3rd ed. New York: Abrams, 1997.

Shapiro, Michael J. *The Politics of Representation: Writing Practices in Biography, Photography, and Policy Analysis.* Madison: University of Wisconsin Press, 1988.

Sontag, Susan. *On Photography.* New York: Farrar, Straus & Giroux, 1977.

Chapter 14

European and Global Culture
in the Late Twentieth Century

The last years of the twentieth century, a boom period for computer technology and all types of digital information storage and communication, witnessed an explosion of cultural production in literature, music, and cinema that was most remarkable for rapid crossing of national boundaries. For some contemporary cultural interpreters, cultural crossings are by definition symptomatic of our "post-" age, perhaps Postmodern, almost certainly Postcolonial. The speeded-up nomadism producing odd cultural juxtapositions that Jean-François Lyotard celebrated more than twenty years ago has become far more pronounced in the age of globalization driven by the Internet and all manner of cyber-industries. To some extent, one need not travel away from one's home to partake of this brave new world.

And yet when we consider European literature in recent years, it is quite striking how many distinguished writers have migrated from other countries, sometimes former colonies of the host European countries. An equally striking feature has been the strength of regional writing (or perhaps we should say writing from areas traditionally dominated or overshadowed by major capitals), for example, Ireland and Scotland. What has been true for literature has been true as well for cinema and music. All of this would appear to represent a revitalization of European culture in newly diverse forms, but these developments have been overshadowed by morbid anxieties concerning a supposedly monolithic American popular culture serving as the major vehicle of economic globalization.

An Expanded Sense of "European" Literature

The British Isles have offered examples in recent years of literary contributions both by immigrants and by writers exemplary of the cultural resurgence of Ireland and Scotland. One of the most acclaimed novelists recently in England has been the Japanese-born Kazuo Ishiguro (1954–), who emigrated with his family in 1960. Although he has written of Japanese cultural themes, his most successful books have been thoroughly European in emphasis, as in his 1989 novel *Remains of the Day*, about a painfully repressed English butler. His 1995 novel *The Unconsoled* explores Central European settings through the baffling experiences of a touring concert pianist.

V. S. Naipaul (1932–) is a prolific novelist and essayist born in Trinidad of Indian ancestry, yet he writes from his adopted country as a fierce defender of European civilization with a very jaundiced view of Third World cultures, as his scathing indictment of Caribbean revolutionaries in *Guerrillas* (1975) makes clear. He turned his withering ire toward Central Africa in his 1979 novel *A Bend in the River*. His more recent books have analyzed Indian civilization and his personal, family relationships. If Naipaul seems to repudiate his Third World origins, the Pakistani immigrant novelist and screenwriter Hanif Kureishi (1954–) portrays his own hybrid culture in a much more sympathetic light. This portrayal has taken on real political urgency as xenophobic "Paki-bashing" politics have menaced the South Asian community on England. Kureishi adapted two of his novels for the screen. Both *My Beautiful Laundrette* (1985) and *Sammy and Rosie Get Laid* (1988), featuring screenplays by Kureishi, were directed by Stephen Frears (1941–). The two films depict the economic and social ambitions of Pakistani immigrants and, in the former case, confront the deeply repressed subject of homosexuality.

By far the most famous literary immigrant in England after 1990 was the Indian writer Salman Rushdie (1947–). The product of a Muslim merchant family, Rushdie's early novels examined the painful history of the partition of India and Pakistan and the violent early history of both countries since independence (the year of Rushdie's birth). In the 1980s he turned his attention to Third World revolutions, especially in Nicaragua. But in 1988 his ambitious novel *The Satanic Verses* brought him fame and attention of an altogether unwanted variety. Islam is the subject of the novel, and some Muslims were deeply offended by what they regarded as the author's irreverent attitude. In Iran, the Ayatollah Khomeini issued a *fatwa*, or formal death threat (urging believers to carry it out) against Rushdie, who went into hiding for a number of years. The Japanese translator of the book was assassinated, and writers throughout the world rallied in support of Rushdie and freedom of expression. After several years Rushdie emerged gradually from hiding, and toward the end of the 1990s, tiring of life in England, he relocated to New York City.

In the face of ongoing political troubles in the North and the terrible economic plight of the 1980s especially, Irish literature showed its vitality through the novels of Edna O'Brien (1932–) and Roddy Doyle (1958–) and the poetry of Seamus Heaney (1939–) and Eavan Boland (1944–). O'Brien nourished the flame of the Joycean tradition in modern Irish writing, both lyrically and in terms of sexual candor. In *House of Splendid Isolation* (1994) and *Down By the River* (1996), her brutal dissection of the hypocritical sexual repression that imprisoned Irish women has made her work controversial in Ireland. *House of Splendid Isolation* also confronted the subject of Irish terrorism, while *Wild December* (2000) examined the anachronistic nature of Irish farm life. Urban life, Dublin in particular, is at the center of Roddy Doyle's often comic novels about the scruffy working-class section called Barrytown. The poems of Northern Ireland-born Seamus Heaney, winner of the 1995 Nobel Prize for Literature, address public concerns and the enduring themes of Irish culture: the land, community, and the burden of history. These themes recall the example of Yeats. Also like Yeats, he has received distinction as a prose author (1980, *Preoccupations: Selected Prose, 1968–1978*) and, in more recent poems, has considered matters of spirituality (1996, *The Spirit Level*). In 1999 Heaney published his new translation of *Beowulf* to great acclaim. Eavan Boland, who has lived in the United States for many years, is nevertheless considered one of her country's major poets. The passage of time, the experience of women, and the poetic imagination are her principal concerns, as displayed in her collections *In Her Own Image* (1980) and *Outside History* (1990).

Prime Minister Tony Blair's Labour government began the process in 1997 of granting autonomy to Scotland, supplying political affirmation of the tremendous creative explosion in artistic expression that has marked contemporary Scotland. Beginning in the early 1980s, such films by Bill Forsyth (1948–) as *Gregory's Girl* (1981) and *Local Hero* (1983) had attracted attention and piqued curiosity about contemporary Scotland. But by the 1990s literature was making the news in Scotland. For some, the themes being revealed were not exactly welcome news. Two novelists, James Kelman (1946–) and Irvine Welsh (1958–), chronicled the depravity of characters in the underworld of, respectively, Glasgow and Edinburgh. A storm of protest greeted the awarding of the distinguished Booker Prize (England's highest literary award) in 1994 to Kelman's novel *How Late It Was, How Late*. This story of a hapless alcoholic's sudden blindness and his attempts to cope with his predicament is remarkable for its relentless obscenity and almost impenetrable Glaswegian dialect. Depravity and patois also combine in Irvine Welsh's novels about the drug culture of Edinburgh.

French literature in the last years of the century featured representatives of former French colonies as well as native-born writers who described the increasingly culturally diverse French scene, although this diversity comes under attack even more so than in England. No doubt the single most celebrated émigré author in France is Milan Kundera (1929–) of Czechoslovakia. A refugee from the Communist Czech regime, he settled in Paris and began to try his hand at writing in French, although the novels for which he became well known (*The Book of Laughter and Forgetting*, 1979; *The Unbearable Lightness of Being*, 1984) were written when his country still bore the name of Czechoslovakia. Still, he remains representative of a general trend by which Eastern European artists are well received in Western Europe.

The most dramatic indication that "French" literature was being redefined to include writing from the broader Francophone world came in 1992 when Patrick Chamoiseau (1953–) of Martinique received France's major literary award, the Prix Goncourt, for his novel *Texaco,* set in the French overseas department and featuring a stylistically innovative blend of French and Créole. Other examples of important new writers in France come from former colonies in Africa and Asia. Marie Ndiaye (1967–) is a Senegalese immigrant who writes of African women caught between their traditional cultures, which often include practices like polygamy and female excision, and the fast-paced culture of contemporary France. She published a number of novels during the 1990s, including *En famille* (1990, *Among Family*), *La Sorcière* (1996, *The Sorceress*), and *Hilda* (1999). An admirer of Baudelaire, Beckett, and Kafka who emulates their dark and contradictory themes (such as the existence of beauty in the midst of evil and degradation), Linda Lê (1963–) emigrated to France from Vietnam at the age of fifteen. Her novels include *Calomnies* (1993, *Slander=Calomnies: Calomnies*), *Les trois Parques* (1997, *The Three Fates*), and *Voix* (1998, *Voices*).

Even when they are not immigrants, members of the new generation of French writers show through their work the impact of the changing face of France. Daniel Pennac (1944–) brings the world of the gritty, often bleak Paris suburbs, with their street slang and the connection of their youth to global hip-hop culture, into his novels. But the writer whose work has most jolted French sensibilities is Michel Houellebecq (1958–). His fictional characters, in such books as *Extension de la domaine de la lutte* (1994, *Whatever*) take for granted the ethnic and cultural diversity of contemporary France, as they dine on Tex-Mex cuisine or listen to African music. What French readers have found most disturbing, however, is the thoroughgoing amorality of characters who stand for nothing beyond acquisitive hedonism, like French versions of American so-called yuppies. Devoid of any feeling more elevated than their animal appetites, they fit the profile that some theorists of Postmodernism have attempted to describe. Extreme examples of such characters populate the pages of *Les Particules élémentaires* (1998, Elementary Particles), Houellebecq's longest novel and one that occasioned a national debate over the morality and politics of literature. More recently, Houellebecq's notoriety has expanded in another direction, as leader of a rock band.

Postmodern European Cinema

Faced always with the daunting commercial challenge of competing with big-budget Hollywood imports, European directors of the 1980s and 1990s wrestled with themes that included new engagements with the horrors of their century's history, the changing roles of the sexes, sexual and ethnic identity, and the decline of the industrial working class. In short: themes central to what most theorists seem to emphasize under the rubric of Postmodernism.

The embrace of Eastern European artists, noted earlier, was especially evident in French cinema, where a number of the most remarkable films of the 1980s and 1990s were directed by Polish immigrants or, in the case of Andrej Wajda (1926–), by a celebrated Polish director contributing to French filmmaking. At the height of Poland's Solidarity movement against the Communist regime, Wajda came to France to direct *Danton* (1982). Ostensibly a historical film about the fall of the French Revolutionary leader based on the sympathetic portrayal given him in Georg Büchner's nineteenth-century play *Dantons Tod* (*The Death of Danton*), Wajda's film, using a combination of French and Polish actors, commented indirectly on the situation in Poland. The severe, forbidding facial features of the actor playing Robespierre clearly referred to General Wojciech Jaruzelski of Poland, and Wajda's choice of the charismatic French actor Gérard Depardieu for the role of Danton was motivated in part by what the director believed was his physical resemblance to Lech Walesa, the Solidarity leader. Wajda's film was an enormous success in France, and helped to set the stage for the observance in 1989 of the Bicentennial of the Revolution (which unfolded over the next decade with a notable lack of sympathy for Robespierre or any of the more radical elements of the Revolution).

One of the significant émigré Polish directors in France was Agnieszka Holland (1948–), whose contribution to the ongoing reexamination of the Holocaust years was her 1990 film *Europa Europa,* based on the astonishing true story of a German Jewish boy's successful attempts to mask his identity during Hitler's regime. More recently she began making films in English. No doubt the major contribution by a Polish director to French cinema in the 1990s was the trilogy of films *Trois couleurs* (*Three Colors*): *Bleu* (1992, *Blue*), *Blanc* (1993, *White*), and *Rouge* (1994, *Red*) by Krzysztof Kieslowski (1941–1996). The second in the series deals with a Polish man living in France, while the others feature French characters. Although each film can be viewed and understood as a separate entity, they tie into each other, with characters from one film appearing in brief vignettes in the others. Also, brief scenes involving extras are repeated in all three films. In this triptych of films, each title refers both to one of the colors of the French tricolor flag as well as to one of the trio of French Revolutionary principles. Thus "Blue" = Liberty, "White" = Equality, and "Red" (blood) = Fraternity.

In 1995 the young director and actor Mathieu Kassovitz (1967–) dropped something of a bombshell on the world of French cinema was his uncompromising, troubling film *La Haine* (*Hate*). Shot in stark black and white, this films takes the viewer into the not-so-pretty world of the Paris *banlieues* (suburbs), where immigrant and minority communities suffer the indignities of poorly maintained public housing, high unemployment, crime, and the hostility and occasional violence of the police. An improbable trio of young friends, one Arab, one black, and one a French Jew, explore a world where young people live their risk-filled lives to a soundtrack of hard-core rap music, clearly identifying with the desperate culture of American inner cities. The film showed a side of France that most French people do not wish to see or acknowledge, one visitors to the country rarely experience. Thus it met with denunciation as well as admiration for its courage. Capitalizing on the success of *La Haine*, Kassovitz turned toward the big-screen thriller genre, including his film *Les Rivières pourpres* (2000, *Crimson Rivers*).

Italian cinema retained many of the characteristics that had marked it during its heyday in the period from 1945 to 1975, while exploring some new directions. Giuseppe Tornatore (1956–) is a director whose earliest films were set in Sicily and extreme southern Italy. Emphasis on that region has enormous political significance for Italy, where bitter North-South tensions remain at the heart of Italian national life. It is also in keeping with what some have seen as a theme of Postmodern culture, that is, renewed attention to more marginal, overlooked areas of a nation. Tornatore's most engaging early film was *Cinema Paradiso* (1988), the story of the central importance of the local cinema for a small Sicilian town. The young boy whose fascination for the projection room takes him there night after night evokes the films of Fellini or even Truffaut, depicting the lifelong love affair the director experiences with cinema. Later Tornatore branched out into working with actors in other countries. His *Une Pure formalité* (1994, *A Pure Formality*), in French, is a brain-teaser of a drama starring Gérard Depardieu and the Polish director Roman Polanski.

Almost the only Italian director of the earlier generation remaining alive or active, Bernardo Bertolucci tackled a subject in his 1998 film *Shanduraï* (*Besieged*) that reflected the new immigration in Italy. Like France, Italy has experienced significant recent immigration from sub-Saharan Africa, especially apparent in such major cities as Rome and Milan. This film tells the story of an improbable affair between a lonely English expatriate pianist living in Rome and his African housekeeper, herself a medical student.

For better or worse, no one in Italian cinema enjoyed greater notoriety at the turn of the century than the comic actor/director Roberto Benigni (1952–). A rubber-faced comic talent well suited to slapstick, Benigni took on the deadly serious topic of the Holocaust in *La Vita è bella* (1998, *Life Is Beautiful*). His film tells the story of an Italian Jewish family deported to Auschwitz. The father (played by Benigni) and the young son are separated from the mother, and the father, seeking to shield the boy from the horrors around him, pretends they are part of an elaborate charade or game, with a prize in store if they "play" successfully. Critics and audiences were divided about this film. Some felt the use of humor was daring and successful, rendering the Auschwitz experience all the more powerful and shattering. Others argued Benigni had trivialized the topic with his unwarranted comic approach.

Unbridled humor and madcap pacing mark the prolific cinematic output of Spanish director Pedro Almodóvar (1948–). Heir to the Surrealist sensibility of Buñuel, Almodóvar documents life in contemporary Madrid (complete with such urban ills as crime and drugs), with particular emphasis on women. Openly homosexual, he extols women and celebrates them in every way in films that include female impersonation and transsexuality, often featuring as main characters actresses, particularly ones whose glory has long since begun to fade. Such films as *La ley del deseo* (1986, *The Law of Desire*), *Mujeres al borde de un attaque de nervous* (1987, *Women on the Verge of a Nervous Breakdown*), *Atame!* (1990, *Tie Me Up/Tie me Down!*), and *Todo sobre mi madre* (1999, *All About My*

Mother), among many others, offer frank eroticism, bracing humor, improbable plot twists, and cliff-hanger dramatic episodes.

Wim Wenders (1945–), the most prominent German filmmaker of the last decade, increasingly crossed national boundaries in terms of casting, location, and languages used in his films. *Der Himmel über Berlin* (1987, *Wings of Desire*) provided unforgettable glimpses of Berlin in its last days as a divided city. It is the story of angels who watch over the city's inhabitants, and achieved powerful effects through its lyrical, at times transcendent, style. Although set in Berlin, it featured actors and conversations in German, French, and English. *Bis als Ende der Welt* (1991, *Until the End of World*) was not just international but global in scope. Its series of episodes circumnavigate the earth. By the end of the 1990s, Wenders, in a move both envied and resented by other European directors, had made the jump to Hollywood, using the English language exclusively and greater Los Angeles as his setting in *The End of Violence* (1997) and *Million Dollar Hotel* (1999). One of the most distinctive features of a Wenders film is his use of music from a wide array of genres, very noticeable in the soundtracks of *Wings of Desire* and *Until the End of the World* as well as in his 1994 film *Lisbon Story*. In 1999 he also directed a documentary film about contemporary Cuban music called *Buena Vista Social Club*.

The Netherlands has seldom figured in the annals of cinema, but Marleen Gorris (1948–) was one of the most important new European directors of the 1990s. Her subject as a filmmaker is women's lives, viewed from a unique perspective that yields new insights into the ways women relate to each other within and across generations and to others in their families and circles of acquaintances. The 1995 film *Antonia's Line* follows its group of characters as they age and as their circle is diminished by death. Gorris narrates a story of love, friendship, and profound ties to the land in a remote part of her country. In 1997 she released her adaptation of Virginia Woolf's *Mrs. Dalloway*, featuring Vanessa Redgrave in a masterful performance in the title role.

Scandinavian cinema produced no director of the stature of a Bergman, although that director began his farewell to his career early in the 1980s. The final scene of his semiautobiographical epic *Fanny och Alexander* (1983, *Fanny and Alexander*) was reminiscent of Shakespeare's Prospero, bowing out movingly at the end of *The Tempest*. Lasse Hallström (1940–) was a notable Swedish director of the newer generation who movingly depicted the world of a foster child in *Mitt liv som hund* (1985, *My Life as a Dog*). By the 1990s he became part of the trend of European directors moving on to the Hollywood film industry, where he made such well-regarded English language films as *What's Eating Gilbert Grape?* (1993) *The Cider House Rules* (1999), and *Chocolat* (2000). One very significant new Danish director was Lars von Trier (1956–), whose powerfully bleak film *Breaking the Waves* (1996)—in English— was set in northern Scotland. He pushed his themes of sexuality and madness to greater and more controversial extremes in *Idiotern* (1998, *The Idiots*). He followed this with another film in English, an extremely controversial musical called *Dancer in the Dark* (2000).

As in the literary field, Ireland figured prominently in late twentieth-century cinema of the British Isles. In the films of Jim Sheridan (1949–) and Neil Jordan (1950–), this often meant confronting the violent modern history of Ireland, especially the "troubles" in the North. Sheridan's *My Left Foot* (1988) featured Daniel Day-Lewis in a remarkable performance as the severely handicapped writer Christy Brown. His *In the Name of the Father* (1993), also featuring Day-Lewis, was based on the true story of a group of Irish young people wrongly imprisoned for seventeen years for a terrorist bombing in London in the early 1970s. His later film *The Boxer* (1997) narrated the story of a former Northern Irish Republican Army supporter trying to fashion a new peaceful life for himself. Jordan's acclaimed 1992 film *The Crying Game* critically examined the tactics and ethics of IRA terrorism while weaving the plot around an improbable love story.

Many of the most striking English films of the 1990s dealt with themes of the embattled working class, as had Bill Forsyth's Scottish films of the 1980s, in the aftermath of Margaret Thatcher's years as prime minister. One of the directors most consistently to portray the terrible challenges faced by working-class families has been Ken Loach (1936–) in such films as *Raining Stones* (1993) and *My Name is Joe* (1998). In his 1997 film *Brassed Off,* Mark Herman (1955–) offered a new approach to theme of workers threatened by Thatcher policies. The film is the story of coal miners, facing impending unemployment, who take part in a national competition of brass bands.

Class is one of several themes found in the films of Mike Leigh (1943–). His 1993 film *Naked* introduced the talented actor David Thewlis in the role of a disagreeable down-and-out young man from Manchester making his way in London. Leigh gained wider attention in 1996 with *Secrets and Lies,* the story of a mixed-race English woman searching for the white birth mother who abandoned her. *Career Girls* (1997) follows the improbable friendship of two women from university days into early middle age. Leigh's 1999 film *Topsy-Turvy,* based on the real-life composers Gilbert and Sullivan, was a significant departure for this talented director.

The lives of immigrants living in England has been and will no doubt continue to be a significant subject for English filmmakers. The South Asian community has commanded much of the attention, and the impact of Stephen Frears's films based on Hanif Kureishi's screenplays has already been noted (in relation to literature). Gurinder Chadha (1960–), born in Kenya to an Indian family, represented the Indian community in Britain from a woman's perspective in *Bhaji On the Beach* (1994), the story of a group of Indian women who book a weekend excursion to the resort coastal city of Blackpool, where they encounter bigotry but much more, quite a lot of it presented in humorous situations.

Totally unclassifiable are the films of Peter Greenaway (1942–), who approaches his hauntingly mysterious, erotically charged films with the eye of a painter, typically employing wide screens on which the camera applies the celluloid equivalent of broad brush strokes. In the deliberately grotesque *The Cook, the Thief, His Wife, and Her Lover* (1989), the horizontally tracking camera appears to follow characters walking through walls from room to room, situation to situation. Greenaway's *Prospero's Books* (1990), starring the legendary English actor John Gielgud (1904–2000), is a visually extravagant, mind-altering experience inspired by Shakespeare's *The Tempest,* although no less faithful to the text of the play for all that. Greenaway's 1996 film *The Pillow Book,* an erotic tale involving Japanese calligraphy, seems almost a direct application, intentional or not, of Roland Barthes's eroticized notions of textuality.

Not all European directors of recent years have been as aesthetically uncompromising as Greenaway. In fact, many have longed for mass audiences even if they cannot expect to approach the global saturation point of Hollywood releases.

Space and Performance in Postmodern European Art

Certainly no form of art in recent decades has been as influential as cinema, but significant developments in European art have been related, in part, with the preoccupation many artists have had with questions of space, including urban public space and the space of the gallery or museum. The recent trends in European art have unfolded at a time when those who see themselves as speaking for the art world have never tired of repeating the claim that New York City remains the global center for the visual arts. Theorists argue that concern with space is a fundamental symptom of Postmodernism, as is a tendency to extend certain energies of the Modernist avant-garde. Recent European art exhibits both of these tendencies, and both intersect in the late twentieth-century art form known as "performance."

Perhaps the major European figure to inspire new art in what might still be called, oxymoronically, the avant-garde tradition was Josef Beuys (1921–1986) of Germany. A Luftwaffe pilot during World War II, he flew a plane that was shot down over the Russian steppes. Nearly dead, he was found by Tartar tribesmen. To halt frostbite and to keep him alive, they packed his body in fat. Beuys was eventually restored to health, but had to wear a felt fedora due to head injuries he had sustained. In his sculptures and other artistic creations, Beuys routinely incorporated globs of fat and bits of felt to refer to his experiences.

He began to exhibit his art in West Germany as early as 1953, but became best known for elaborately staged performances accompanied by explanatory texts and manifestos, and later preserved on videotape. His performances usually incorporated natural elements, including animals both living and dead. The line between sculpture and landscape gardening was crossed in his series of oak trees planted at the Dia Art Center in New York City's Chelsea District. The position of Beuys vis-à-vis the art establishment was never a comfortable one. He was dismissed from his position as a professor at the Düsseldorf Art Academy in 1972, although this eventually was reversed. He did represent Germany at the Venice Biennale in 1976. He remains an important founding figure of so-called performance art, particularly important in New York City during the 1980s and 1990s, but also an influence on European arts. Dance has been one area of the performing arts to show this influence, as in the genre-defying productions of Pina Bausch's Tanztheater Wuppertal, an acclaimed German dance company.

Hans Haacke (1936–) is a contemporary German artist specializing in what has come to be called "installation art," usually a combination of sculpture with posters or other texts that intervene in gallery space in ways similar to performance art. What Haacke does is to use his installations to call attention to the role art institutions such as major museums play in the corporate world. Often he deliberately exposes the links museums have, through their governing boards, to corporations whose practices would seem to have little to do with artistic creativity or expression. His effort is always to challenge the claim art as an institution makes about its political or social neutrality, or that some make for the supposedly subversive character of modern art. Haacke charges the art establishment with being exactly that—part of the established social order that perpetuates social injustice. His art is a spatial intervention meant to foster a critical perspective on the museum as institution.

Some of the most striking European art of the contemporary era has been an effort strategically to make use of or intervene in space, from the space of a gallery to a familiar public square. Mario Merz (1925–) is the leading artist associated with the Italian Arte povera ("poor art") movement, whose members stand for the use of ordinary (albeit very twentieth-century) materials in making art. In Merz's case, he assembles curious igloolike structures from shards and panes of glass or Plexiglas, to which he sometimes adds rope or other materials, often lengths of neon tubing kept illuminated as part of the piece. He is fascinated with Fibonacci numbers, which he often represents with the neon tubes. These numbers are named for an Italian mathematician, and are formed by adding the preceding numbers in the series (e.g., 1, 2, 3, 5, 8, 13, 21) to arrive at the next number. The result in Merz's art is a curious blend of very primitive elements with very modern ones.

At least since the completion of the controversial Centre Pompidou in 1977, Paris has provided the setting for some notable intrusions of new art work into some very old public spaces. For example, just south of Centre Pompidou is the Fontaine Stravinski, filled with floating sculptures designed by the French artist Niki de Sainte-Phalle (1930–). The moving sculptures pay homage in part to the artist's husband Jean Tinguely (1925–1991), the Swiss master of kinetic sculpture famous for the auto-destructive character of his pieces. And nearly as famous and, for some, as controversial as the American architect I. M. Pei's glass pyramid slicing through the courtyard of the Louvre Museum are Daniel Buren's (1938–) short black-and-white columns jutting up through the courtyard of the nearby Palais Royal.

Installation art has also thrived in Paris. Christian Boltanski (1944–), for example, fills galleries with photographs of himself in elaborate sequences, dispersed among other objects and materials, in a combination of art and autobiographical narrative. A form of installation art that evokes the ethnographic displays of the Musée de l'Homme was introduced by Gérard Titus-Carmel (1942–) in his *Le Cerceuil Tlingit de poche* (1975, *The Pocket-Sized Tlingit Coffin*). This work attracted the critical attention of Jacques Derrida in his essay *La Vérité en peinture*. The Tlingit were native to the Pacific Northwest coast of British Columbia and the subject of commentary by modern anthropologists interested in gift economies. Titus-Carmel fashioned tiny replicas of the coffins and then filled a gallery with reproduced images of his replicas. The proliferation of copies, almost à la Warhol, evokes the extravagant squandering of the potlatch ceremony.

Any visitor to art museums in recent years is as likely to encounter photography as painting or sculpture, and modern art museums regularly feature exhibitions of a single photographer or groups of similar ones. One European photographer who has been well recognized in this way is Thomas Struth (1954–) of Germany, a photographer whose subject is the temporary transformations of spaces caused by the passage of people through them, especially the space of museum galleries. The subjects of his enormous color photographs include crowds gathered in front of celebrated paintings in such museums as the Louvre in Paris or the Uffizi in Florence, or in such major tourist destinations as St. Peter's Basilica in Rome. A similar approach can be seen in the work of the Swiss photographer Beat Streuli (1957–), who produces equally large color prints taken candidly (in fact, furtively) of crowds in streets of major global cities. Gabriele Basilico (1944–) of Milan, Italy, is also preoccupied with cities, but his photographs display scenes of urban desolation with not a human figure in sight. Amsterdam's Stedelijk Museum organized an exhibition in 2000 that juxtaposed the work of Basilico and Streuli.

Contemporary European art also provides variations on the persistent Postmodern themes of the decentered or fragmented subject as well as the those of sexuality and the body, the latter related to questions of representation. So-called Neo-expressionism reasserted the primacy of physical representation in art. The German artist Anselm Kiefer (1945–) used photographed images, sometimes incorporated in huge paintings, to explore themes of Nazi culture and its aftermath. Later, he adopted installation art, especially to explore Jewish mysticism and other esoteric traditions of ancient cultures. The Italian painter Francesco Clemente (1952–) employed stark colors and startling images to portray dreamlike, often hallucinatory images featuring human heads and figures. Josef Beuys strongly influenced both artists. Schizophrenia or at least the divided nature of the subject achieves violent expression in the work of German artist Thomas Schütte (1954–). Much of his work consists of doll-like figures clad in elaborate print fabrics. Typically, each figure has two heads, each facing off in different directions. Their hideous grimaces suggest joined bodies in the act of wrenching themselves free of each other. Schütte then takes several color photographs of each "pair," exhibiting large-size prints along with the figures standing on pedestals and protected by plastic domes, much as would be used by a collector of precious dolls.

The French artist Gilles Barbier (1965–) fills galleries with figures that proliferate at least as much as Schütte's, and in his case they are identical, despite differences in pose and posture. Barbier seems to have taking "cloning" to heart in his midget-size eerie wax figures whose facial features manage simultaneously to resemble infants and elderly men. Other artists insert their own bodies into their art. The Austrian painter Arnulf Rainer (1929–) has produced a voluminous, varied body of work that includes large black-and-white photographs of his contorted body on which he has layered paint. He also directly inflicts his body on the surfaces of his works by painting with his fingers, hands, and feet, often in obsessively repetitious patterns.

Sexuality and the ambiguity of identity are central to the large-scale pop-influenced paintings of two openly homosexual English artists who call themselves simply Gilbert (1943–) and George (1942–). Their work is playful and irreverent, often including stiffly posed self-portraits in which they look like eternally youthful representatives of Eton or some other elite British school. Since the early 1980s, however, it has taken on a tone of urgency due to the AIDS epidemic, which they have made one of their main topics. Another pair of performance artists from Germany present their personal appearance as their art, accompanied by the slogan "wherever we are is museum." Eva and Adèle, as they are called, appear dressed as women but with shaved heads painted white and with elaborate clownish makeup. One actually is a woman and the other is a preoperative male transsexual. They always appear in identical outfits, carry dainty purses, and stage "campy" interviews in conjunction with their art exhibitions. They claim to come "from the future."

While European art has retained its vitality, European artists of this recent period do not stand out as "European" in essence. The art world has become global, and especially since 1945, the United States has been a constant point of reference.

European Music since 1980:
Mixed Genres, Mixed Ethnicity

Any visitor to a well-stocked record store in a major European city cannot fail to be impressed by the tremendous variety of choices, from regional European folk music to Western pop hits and everything in between, often with a far greater depth in such genres as jazz and blues than would be found in a comparable American store. Contemporary European music has asserted itself forcefully even while entering into combination with a variety of forms and styles from around the globe. Much of this new hybridity has stemmed from the newer immigration of African and Asian populations into Western and Central European nations.

Recorded music can be terrifically expensive in European countries, where heavy leisure taxes are added into the retail cost. Thus, for many listeners, the numerous annual music festivals held throughout the Continent provide a means of exposure to music they might not otherwise hear. The opportunity to hear music otherwise unavailable applies especially to "classical" music (here taken to include contemporary compositions), by definition an increasingly selective and narrow sector of a music market dominated by pop music. Few Western European composers became well known in recent years outside their own countries. One who achieved relatively greater prominence was Louis Andriessen (1939–) of the Netherlands. He was active as a composer by the 1960s, but most of his works date from the 1980s and 1990s. He is an intensely cerebral composer who uses ideas from all of the arts and brings compositional elements from serial music and jazz to bear on his music. To most ears, his music would seem "minimalist," but it is replete with ideas. In 2000 he composed an opera called *Writing to Vermeer,* based on the life of the seventeenth-century Dutch painter. The English filmmaker Peter Greenaway wrote the libretto and contributed his unique visual concepts to the opera's staging.

The general European interest in Eastern European artists has made some composers from the former Eastern Bloc quite popular in the West, often because of the intense spirituality in their music. Such musical emphasis is in keeping with a renewed interest in spiritual topics often found in recent years, especially among young people. The Polish composer Henryk Gorécki (1933–) probably has enjoyed the greatest success with such somber, brooding pieces as his *Symphony No. 3* (Symphony of Sorrowful Songs). His work is redolent of the strong Polish identity with Roman Catholicism, felt especially during the papacy of John Paul II, formerly Karol Wojtila of Poland. A far more mystical composer is Arvo Pärt (1936–) of Estonia, whose compositions are profoundly religious in tone (as in his *Te Deum*) and employ orchestras and choirs of enormous size in order to achieve an overwhelming effect.

By the 1990s rock music no longer enjoyed the massive allegiance it had in preceding decades, although certainly any number of rock-influenced genres proliferated throughout global pop music. The punk movement in England had given way to what some called "New Wave," a less confrontational form of rock 'n' roll that ranged from the strict traditional formula of guitar/bass/drums to growing experimentation with electronic music. As for electronic enhancements of recorded performances, it became increasingly common for groups to release dance-oriented remixed versions of their most successful songs, a practice originally associated with Jamaican reggae music.

A few of the bands formed in the punk era soldiered on in keeping with their original oppositional stance and radical political vision. Two of the most important were The Fall, of Manchester, and the Mekons, from Leeds in the North. Both continued to perform in the year 2000 and on into 2001, depending on a prolific recording catalog and a devoted fan base to compensate for their lack of commercial standing or major-label affiliation. For a while in the early 1980s, a politically outspoken band with punk roots called the Gang of Four made significant music that managed to be both articulate and danceable. One English band that made the transition from punk to new wave was Joy Division, which changed its name in 1981 to New Order, after the suicide of their lead singer. They were controversial because of the Nazi association of their name, but they were successful as they moved steadily toward electronic music, whose effects eventually overwhelmed the rock instrumentation with which they began. They pioneered in the use of computer programming of recorded music, becoming in the process an important influence on the development of what came to be called "techno" music.

Two of the most successful English bands of the 1980s were The Cure and the Smiths. Both bands featured lead singers trading on the kind of gender ambiguity made fashionable in earlier rock music by singers like Mick Jagger and David Bowie. Robert Smith of The Cure appeared often in lipstick and eyeliner, striking a decadent pose with music that moved from mournful and dirgelike into the kind of electronically flavored style pioneered by New Order. The lead singer of The Smiths called himself simply "Morrissey." His songs contained references to great English poets like Keats and Yeats, and he expressed his allegiance to the openly flaunted homosexuality of Oscar Wilde. The Smiths hailed from Salford, a rough Manchester neighborhood known for its forbidding boys' reform school. An even more commercially successful English band of the 1980s that featured an ambiguously gendered lead singer (in this case a woman) was the Eurythmics, essentially a duo consisting of a talented guitarist and musical arranger named Dave Stewart and a gifted singer named Annie Lennox. Lennox's striking looks and "butch" haircut made her one of the first stars of MTV, the Music Television network that emerged in the United States and soon spawned imitators throughout the world. The network also helped promote the career of the very successful Irish band U2, known for their highly romantic, visionary stance. They were part of the renaissance in Irish pop culture, along with the raucous traditionally based rock band The Pogues.

By the mid-1980s, as the vinyl record album was beginning to be overtaken by the new technology of compact discs, an enormous profusion of both English and American bands were recording. The seeming explosion of new bands recording their music was due almost completely to a thriving recording industry of independent companies, companies that were willing to promote music that had more critical appeal than chance of commercial success. One of the most important companies was Rough Trade, actually a network of small independent companies for which many critically respected bands recorded in the late 1980s. On the European continent, a significant label recording adventurous avant-garde artists was Crammed Discs of Brussels. The position of these companies was perilous by then due to a combination of factors. Some companies were threatened by the new digital technology of compact discs or were slow to adapt to them. The spread of music television gave enormous exposure to a limited number of recording artists, and the major record companies geared themselves more than ever to selling extraordinary numbers of copies of a few select discs. They remained indifferent about promoting other artists on their labels. Finally, as the major multinational companies such as Sony and Polygram consolidated their power, they were able to overwhelm the market position of the independent companies. When Rough Trade, the most conspicuous such company, folded in 1990, it signaled the end of an era in recorded music.

But while the independent labels flourished, they made possible the emergence of new musical genres throughout Europe and the world, sometimes in surprising locales. During the 1980s Paris became a major center for the recording, producing, and marketing of new forms of pop music by the African musicians who were part of a new wave of immigration that began when the newly inaugurated president François Mitterand relaxed entry restrictions in 1981. As the network of recording studios and performance halls became more established, more and more musicians were attracted to Paris, even if only for temporary stays. By the end of the decade, Paris could claim to be the center of so-called World Music, somewhat loosely defined as rock-based pop music adapted to the traditional styles of musicians especially of Third World origin.

Algerians and other peoples of the North African Maghreb (the northwest region that includes parts of Morocco, Algeria, and Tunisia) made up the largest proportion of the recent immigrants, and a new form of Algerian pop music called "raï" was the first type of African music to become popular in France. Raï was an upbeat, fast-paced, dance-oriented music featuring a combination of jazz and rock instrumentation and sometimes incorporating traditional North African instruments such as a type of lute named oud. Popular raï singers were known by names preceded by *Cheb* ("boy") or *Chaba* ("girl"). Their songs were songs of physical pleasure, including the joys of wine, forbidden to strict Muslims. Themes such as these were abhorrent to the militant Islamic party that controlled much of Algeria after the beginning of the civil war there in the early 1990s. As a result, Paris was more than merely a musical haven for many Algerian musicians. One of the most spectacularly popular and successful singers was Cheb Khaled (1960–).

At times France has been far from hospitable to its recent immigrant population. Periodically new restrictions have been imposed, and deportations of those without proper papers have begun, and the xenophobic, neofascist National Front Party of Jean-Marie Le Pen that calls for a ban on immigration and the return of immigrants to Africa has regularly polled between 15 and 20 percent of the vote in regional elections. Due to the burden of French history (its 1954 to 1962 Algerian war) and the fierce prejudice many hold against Islam (especially against outward expressions of its observance in this avowedly secular republic), Algerians have borne the brunt of anti-immigration policies and attitudes.

The younger generation of France's Arab population has been especially politicized by these developments. Many claim French citizenship (although the government by the 1990s had done away with the automatic granting of citizenship based on birth in France) and see themselves as French, yet they maintain pride in their Arab heritage. Theirs is a deliberately hybrid identity. By the early 1980s young people of North African descent living in Paris, Lyon, or Marseille had evolved their own unique argot called *"verlan,"* which was based on reversing the order of syllables in words. Hence *verlan* is formed by reversing the French *l'envers*. Soon they were calling themselves *beurs,* a word deriving from an approximation of the sound made by reversing the syllables in *arabe. Beur* culture came to refer to the music, clothing, or other styles and preferences of the generation born in France, whether their parents came from Algeria, Morocco, or Tunisia. For several years there was an influential underground radio station in Paris called "Radio Beur" playing the music of the new generation. One example was the group Carte de Séjour (named for the official French temporary residence permit), whose music was an interesting blend of a punk rock sound with North African influences and themes. Lead singer Rachid Taha (1958–) went on to enjoy a successful solo career.

In 1985 a record produced by the Cameroonian émigré musician Manu Dibango (1933–) called *Tam-Tam pour l'Ethiopie* was recorded in

Paris, with sales to benefit famine relief in Ethiopia. Musicians and singers included the biggest names in contemporary African music, that is, music of sub-Saharan Africa. This event made evident what had been emerging during the previous four years: that Paris was now the center of African music, especially by performers coming from former French or Belgian colonies. The sounds they were producing bridged traditional African styles and Western-style heavily electronic pop music. This hybrid actually had been emerging on the African continent for some time. Dakar, Senegal, had long been a center of musical cross-fertilization, with jazz, rhythm and blues, and other Western forms coming into contact with African genres. Congolese musicians, heavily influenced by Caribbean sounds, had invented a guitar-based form of pop music called "*soukous.*" In turn, musicians from the Antilles responded to the new African sounds by fashioning a new heavy electronic sound called "*zouk.*"

These styles and more converged on Paris, where a traditional kora (twenty-one-stringed African harp) player from Guinea named Mory Kanté (1950–) had begun recording with musicians playing amplified instruments. Kanté was an example of the traditional West African *griot,* a combination performer and oral historian descended from a family line. The Senegalese trio Toure Kunda became extremely popular in Paris, the first example of an African band to enjoy great commercial success in Europe. By 1985 a brilliant Zairean musician and musicologist named Ray Lema (1946–) had established himself in Paris, recording traditional African sounds using electronic instruments. And a very successful zouk band called Kassav', made up of members from Martinique and Guadeloupe, took Paris by storm, performing especially at Antillean carnivals throughout the city between 1985 and 1987.

Paris did not just embrace African music overnight, however. Much of the groundwork had been accomplished by a Senegalese immigrant named Mamadou Konté (1948–). In 1978 he announced the formation of an organization called Africa Fête, which would be an annual music and cultural festival promoting African arts, designed to educate French people about the African presence in their midst. By the mid-1980s, Africa Fête (which still exists) had become a thriving yearly enterprise that profiled the best African musicians. By the following decade it was beginning to tour other major world cities. The Mitterand government, especially its culture minister, Jack Lang, welcomed these artistic developments. Lang brought substantial government backing to annual music festivals at which the new World Music was spotlighted. One of the most important was the event in central France known as *Le Printemps de Bourges.* In 1989, Lang saw to it that African musicians and dancers were featured prominently in the July 14 bicentennial parade down the Champs-Elysées.

That moment of good feeling gave way in subsequent years to resentment, contradiction, and confusion as immigration restrictions increased (first in 1992 and again in 1996) and the demise of several of the independent record companies that had championed African music meant that opportunities for African musicians in Paris were reduced. Paris remained the principal center for such music, but new difficulties presented themselves. For example, musicians from African countries requesting visas for the purpose of recording or performing began to be refused, whereas in the previous era they would have faced few obstacles. Some well-established musicians, such as the famous Malian singer Salif Keïta (1949–), became fed up and returned to Africa.

Then there was also the issue of language. By the 1990s, French culture was in full cry against the incursion of English words and American influences, and any language other than French in songs encountered obstacles, including the demand the radio stations play a substantial percentage of French-language songs. But there was one additional factor: Like rock 'n' roll before it, African pop music began to lose out to rap music and the "hip-hop" culture surrounding it.

The *beurs* as well as the second generation of sub-Saharan African immigrants embraced hip-hop style, as portrayed memorably in Kassovitz's film *La Haine.* Rap in French was a growth industry, and ran the gamut from silky-smooth vocal styles that incorporated quintessentially French *chanson* to the confrontational slamming beats of "gangsta" rap. By far the most prominent French rapper was Claude M'Barali, a. k. a. "MC" Solaar (1969–), the French-born son of Senegalese immigrants who was known as much for his articulate interviews and political pronouncements as for his songs. He supplied an eloquent rebuttal of the hate-mongering politics of Le Pen.

France was not the only example of a country whose popular music gravitated toward hip-hop styles. Italy, where anti-immigrant feeling would run perhaps even higher by the end of the 1990s, was home to pop music styles that made contact with a variety of influences around the globe. Inspired by American rap music, "Posse" was a musical genre that emerged in the late 1980s, linked to the radical student movement known as La Pantera (The Panther). Posse and rap groups in Italy frequently have used regional dialects. An example is I Nouvi Briganti from Sicily. They are also often political in their themes, as is the case with Sud Sound System from Puglia, who sing about the Mafia. Proclaiming a southern identity is itself a political act, for ever since the days of unification in the 1860s, anti-South prejudice has been part of the Italian political scene. Sa Razza Posse is a group from Sardinia that sings about their southern heritage, with all its disadvantages.

As in France and in other countries where hip-hop styles have taken root, Italian musical hybrids have been created that have implications for racial mixing and solidarity. One style came about as a result of interest in African *griot* influences and the Jamaican reggae/rap dancehall style known as raggamuffin. The meeting ground was *tarantolati* music and dance tradition of the South, where tarantula bites are a serious threat. The resulting style called itself *tarantamuffin*. Themes of race and immigration also appear in the urban-based music of northern Italy, where one example is the mixed-race group from Turin who call themselves Mau Mau. Political themes in northern-based Posse music have included the opposition expressed to the Gulf War of 1991 by the Bolognese group Isola Posse, with their song "Stop al panico." Finally, just as French hip-hop artists seem united in their denunciation of Jean-Marie Le Pen, Italian groups regularly scorn the very wealthy Rightist politician Silvio Berlusconi, who plays a similar role in Italian politics.

Jamaican raggamuffin was appropriated generally throughout Europe, where it appealed to rap fans but nevertheless constituted a separate category, with a special appeal to dancers. One of the most unusual adaptations of this music unfolded in early 1990s' England, where Indian and Pakistani immigrants worked it into a dance-oriented style based on a traditional Punjabi music called *bhangra*. *Bhangra* had always been a festive music, associated with the harvest and especially favored at weddings. It was also ubiquitous in soundtracks of Indian films. Like Jamaican "dub" of "version" music, where tunes were remixed to accentuate their most danceable rhythmic qualities, *bhangra* music was bass-heavy, using a two-sided drum called the dhol to provide repetitive percussive tracks over which DJ-style performers improvised lyrics.

The most successful performer in this genre was a young Indian immigrant named Don Raja. He called himself Apache Indian, the "Apache" part of the name being a tribute to Wild Apache Productions, a Brooklyn, New York–based company founded by a Jamaican/American performer called Super Cat. Apache Indian's songs were unique amalgams of Jamaican rhythms accompanied by lyrics that described the lives of the Indian immigrant community in England, from their food preferences to their desire for arranged marriages. Another performer called Bally Sagoo remained closer to the traditional *bhangra* sound, but with very heavy electronic amplification.

This was a musical style evolving in relation both to hip-hop and to the enormously popular (in England and throughout the world) music called techno, a fully electronic form of dance-oriented music. Structured around repetitive but often complex layered beats and making use of the "sampling" techniques (i.e., where a bit of recorded sound from another source is incorporated, often as a repetitive motif, in a new performance) pioneered by hip-hop music, techno music in England and elsewhere evolved in relation to the "rave" scene, associated for a while in the early 1990s with Manchester, England. "Raves" were all-night dances featuring DJs more often than live bands and using a combination of drugs and overwhelming volume in the music to induce an ecstatic state in the audience.

One of the most successful groups in techno music was a duo from Manchester called the Chemical Brothers. They were masters of the use of repetition in their complicated audio mixes, but repetition with ever so slight variation, calling to mind some of the compositions of American minimalist (e.g., Steve Reich, Philip Glass) music. Another prominent figure in the field was Norman Cook, a.k.a. "Fatboy Slim," who excelled in using very obscure forgotten pop songs as the basic framework for his techno explorations. The rave scene inspired a new low-key style called "ambient" music, one purpose of which was to soothe weary revelers spent from their night of raving. Brian Eno (1948–), an English rock musician who was a founder of the group Roxy Music, had first used the term to describe a form of electronic minimalist music he began to compose in the late 1970s, but the concept of music that is to create an ambiance rather than demand close listening goes back a long way, at least to the early twentieth-century musical aesthetic of Erik Satie. The most prominent English "ambient" artist was Alex Patterson, a.k.a. "The Orb." He made use of nature sounds, fragments of broadcast speech, sampled bits of recorded music, and soothing repeated phrases of electronic music to weave elaborate ambient spells.

So-called industrial music was a genre related somewhat to techno, although it often featured groups using more conventional rock instrumentation than computer-based instruments. The goal of industrial bands was to simulate machine sounds, creating a discordant sonic atmosphere that suggested urban alienation and anxiety. Deliberate use of such sounds was not dissimilar to the Futurist aesthetic and their embrace of "noise music" (*bruitisme,* as it came to be known in France). While many industrial musicians were American, one of the leading acts was the Berlin-based band Einstürzende Neubauten (the name means "collapsing new buildings"). The members of this group, led by writer/artist/musician Blixa Bargeld, had close ties to the German avant-garde. Their music often altered between subtle, understated passages and violent crescendos.

We have encountered previously the idea that Postmodern culture includes renewed interest in regional, obscure, often overlooked forms. One noticeable feature of the vogue for what, in an unsatisfactory phrase, the music industry called World Music has been the attention accorded music from almost forgotten corners of Europe. Sometimes this means strictly traditional sounds, such as Irish folk music or the Gallic/Celtic sounds of ancient Breton music. The Spanish region of Galicia, which also received some recent attention, is another area where a form of bagpipe music suggests kinship with Celtic styles. The 1990s saw a resurgence of interest in ancient forms of polyphonic singing, still found in Corsica and Sardinia. One of the most popular forms of vocal music, which struck most ears as utterly traditional, was the female choral music of Bulgaria, which makes use of call-and-response patters that suggest African singing at times. A series of recordings called *Les Mystères des Voix Bulgares* began to be released in Paris in 1987 and popularized Bulgarian music to a considerable degree. Actually, the singing was a significantly urbanized, modernized version of more traditional styles.

Portugal and Spain have been sources of some extremely varied and adventurous pop music in recent years. The mournful, African-influenced Portugese *fado* genre is popular throughout Europe, and one of the most successful Portugese musical acts is a band from Lisbon called Madredeus. Theirs is a haunting guitar-based sound, also featuring female vocals and drawing on traditional Portugese styles. They were featured in Wim Wenders's film *Lisbon Story*. A number of Spanish groups, especially those from the southern part of the country just across the Straits of Gibraltar from Morocco, achieve a blend of styles that are as much African as they are Spanish. Radio Tarifa, based in Madrid, is an example of a band that uses Spanish Flamenco influences, Moroccan trance music, and the piercing flute sounds of the Maghreb to create a truly multiregional style. They serve as a reminder that the real meaning of World Music would be the end, once and for all, of boundaries and sharp distinctions obtaining between one style or genre and another.

Something Other Than a Conclusion

No one person can confidently assess all that exists at the beginning of the twenty-first century within European culture, and certainly no one cultural theorist has emerged within the ranks of the Postmodernists who offers an encompassing, persuasive framework for interpreting what seems to be afoot. For one thing, such an attempt at a "master narrative" would be strongly antithetical to the Postmodern sensibility. But one prominent French theorist who at least has commented on an impressive array of topics—sociological, legal, economic, ethnic (emphasizing immigrants and minorities), and aesthetic—is Pierre Bourdieu (1930–), a sociologist and anthropologist who holds a chair at the Collège de France, is director of studies at the École des Hautes Etudes en Sciences Sociales, and is head of a Paris-based, Europe-wide institution called the Centre de Sociologie Européene.

Bourdieu's early work as a social theorist, deriving from his anthropological fieldwork in Algeria, focused especially on what he termed the *habitus,* referring to the way human experiences of such basic things as their dwellings shape their social behavior and limit what they are able to imagine in terms of social reality. Typical of French social theorists, he strives always to address themes of social control and domination without recourse to a Marxist lexicon that would include such concepts as ideology or alienation. But, like Gramsci before him, Bourdieu has preoccupied himself with the ways in which domination operates often through cultural institutions, and often hidden from view, as he puts it "in the wings," as if society itself is the stage. Himself a product of elite French schools who was made to feel embarrassed by his humble background, Bourdieu has analyzed (in a 1984 work called *Homo Academicus*) the intricate ways the French *grandes écoles* reproduce the hierarchical structures resistant to change in French cultural life.

Also like Gramsci (and again he would chafe at the comparison), Bourdieu takes the cultural sphere very seriously, something missed by those who look exclusively at political or economic life. One of his most important studies is called *La Distinction* (1979, *Distinction*), and it explores the way "taste" plays a determining role in cultural life. He points out, for example, that the way children of elite families feel perfectly at home touring an art museum is enormously revealing of ongoing processes of acculturation that ensure continued domination of social elites. More than most French intellectuals, Bourdieu pays close attention to popular culture, and accepted the invitation from the influential pop music magazine *Les Inrockuptibles* to be guest editor of one issue.

One of Bourdieu's most important and ambitious projects, a huge collaborative work of which he was the general coordinator, was *La Misère du monde* (1993, *The Misery of the World*), a collection of interviews with workers and unemployed people about their jobs, their attitudes toward work, and their hopes and aspirations. It was a real pulse-taking of the French populace at a time of troubling high unemployment and convenient scapegoating of immigrants, another population for whom Bourdieu has great sympathy. He regularly speaks out against anti–immigrant attitudes and policies. Most recently, his has been the leading voice in criticism of American-style economic globalization that threatens French republican values and the guarantee of protections for workers built into the very structures of French laws and political institutions.

Probably it will not be long before a new name emerges to shape perceptions of European cultural realities. When we are all struggling to imagine a new century at a time of unprecedented change, the point is not to give Bourdieu the last word. But perhaps he will have had some of the first words.

Suggestions for Further Reading

Forgacs, David, and Robert Lumley, eds. *Italian Cultural Studies: An Introduction.* New York: Oxford University Press, 1996.

Gilroy, Paul. *"There Ain't No Black in the Union Jack": The Cultural Politics of Race and Nation.* Chicago: University of Chicago Press, 1991.

Goldberg, RoseLee. *Performance Art: From Futurism to the Present,* revised ed. New York: Abrams, 1988.

Goldberg, RoseLee. *Performance: Live Art Since 1960.* New York: Abrams, 1998.

Hargreaves, Alec, and Mark McKinney, eds. *Post-Colonial Culture in France.* London: Routledge, 1997.

Lipsitz, George. *Dangerous Crossroads: Popular Music, Postmodernism, and the Poetics of Place.* London: Verso, 1994.

Shusterman, Richard, ed. *Bourdieu: A Critical Reader.* Oxford: Blackwell, 1999.

Index of Names

CPSIA information can be obtained at www.ICGtesting.com
Printed in the USA
LVOW07s0259310815

452165LV00003B/242/P